Twayne's English Authors Series

EDITOR OF THIS VOLUME

George D. Economou

Long Island University

Robert Henryson

TEAS 274

James III of Scotland

ROBERT HENRYSON

By ROBERT L. KINDRICK

Central Missouri State University

TWAYNE PUBLISHERS

A DIVISION OF G. K. HALL & CO., BOSTON

Published in 1979 by Twayne Publishers,
A Division of G. K. Hall & Co.
All Rights Reserved

Printed on permanent/durable acid-free paper and bound
in the United States of America

First Printing

*Frontispiece of Trinity Altarpiece
(James III) by Van der Goes, printed
by permission of The Lord Chamberlain,
copyright reserved*

Library of Congress Cataloging in Publication Data

Kindrick, Robert L
Robert Henryson.

(Twayne's English authors series; TEAS 274)
Bibliography: p. 201–209
Includes index.
1. Henryson, Robert, 1430?–1506?—Criticism and interpretation.
PR1990.H4Z68   821'.2   79–15377
ISBN 0–8057–6758–4

For Carolyn
and Robert W. Kindrick

Contents

About the Author

Robert L. Kindrick received his Ph.D. from the University of Texas at Austin. He is Professor and Head of the Department of English at Central Missouri State University, where he has taught since 1967. He serves on the Board of Directors of the Missouri Committee for the Humanities. His previous publications have appeared in *MidAmerica*, *Medievalia et Humanistica*, and *Studies in Scottish Literature*.

Preface

Most students of the works of Robert Henryson find themselves becoming the poet's advocates. Henryson's broad erudition, practical wisdom, and humane tolerance invite the modern reader's sympathetic attention. His stature as a literary figure has led those who know his verse to express regret that he is not more widely appreciated. Only in the last thirty years has he begun to receive the scholarly and popular recognition he deserves.

The purpose of this volume is to provide an overview of Henryson's poetry, along with an introduction to his cultural and social milieu. Since there is only the scantest biographical data, I have tried to examine Henryson's philosophy, politics, and religion by comparing his attitudes with traditional medieval patterns of thought and developing Renaissance ideals. Henryson was influenced by Patristic exegesis, chivalric values and courtly love, but he also felt the effects of the courtier's ethics and the new humanism being transported to Scotland from Italy. By considering Henryson's poetry in terms of earlier conventions and fifteenth-century change, I have tried to explain the entire range of beliefs about life and art embodied in his poetry. The cultural turmoil of the period, when medieval attitudes were being displaced by humanistic values, often led to contradictions and inconsistencies. Yet Henryson managed to forge a systematic and humane set of values out of the sometimes erratic patterns of thought that were his birthright.

A few points about my methodology may assist the reader who uses this book. The organization of the poems for purposes of critical discussion does not reflect a theory about their chronology. Our knowledge of Henryson's life is too sketchy to permit any but very broad generalizations about when the poems were written. It seems likely that *Orpheus* is an early work and that some of the fables may be dated in the 1480s, but we can be certain of very few facts in the matter. My method of organization, then, reflects some convenient principles of structural division similar to those Charles Elliott has used in his edition of the texts. I should also add that the bibliography is highly selective. Considerations of space led me to exclude reviews, dissertations, survey and background material, and many brief notices now superseded by other works listed. Moreover, Florence Ridley's "Middle Scots Writers" is a thorough and reliable bibliographical guide to all but the most recent material.

In the preparation of this book, I incurred a long list of debts. I have profited from the work of numerous Henryson scholars whose volumes and articles have contributed to the "Henryson revival" now in progress. Among others, Marshall W. Stearns and Denton Fox have provided valuable insights into Henryson's social and cultural concerns. John MacQueen, whose broad knowledge has helped the cause of all Scottish literature, has performed a vital service by showing how Henryson's humanistic education influenced his writing.

I am also most grateful to those more immediately involved in this project. The staffs of the British Library and the libraries of the University of Kansas, the University of Missouri, and Central Missouri State University provided kind and generous assistance. It is impossible to repay Frank M. Patterson, Ronald W. McReynolds, Robert V. Graybill, Larry Olpin, and Steve Khinoy for their comments on various portions of the text. George Economou has been a wise and patient editor, whose generous concern has made my task much easier. Finally, I must express my thanks to William M. Ryan and Robert H. Wilson, whose enthusiasm about medieval literature led me to Henryson.

ROBERT L. KINDRICK

Central Missouri State University

Acknowledgment

Portions of chapter three originally appeared in *Studies in Scottish Literature XIV* (Columbia: University of South Carolina Press, 1979).

Chronology

CHAPTER 1

Henryson and His Times

I *Biography*

THE life of Robert Henryson presents a series of fascinating puzzles. The source of the problems is not a dearth of facts: indeed, there are too many facts about late fourteenth- and early fifteenth-century people bearing the name of Robert Henryson. The major difficulty is attempting to decide which facts pertain to the life of the author.

One of the most widely accepted pieces of information about Robert Henryson the poet comes from the 1570 edition of *The Morall Fabillis*, printed almost seventy years after the presumed date of his death. On the title page he is described as "Scholemaister of Dunfermeling," a position of considerable importance. There is, however, no authentic record of his academic training or of his work in that position. Henryson's acquaintance with Dunfermline may also appear in possible references to Dunfermline Abbey in "Abbey Walk."

It is likely that Henryson attended one of the grammar schools of Scotland established before 1400. The list includes Abernethy, St. Andrews, Roxburgh, Perth, Stirling, Lanark, Linlithgow, Ayr, Aberdeen, Glasgow, Kelsow, Montrose, Cupar, Haddington, and Tranent, and there may have been others unrecorded.[1] It is possible to be a little more sure of the curriculum that Henryson would have followed in such a school. Most of his time would have been devoted to the study of the *trivium*, comprising grammar, rhetoric, and logic. He would probably have studied works including Aesop's fables, Cicero's *De amicitia* and *De inventione*, Horace's *Ars poetica*, and Geoffrey of Vinsauf's *Poetria nova*.[2]

The location of Henryson's university training is equally enigmatic. There were two universities in Scotland he might have attended, St. Andrew's University, founded in 1411, and, less likely, the University of Glasgow, founded in 1451. Henryson's name appears in the registry of neither. Scotland's unstable relations with England during the fifteenth century make it quite unlikely that he would have gone to either Oxford or Cambridge. The most likely alternative at present is that he attended a continental university.[3] Since the reign of Robert I, Scots had traditionally attended the University of Paris. Charles Elliott believes that the University of Louvain or the University of Cologne is the most likely, but his inquiries have yielded no proof.[4] R. D. S. Jack speculates that Henryson had a close association with the University of Bologna and "returned from time to time to Italy," while John MacQueen has found strong evidence of Henryson's knowledge of Florentine Platonism.[5]

Henryson's university curriculum is more readily available. His training would have included study of grammar, logic, and rhetoric, with additional work in the *quadrivium*: geometry, arithmetic, music, and astronomy. He would probably have studied Boethius' *Consolation of Philosophy*, Boccaccio's *Genealogia deorum*, Aristotle's *Metaphysics*, St. Thomas's *Summa Theologica*, and Hugh of St. Victor's *Didascalicon*. The result of his grammar school and university training would have been a firm command of the arts of communication and a thorough knowledge of the best of the medieval traditions in science and humanities.

We have more concrete information about the possible nature of his life in Dunfermline. Under James III and James IV Dunfermline flourished. The city developed around a Benedictine monastery founded by St. Margaret around 1074. During the reign of David I, the monastery was changed to the Abbey of the Holy Trinity (1124) and the city became a royal borough. Later it became a royal residence, and James I was born in the royal palace there. MacQueen notes the number of royal interments in the church and suggests that it had almost become a "Scottish Westminster Abbey." Henryson's position in Dunfermline would have provided him substantial prestige. He would most likely have taught the same material that, as a youth, he had been taught in one of the grammar schools of the country.

There is less specific information about Henryson's other adult activities. We have no record about his marital status or any possible descendants, despite the efforts of John Henderson.[6] From the poems we learn other facts about Henryson's life. If we believe his personal comments in stanza 33 of *Orpheus and Eurydice*, we know that he "cowth nevir sing a noit" [7] despite his detailed explanation of music theory. It also seems likely from the technological detail in "The Preaching of the Swallow" that he had some acquaintance with the flax industry. As vital as this was for international affairs, however, there seems little need to suggest an exceptional interest on the part of the poet. David Laing, the major source of modern biographical information, identifies two fourteenth-century refer- ences to the poet, but his evidence is inconclusive. Laing believes that Henryson was the "Magister Robertus Henrison notarius publicus" who witnessed three deeds recorded in the *Registrum de Dunfermelyn*.[8] These grants were made by Henry Abbot to George de Lothreisk, and Patrick Barone and his wife Margaret between 1477 and 1478. Laing speculates that Henryson's position would make it quite likely that he was either one of the ecclesiastics permitted to carry on such duties before 1469 or one of the literate laymen who were permitted to assume the duties after the royal decree which transferred such authority in the secular world to the king. MacQueen agrees with Laing that the poet is the "Magister Robertus Henrisone in Artibus Licentiatus et in Decretis Bachalar- ius" who became a member of the University of Glasgow in 1462.[9] Laing further argues that the title "Decretis Bachalarius," a law degree, indicated that the schoolmaster of Dunfermline was also involved in legal activities.

Attractive as Laing's speculations are, they are no more than speculations. Laing himself lists no fewer than six Robert Henrysons who lived in the late fourteenth and fifteenth centuries. He does not suggest the list is complete, and there is no reason to believe that the number could not be easily tripled or quadrupled. To suggest that the poet and he alone is the subject of any or all these references is untenable unless further evidence is available. Moreover, Laing's suggestion of a legal career is belied by the poet's professional title in the 1570 edition of the *Fabillis* and possibly his interest in medicine which appears in "Sum Practysis of Medecyne" and *The Testament*.

There is one last tale about Henryson's life that deserves mention. By 1639, Sir Francis Kinaston had completed a Latin translation of Henryson's *Testament of Cresseid*, "which may passe for the sixt & last booke" of Chaucer's *Troilus and Criseyde*. He included a story about Henryson's old age, apparently confirming Henryson's own designation of himself as "ane man of age." Kinaston's tale is:

For the Author of this supplement called the Testament of Creseid, which
may passe for the sixt & last booke of this story I haue very sufficiently bin
informed by S^r [Tho:] Eriskin late earle of Kelly & diuers aged schollers of
the Scottish nation, that it was made & written by one Mr Robert
Henderson sometimes cheife schoolemaster in Dumfermling much about
the time that Chaucer was first printed & dedicated to king Henry the 8th
by Mr Thinne which was neere the end of his raigne: This Mr Henderson
wittily obseruing, that Chaucer in his 5th booke had related the death of
Troilus, but made no mention what became of Creseid, he learnedly takes
vppon him in a fine poeticall way to expres the punishment & end due to a
false vnconstant whore, which commonly terminates in extreme misery,
about, or a litle after his time the most famous of the Scottish poets Gawen
Douglas made his learned & excellent translation of Virgils AEneids, who
was bishop of Dunkeld, & made excellent prefaces to euery one of the
twelue bookes: For this Mr Robert Henderson he was questionles a learned
& a witty man, & it is pitty we haue no more of his works   being very old he
dyed of a diarrhea or fluxe, of whome there goes this merry, though
somewhat unsauory tale, that all phisitians hauing giuen him ouer & he
lying drawing his last breath there came an old woman vnto him, who was
held a witch & asked him whether he would be cured, to whome he sayed
very willingly. then quod she there is a whikey tree in the lower end of your
orchard & if you will goe and walke but thrice about it, & thrice repeate
theis wordes whikey tree whikey tree take away this fluxe from me you shall
be presently cured, he told her that beside he was extreme faint & weake it
was extreme frost & snow & that it was impossible for him to go: She told
him that vnles he did so it was impossible he should recouer. M^r
Henderson then lifting upp himselfe, & pointing to an Oken table that was
in the roome, asked her & seied gude dame I pray ye tell me, if it would not
do as well if I repeated thrice theis words oken burd oken burd garre me
shit a hard turde. the woman seeing herselfe derided & scorned ran out of
the house in a great passion & Mr Henderson within halfe a quarter of an
houre departed this life. . . .[10]

Delightful as Kinaston's tale is, it is hardly reliable. The authority is
too uncertain; the events too dramatic and too much the standard
fare of Scottish folklore.

An attempt to fix precisely the dates of Henryson's life, the last of
the biographical enigmas we shall consider here, meets with as
much frustration as Laing's attempts to trace his adult activities in
Dunfermline or Kinaston's effort to investigate the eccentricities of
the later years of his life. From Dunbar's "Lament for the Makars,"
published by Chepman and Millar in 1508, it is clear that Henryson

was dead before the printing. Speaking of death in his catalog of Scots poets, Dunbar says: "In Dumfermelyne he has done roune/With Maister Robert Henrisoun . . ." (ll. 81–82). Unfortunately, however, there is no date established for the writing of the "Lament." General consensus places the date of Henryson's death between 1500 and 1506.

Establishing a general date for Henryson's death makes possible an educated guess at the date of his birth. There is evidence in the popular tradition, reflected in Kinaston's story and in Henryson's own works, to believe that he led a long life. It seems impossible to date his birth as precisely as 1425, as Laing did, but there is sufficient information to place his birthdate between 1420 and 1435. How any date in this range reflects on Henryson's private life and the external conditions of his poetry often depends on how much credence is to be lent to the Laing and Kinaston material.

Even as deprived of facts as we are, we may still construct a portrait of the poet. Born in the early years of the fifteenth century, he was well-educated in the basic intellectual traditions of the Middle Ages. His humanism and his lack of turgidity in style are revealed in his writings. His works also reveal a man who is primarily a teacher. This is not to say Henryson is a pedant. He is a student of life; he sees meaning in the universe and attempts to tell others about it. Although perhaps the most didactic of the Makars, he is also "humanitarian, democratic, and independent." [11] As he lived out a long and probably very full life, his achievement received recognition among the brotherhood of poets.

II *Fifteenth-Century Scotland*

Henryson's society was dangerous and turbulent. M. W. Stearns sums up the startling contrast between the accomplishments of Scottish art and politics in the fifteenth century: "Although the fifteenth century in Scotland was a golden age of Scottish culture, it was also an age of transition, of political turmoil and civil war, of unscrupulous violence, and bloody treachery." [12] Political life was uncertain and constantly shifting. Despite the strong patriotism that had continued to develop after Robert I and David II, relationships between the king and his barons were in a constant state of flux. International relations offered no consolation for the fifteenth-century Scotsman. Constantly at odds with England over questions of feudal superiority and territorial boundaries, Scotland found herself forced into a series of alliances with France and Burgundy. Although often no more than a pawn in the political games played by the aspiring monarchs of England and France, Scotland sometimes determined the outcome of the game. Domestic affairs and social policies were just as uncertain as monarchical relations and international affairs.

Largely dependent on strong feudal ties with recalcitrant nobles, the Scottish peasant found his life harsh and unstable. The Highlands clans managed to maintain their independence partially because of their inaccessibility, but their lack of contact with other parts of Scotland and with other countries resulted in few of the benefits from trade and the exchange of information. To the South, peasants were racked by the constant wars of the barons with each other and of the state with England. While the burgesses were generally prosperous and gained greater prestige throughout the century, they too often found their treasuries depleted by heavy taxes under both James I and James II and by numerous loans to the royal family, some of which were very slowly repaid. The church was unable to perform either its spiritual or social duties efficiently because of its involvement in domestic politics and the schisms that weakened papal and ecclesiastical authority prior to the Reformation.

III   *Politics*

Any study of the politics of fifteenth-century Scotland must take account of the relationship that existed between the monarchy and the notoriously rebellious Scottish barons. A trend persisted throughout the century involving the consolidation of power in the hands of the king. When James I returned from imprisonment in England (which had been prolonged by his uncle, the Duke of Albany), he applied himself to the subjugation of nobles who tried to maintain their own power at the expense of the king. His imprisonment of Duke Murdoch and his family along with Sir John Montgomery and Allan Otterburn and his beheading of Walter Stewart broke the power of the barons. Through manipulation of relations between Scotland and France, James managed to make the country relatively secure from international disruption, while he depleted the power of his rivals through arrests, imprisonments, and heavy taxation. James' interests could best be served by the maintenance of peace. Moderately successful in curbing the power of even such nobles as the Lord of the Isles, the most independent of all the barons, James ultimately died at the hands of a group of conspirators who objected to his policy of royal consolidation. Though considered an unreasonable tyrant by some of his contemporaries, "there is no doubt that he endeavored with varying degrees of success to improve every department of Scottish political life." [13] Scotland was more politically stable than it had been since the time of David II.

Much of James' work was undone at his death. James II was crowned on March 25, 1437, at the age of six. He at once became a prize in a highly complicated contest for royal authority during his minority. Two power-seeking nobles, Sir William Crichton and Sir Alexander Livingston, boldly began gathering the perquisites of royal power, even going so far as to imprison the queen mother. Ruthless suppression of the Douglasses resulted in the maintenance of power in the hands of the Livingstons and the Crichtons until 1449, when James married Mary of Guelders. Immediately after his marriage, the king began to assert his own authority. Initiating an attack on the Livingston family, James set about the task that his father had begun after the death of Albany. His skillful dealings with both the Lancastrian and Yorkist factions in England permitted him to devote a good deal of his time to domestic policies. He completely suppressed the Douglas clan and even regained Berwick, which had been lost to the English. Unhappily for Scotland, James died before he was thirty. At a ceremony on Sunday, July 3, 1460, to welcome Mary to the siege of Roxburgh, a cannon burst and James was mortally wounded in the thigh.

The death of James II once again placed Scotland under the rule of a monarch in his boyhood. At the time of his father's death, James III was eight years old. The usual period of tumult after a king's death was followed by more extensive challenges to royal authority by the earls of Douglas and Ross. Deprived of the counsel of his mother and his uncle by their untimely deaths, James found himself the object of factional dispute. Although he did indeed show "a remarkable talent for political survival," [14] he was not as shrewd as his father or grandfather. He found himself involved in baronial disputes and an English war. Occasionally, James seems to have simply withdrawn from the tough and vicious world of fifteenth-century Scottish politics. Extravagant in his personal tastes, James was lax in the administration of justice. He was inconsistent and capricious. He would award court favorites such as Thomas

Cochrane and Thomas Preston with large gifts of cash or land but
ignore the advice of his official councillors. He was even berated by
Bishop Elphinstone for his lust. Harassed by his own barons, James
found himself forced to rely on the strength of public sentiment to
regain his position. Confronted with a rebellion by his own son and
influential barons such as Angus, Argyll, and Hailes, James
ineffectually led an army against them at Bannockburn in June,
1488. According to the Pitscottie chronicler, he fell in the midst of
the battle. Severely wounded, he was taken to an old mill. When
James asked for a priest, a mysterious stranger appeared who
stabbed him in the heart.

The accession of James IV was marked by a purge of the
supporters of the old king. Even so, however, the new monarch was
able to reestablish the political unity that had evaded his father. He
avoided the capricious favoritism that had caused James III to fall
into disrepute. Bolstered by the establishment of a court party,
James was able to arrange peaceful relationships with England and
even used his own matrimonial prospects as a means of solidifying
international relations. As Nicholson says "James acquired, and
kept, an easy popularity," [15] which, along with his skill in
international relations, ushered in a remarkable period in Scottish
culture. At long last, many of the independent barons were
subdued. The ensuing peace gave Scottish society time to pursue
art, architecture, and literature. Until the battle of Flodden,
Scotland enjoyed a "golden age."

IV *The Church*

Vital to the organization of Scottish society as to that of every
other Christian country during the Middle Ages was the church. At
its best the most significant force for social change and public
welfare in the period, the church at large often found itself
weakened by internal disputes and the corruption of its members.
The Scottish church suffered the same problems. Divided at the
beginning of the fifteenth century by the Great Schism, the church
had already been weakened by the internal policies of David II,
Robert II, Robert III, and the Duke of Albany.

Church benefices were an important part of the monetary and
social structure of medieval Scotland. They were also, however, a
major source of contention among the Scottish clergy, the crown,
and the pope. The crucial issue was the question of authority to

settle benefices. The Scottish church believed that, ideally, they should have been under local control as much as possible. But the incomes from church occupations were too significant to go unnoticed by the king of Scotland, who was constantly in need of money. As a result the crown made inroads on the clerical control of church offices. Partially because of avarice, partially because of concern, and partially because of a desire for stricter control, the pope attempted to "reserve" not only bishoprics but lesser benefices for his own designation. Urban VI, Clement VII, and Benedict XIII had all used clerical benefices to maintain tight control over the Scottish church.

Problems created by internal dissension and greedy monarchs were not the only ones the church confronted. On occasion, its own role in politics led to trouble. Bishop Kennedy, for instance, was nephew to James I and uncle to James III. He was a dominant and forceful figure: after the death of Mary of Guelders, in 1463, he was perhaps the most influential political advisor in the nation. Yet he was not above the factionalism that pervaded Scottish politics during the reign of James II. As a political figure, he was subject to attack and harrassment from rival factions such as the Black Douglases. Attacks on him and his authority depleted the resources and prestige of the church.

Another major factor that contributed to the predicament of the fifteenth-century church was the widespread corruption among its members. Churches practised the custom of selling corrodies, or lifetime board and room, to enrich their coffers and serve their immediate ends. That the fees for corrodies did not always meet the expenses of corrodians seemed inconsequential to clergymen who sold them. The private lives of clerics reflected extensive examples of hypocrisy and corruption. Numerous attempts at reforming both regular and secular clergy were initiated during the period, and from the kinds of restrictions enforced we may gain an estimate of the abuses practised. Among other regulations, clergymen were enjoined from keeping concubines, gossiping about their parishoners and superiors, drinking and swearing, and using church funds for their own purposes. The use of church funds for personal pleasure was apparently sufficently common that services were sometimes abridged for want of oil, wine, and candles. Most shocking of all to many church investigators was the sexual conduct of monks and nuns. Numerous children granted dispensations from illegitimacy attest to the sexual activities of clergymen. Unwilling to

remain as cloistered as their vows dictated, many nuns "wandered,"
even on occasion to the monks' quarters. In 1466 the Prior of
Whithorn had been confronted with charges that included fornica-
tion and was forced to resign.[16] Among their other excesses,
clergymen were also known to keep numerous servants.

Finally, the church found itself in conflict with the developing
towns. Early in the fourteenth century the burgesses of towns such
as Montrose and Dundee had passed acts against ecclesiastical
institutions in their area to protect both their commerce and their
legal authority. Developing in power and responsibility throughout
the fourteenth and fifteenth centuries, the burghs felt their own
independence challenged by church policy. Besides attempting to
usurp some of the commercial powers of the burgesses, the church
even attempted to extend clerical prerogatives and immunity from
prosecution by secular authorities. Moreover, there was a threat of
territorial usurpation from some religious institutions, and town-
gown disputes often exploded over boundaries of church land and
right-of-way privileges.

Debilitated by internal corruption and disputes over control of
church policy, the church was compromised even more by attacks
from the king and the burgesses. Unable, and often unwilling, to
carry out its social function with efficiency, it aroused the ire of
literary men such as Henryson and Dunbar. If social critics saw the
proud nobles as one threat to the commonweal, they often saw the
church as yet another.

V *Social Structure*

Many of the social problems of late medieval Scotland can be
understood through economic and social changes that were transforming the basic substructure of Scottish society. I have already
commented on the tendency toward concentration of political
power in the hands of the monarch, and this centralization struck at
the very core of long cherished feudal institutions. Even in the
fifteenth century, the old feudal relationships between the lords and
their men were perhaps the major cohesive bond in Scottish
society. Highlands Scotland remained enmeshed in a series of
strong tribal alliances even as Lowlands Scotland was entering the
modern age. Powerful nobles such as John of the Isles were able to
rule their own territories often without royal interference because

they had developed small independent kingdoms of their own. These tribal loyalties actually often replaced national patriotism or national commitment.

When Scottish monarchs attempted to garner control of state policy into their own hands, they were effectively challenging the power of the nobles and the whole structure of clan alliances that had been the basis of Scottish political power for hundreds of years. Their challenge to feudal relations was not the only one posed during the century. Feudal relationships were best suited to a largely agrarian economic system, such as that existing in Scotland during the earlier Middle Ages. The lack of national feeling was perhaps concomitant with the reduced need for national governmental structure. As the economy of Scotland grew and as the burghs began to develop international commerce, the need for strong centralized authority and consistent governmental practice was keenly felt.

By the fifteenth century the distinction among royal, baronial, or ecclesiastical burghs was beginning to be conscientiously drawn. The royal burgesses, who held their burghs as tenants of the king, felt themselves superior to the baronial or ecclesiastical burgesses, who derived their authority from less important sources. During the fifteenth century, however, generally all burghs prospered as part of "the growing importance of the new Third Estate." [17] While still subject to the intrusion of foreign authority, they shared in the general urban growth that permeated Europe at the end of the Middle Ages. Part of their development was due to their growing importance as sources of commerce. Although subject to the vicissitudes of war and baronial or royal displeasure, the burghs served as the major commodity exchange centers for wool and cloth products, a key export during the late fourteenth and fifteenth centuries. During the 1450s Edinburgh, for instance, controlled almost two thirds of Scotland's export. The growth in importance of the burgesses was not due solely to their role in international trade. Many of the individuals themselves had acquired sufficient personal wealth and power to be important men nationwide. They were especially important to governmental policy. Throughout the fifteenth century monarchs did not hesitate to borrow large sums from the burgesses to finance wars, marriages, and personal indulgences. For example, in 1457, the burgesses of Edinburgh loaned James II well over 225 marks. The very fact that the king

could depend on the burgh for money when he needed it made
town leaders an ever more important force in the formation of
national policy.

Of course, the growth of the towns did not completely undermine
rural political authority. The powerful nobles, owners of estates,
made a strong effort to maintain the relationship between authority
and land. The basis of much baronial power was the Scottish
peasant. Sometimes betrayed by his clan or national leaders, the
peasant still remained strongly committed to Scottish interests. He
was often able to eke out only a subsistence standard of living
through shared labor and resources. His land might be reduced to
mud by the feet of invading armies, and his crops might be
destroyed by either the enemy or his allies. Adding to his difficulties
was the tendency for the feudal nobles to try to consolidate their
lands at the expense of the farmers. Although a key aspect in any
feudal relationship is keeping the peasant tied to the soil so that he
may fullfill his feudal obligations, many nobles were dispossessing
their farmers. The eviction was often designed to increase the lord's
income. Tenants paid their rents at the beginning of a rental term.
When they were evicted, their rent became the property of the
landlord, who was then free to rent out the land again. Unfortunately, peasants were also often unsure precisely who their lords
were. The seizure of baronial lands by the crown, such as that which
occurred in 1450 when James II moved against the Livingstons,
must have made tenancy a complicated matter indeed. The acts of
revocation, such as that passed by Parliament in 1455, not only
aroused the ire of the nobles but once again placed lands previously
in baronial hands back into the possession of the crown.

As Scotland made the transition from an agrarian to a mercantile
economy, massive changes were slowly being wrought in the social
structure of the country. The old feudal relationships were breaking
down. In their stead, national loyalties and a mercantile economy
grew up as concomitants to the developing importance of the burghs
and the growing power of the burgesses.

Such were the conditions of Henryson's world: Political intrigue,
internal dissension, clerical corruption, and a rapidly changing
economic and social system. He could not avoid being influenced by
political and social conditions and responding to them in his poetry.
Yet political and social polemic is not the substance of Henryson's
work. He sees social abuses and abhors them; but he does not
attempt to promulgate a specific political or social doctrine. Instead,

Henryson views social and political events in the broader context of *caritas*. It is his broad sympathy for human nature and love of mankind that infuses his political doctrines and historical perspectives.

CHAPTER 2

Henryson and Literary Tradition

ALTHOUGH the brilliance of Henryson's poetry is the result of his individual genius, two earlier—and sometimes contradictory—literary traditions have been recognized as major influences on his work. On the one hand, there was the powerful attraction of the developing Southern tradition, a relatively modern and sophisticated movement at the time that Henryson started to write. A less aristocratic and somewhat less learned set of conventions made up the tradition of native Scots verse, an influence more pervasive in Henryson's poetry than generally recognized. In addition to these two major influences, elements of the literature of France and Italy also appear in Henryson's poems.

I *Chaucer and the South*

Henryson's indebtedness to the Southern literary tradition, so closely identified with Chaucer that it is often called the Chaucerian tradition, has been extensively examined and hotly debated. The arguments have ranged from G. Gregory Smith's statement that "the North deliberately put itself to school" in following Chaucerian models [1] to Florence Ridley's assertion of Henryson's independence by showing "how misleading 'Scots Chaucerian,' with its connotations of dependency, really is." [2] Those who emphasize Henryson's debt to Chaucer point to his direct references to *Troilus and Criseyde* in the prologue of *The Testament of Cresseid*, his metrical borrowings, his use of allegory, the nature of his humor, and his "grave eloquence" [3] which he putatively learned from Chaucer. Those who stress Henryson's individuality draw attention to the native Scots tradition strongly evident in his work, the differences in style and tone between his work and Chaucer's, his knowledge of the literatures of France and Italy, and the effects of his own talent which earn him an independent place in literary history. [4]

There can be no doubt that Henryson was influenced by some of the same elements of Southern literary tradition which influenced Chaucer. J. A. Burrow has attempted to analyze the characteristics of the late fourteenth-century literary milieu in England, which he designates as the Ricardian tradition.[5] Burrow has found elements of style, narrative technique, and philosophy which are common to Chaucer, Gower, Langland, and the Gawain Poet. Chaucer developed from this literary tradition and in turn contributed to it through his work. If it is understood that Henryson was influenced by this same tradition and therefore by Chaucer as the outstanding representative of the tradition, some of the difficulties which have given rise to the debate about Chaucer's influence on Henryson will vanish. Chaucer was indeed an influence but primarily as the exemplar of the fourteenth-century tradition of the South. Excepting those instances when Henryson makes direct reference to Chaucer, we can understand a good portion of his debt in terms of the influence of the more general Ricardian tradition of England. Some of the majors points of contact between Henryson and this tradition include verse forms, diction, irony, literary realism, and allegory.

Henryson owes the Chaucerian tradition so much in his use of verse forms that G. Gregory Smith suggests that he "is one of the forerunners of the band of poets who broke with the older habits of Northern verse and established that more or less artificial style which, expressed in a language modified to its own purposes, ruled for over a century." [6] Although Henryson makes more use of native traditions than Smith recognized, there is no doubt that in his use of metric patterns and stanzaic forms, he came under the influence of "worthie Chaucer." The use of rhyme royal in *The Testament of Cresseid* is to be expected as part of the general debt to *Troilus and Criseyde*. Cresseid's complaint and that of Orpheus are written in the six-line stanza of Chaucer's "Anelida and Arcite." Fewer critics have noted that many of the *Morall Fabillis* are written in this same stanza, a possible indication that their date of composition followed *The Testament*.

Although Henryson tends to be more concise than Chaucer,[7] he has a direct and pervasive debt to the Southern tradition in matters of rhetorical tone and literary technique. A portion of this debt appears in his diction. Although not as substantially influenced as Dunbar, occasionally Henryson too uses the "aureate" diction which became a hallmark of Chaucer's "followers." Defined by

Stephen Hawes, an acknowledged disciple of Chaucer, as the use of
"termes eloquent . . . Electynge wordes whiche are expedyent /
In Latyn or in Englysshe after the entent," [8] aureate diction soon
developed into a series of rhetorical formulae and stock phrases.
Although closely associated with the school of Chaucer, its origin is
much more complex, and, as we shall see, it had a strong hold on
the Scots tradition through other sources. [9]

Whatever their source, there is no doubt that aureate conventions exercised a strong influence on much Scots poetry. Their
effects are clearly evident in the following passage from Dunbar's
Goldyn Targe:

> O reverend Chaucere, rose of rhethoris all,
> As in oure tong ane flour imperiall
> That raise in Britane evir, quho redis rycht,
> Thou beris of makeris the tryumph riall;
> Thy fresch anamalit termes celicall
>   This mater could illumynit have full brycht . . . .
> ....
> O morall Gower, and Ludgate laureate,
> Your sugurit lippis and tongis aureate
>   Bene to oure eris cause of grete delyte;
> Your angel mouthis most mellifluate
> Oure rude language has clere illumynate. . . .
>
>   (ll. 253–58, 262–66)

The high proportion of elegant Latin and French cognates creates a
tone markedly different from what is most often found in Henryson's work. However, Henryson occasionally writes a more aureate
passage, such as the opening lines of *Orpheus and Eurydice*, which
contain a definition of nobility:

> The nobilnes and grit magnificens
> of prince and lord, quhai list to magnifie,
> his ancestre and lineall discens
> Suld first extoll, and his genolegie,
> So that his harte he mycht inclyne thairby
> The more to vertew and to worthiness . . . .

Similar passages are found in "The Complaint of Orpheus," the
digression on music, and in the introductory passages of *The
Testament of Cresseid*. Yet, in this respect, Henryson is generally

acknowledged to be the least indebted to Chaucer of all the Scots Chaucerians. Even in the most aureate passages of his poetry, few of his words seem self-consciously elegant or simply inappropriate and pretentious as they sometimes do in the poetry of Dunbar. The relative "ease" of Henryson's vocabulary is in part because most of his words were already well-established in the language before he used them.[10] Proportionately, in fact, Henryson's use of the Southern aureate vocabulary is slight. Most of his language is derived from common Southern literary English or spoken and literary Scots. If this means that Henryson's poetry has a technical interest different from that of Dunbar, it also means that he forged a poetic language closer to the patterns of colloquial speech. Any age that values the technique of Donne over that of Milton will always prefer Henryson to Dunbar. Although the aureate influence of the Chaucerian and Ricardian tradition is present in Henryson's vocabulary, its effect is minimal.

Another rhetorical device that Henryson may have borrowed from Chaucer is a particularly concise gift of irony. Wood suggests that it is Henryson's "most Chaucerian gift" and that it appears in "his power of turning from pathos to humour, from the sublime to the ridiculous," [11] in a single line or short phrase. In Chaucer, these terse ironic comments appear primarily in the descriptions of the characters in the general prologue of *The Canterbury Tales*. The Prioress, for example, speaks French "ful faire and fetisly" but "After the schole of Stratford atte Bowe" (l. 125), a comment on her pretensions to sophistication. The Sergeant of the Law is a great "purchasour": "Nowher so bisy a man as he ther nas, / And yet he semed bisier than he was" (ll. 321–22), an ironic and revealing comment on his self-image as a man of great affairs. This type of characteristic Chaucerian irony appears in other descriptive details in the portraits of the Cook, the Wife of Bath, and the Monk, to name only a few. Jill Mann has recently emphasized the importance of Chaucerian irony and ambivalence by demonstrating how Chaucer uses it in portraits drawn from medieval estates satire.[12]

Henryson uses such ironic touches to good effect. Sometimes he uses ironic understatement, as in "The Trial of the Fox" in which Lawrence, the fox, taunts the wolf, who is a clerical advisor to the lion, a symbol for the king. Deceived by the fox's arguments, the lion drolly agrees "The grettest clerkis ar nocht the wyssest men" (l. 225). The irony is double-edged. Sometimes it also appears in his use of humorous proverbs and is occasionally even self-effacing, as in his digression on music in *Orpheus*. Having launched into a technical discussion of music, Henryson abruptly corrects himself and changes direction:

> Off sic musik to wryt I do bot doit,
> Thairfoir of this mater a stray I lay,
> For in my life I cowth nevir sing a noit. . . .
>
>   (ll. 24042)

Henryson is also capable of tragic irony of the sort that we find in *Troilus and Criseyde* when Troilus ascends into the eighth sphere, looks down, and laughs. It is a vital part of the most touching scene in *The Testament of Cresseid*. After Cresseid's appearance has been disfigured by leprosy, she and Troilus meet on a street. Prince Troilus looks directly in her face and she casts both her eyes upon him. Yet Henryson shows that their recognition of each other is only vague: "And nevertheless not ane ane uther knew" (l. 518). This same sort of tragic irony appears in *Orpheus and Eurydice*, a tale that Henryson must have found irresistible. After his great effort to win Eurydice, Orpheus looks back "blindit . . . with grit effectioun" and loses his lady. Henryson laments with him because his lady "that he had bocht so deir, / Bot for a luk so sone wis tane him fro" (ll. 396–97).

Whether Henryson's irony is specifically Chaucerian or not is open to debate. J. A. Burrow suggests that a mark of all the great poets of the late fourteenth century is that their sense of humor is their "most intimate and persuasive quality." [13] There is certainly no doubt that Henryson could have become aware of the value of such irony from any of a number of sources, but we may assume that he was most familiar with this technique from the Chaucerian tradition. It is one of the qualities of late fourteenth-century English poetry that he blends with native traditions of humor in a masterly fashion.

Henryson's techniques of literary realism may also show Chaucerian influence. Certainly Chaucer has generally been appreciated for his comic and realistic manner. [14] The extent of this realism appears best in his lifelike character portraits. The Knight's dirty smock, the Pardoner's hair, and the Miller's drunkenness are all details that fit in with the level of the dialogue and the social class of these characters on the pilgrimage. Indeed, it is easily believable that Harry Bailey and the Man of Law are drawn from life. [15] However, most of Chaucer's followers in the fifteenth century were not interested in imitating this aspect of his work. They were more concerned about Chaucer's allegorical method than his realism. If Henryson borrowed Chaucer's techniques of realism, he was drawing on an aspect of Chaucer's work often ignored by his contemporaries.

Henryson's realism in character portrayal is most clearly evident in *The Testament of Cresseid*. Stearns has explained Henryson's use of Aristotelian psychology in the final scene between Troilus and Cresseid. The subconscious recognition of Cresseid by Troilus, far from being a piece of literary chicanery, is clearly based on principles in Aristotle's *De anima* and *De memoria*. The function of the reproductive imagination operates when Troilus sees the leper woman, actually Cresseid, and is moved to give her a bag of gold because "with ane blenk it come into his thocht/ That he sumtime hir face befoir had sene" (ll. 499–500). There is no contradiction when Henryson informs us that they did not know one another. Stearns terms Henryson's use of Aristotelian psychology "the most sophisticated that I have discovered." [16]

The use of Aristotelian psychology is not restricted to this poem. The allegorical *Orpheus and Eurydice* focuses primarily on the relationship of the appetitive and rational parts of the mind. While the interpretation is traditional, the poem is, in one sense, an extended psychological treatise. Without an understanding of medieval theories about how the mind functions, the allegory in the poem is lost. Granted that certain motivations of characters, such as Eurydice's fleeing Aristaeus, may seem artificial and inconsistent to moderns, the major thrust of the poem is psychological. Through the allegory, Henryson's interest in his characters is quite evident.

One of the most remarkably rich portions of Henryson's work for characterization is *The Morall Fabillis*. As in *Orpheus*, Henryson's modernity in character portrayal may be easy to overlook because of the obviously didactic nature of the poetry. But Henryson has endowed his animal protagonists with realistic elements. The two mice in their fable have individual characteristics that reflect both their social classes and their sense of competition. Henryson creates a masterful portrait of benevolent concern in "The Preaching of the Swallow." The psychology of the bully and the hesitant humility of the righteous are also clearly portrayed in "The Wolf and the Lamb." At his best, Henryson may be favorably compared with any writer of the Middle Ages in his use of contemporary psychology and his shrewd observation of his fellowman.

Another aspect of Henryson's realism is his depiction of social

classes, which is most apparent in *The Morall Fabillis*. The
characters are drawn from all levels of Scottish society. Nobility is
represented—just as on the Canterbury pilgrimage—but Henryson's perspective on nobility differs from Chaucer's. In his
description of the upper classes, Chaucer largely accepted the ideals
of the chivalric code and paid lip service to the code of
knighthood.[17] Henryson's portraits of the nobility are far less
idealistic. Henryson's use of the wolf as a symbol for both nobility
and clergy gives a clear indication of his perspective on two of the
estates. Indeed, in "The Trial of the Fox" it is the wolf who
represents the clergy in Henryson's attempt to prove the dullness of
some clergymen. The wolf also appears as a representative of men of
law, "mychty men" and "men of heretege," all of whom are "fals
pervertaris of the lawis" (l. 100) in "The Wolf and the Lamb." In this
fable the wily wolf greedily devours the lamb for ancient and
suspect offenses, acting in much the same way as the lawless Boyds
and Livingstons did in fifteenth-century Scotland. Henryson's
wolves, both clerical and noble, are associated with social pretense,
arrogance, stupidity, cruelty, avarice, and injustice. The poet's
solution for coping with both the wolfish nobility and the avaricious
clergy is a strong king,[18] and his social idealism appears clearly in his
attitudes toward monarchy. Like many of his countrymen, peasants
as well as intellectuals, Henryson must have looked to the Lion, a
figure of wisdom and justice in "The Trial of the Fox," as a remedy
for social ills.

In the portrayal of his other animal characters, there is no doubt
that Henryson draws from all classes of society. He represents the
urban upper middle class in the burgess mouse, the lower clergy in
the sheep in "The Sheep and the Dog," and simple countrymen in
"The Fox, the Wolf, and the Husbandman." Instances of social
injustice are always the result of acts by the unjust courts or nobles
against the lower classes. If the Parson is the ethical standard of *The
Canterbury Tales*, the Swallow and the Sheep usually embody the
moral standards of Henryson's *Morall Fabillis*.

Besides drawing his characters from all levels of society,
Henryson proves himself a realist in his use of detailed description.
In "The Preaching of the Swallow" he provides an accurate
description of the flax industry, leading some scholars to believe
that he must have had a special interest in the business: [19]

> This Lint rypit, the carle pullit the lyne,
> Ripplit the bowis, and in beitis fett,

> It steipit in the burne, and dryit syne,
> And with a bittill knokit it, and bett,
> Syne scutchit it weill, and heclit it in the flett;
> His wyffe it span, and twane it into freid,
> Off quhilk the foular nettis war maid indeid.

> (ll. 204–10)

This detailed description of technology is unusual in medieval poetry.

Henryson is just as adept at drawing physical detail of his characters. The very nature of the best fable limits the amount of physical realism we might expect. Even so, in "The Sheep and the Dog," there is detailed description of the members of a fifteenth-century consistory court. A realistic description of fifteenth-century ladies' dress is found in the allegorical "The Garmont of Gud Ladeis." But the outstanding example of physical description is to be found in *The Testament of Cresseid*. Although Cresseid is described as the *a per se* of Troy and Greece, and Troilus is portrayed simply as a noble youth, the description of Cresseid's disease provides the utmost in naturalistic detail:

> 'Thy cristall, ene mingit with blude I mak,
> Thy voice sa cleir unplesand hoir and hace,
> Thy lustre lyre ouirspred with spottis blak,
> And lumpis haw appeirand in thy face!

> (ll. 337–41)

Henryson has provided such detail that in 1841 Sir J. A. Y. Simpson was able to identify Cresseid's disease as elephantiasis.[20] Henryson's detailed description is in the same tradition as the vivid portraits of the general prologue of *The Canterbury Tales*.

Allegory plays a major role in Henryson's poetry. Henryson could have become familiar with allegorical techniques through his own religious training or his acquaintance with continental literary traditions. But allegory is such an integral part of the Chaucerian tradition that Henryson might very likely have learned about the broader applications of allegorical techniques from his English precursors. Although now considered a literary mode, allegory is listed as a figure in Bede's *De Schematibus et tropis*.[21] Its role in the literature of the later Middle Ages has engendered controversy. It is obviously a controlling mode in works such as the *Gesta Romanorum* and *Piers Plowman*, but D. W. Robertson's argument that *The Canterbury Tales* must be read as Christian allegory illustrating the

doctrine of charity has sparked significant debate.[22] Allegorical
interpretations from the twelfth through fifteenth centuries developed from a tradition of biblical explication that extended back
through Origen and Philo, but the primary influences on the period
were, among others, the works of St. Augustine, Hugh of St. Victor,
and Robert Holcot.[23] Hugh of St. Victor distinguished three
different levels at which Holy Scripture may be interpreted—
history, allegory, and tropology—while other writers added a fourth
level of interpretation—the anagogical.[24] Perhaps one of the
clearest expositions of the four-fold level of interpretation is to be
found in Dante's *Convivio*, where the method is applied to secular
writings as well.[25]

Dante begins with the literal level, "the level which does not
extend beyond the letter of the fictive discourse, which is what the
fables of the poets are." [26] Interpretation at this level is simply
understanding the course of narrative events, the surface plot. This
level is basic, because the *sentence* or spiritual meaning follows
directly from it. The second level is the allegorical, sometimes also
called the typological. Dante says of this level that it "is hidden
under the cloak of these fables, a truth disguised under a beautiful
lie. . . ." [27] While Dante chooses to interpret this level in a more
secular fashion, he notes that it has a different meaning for
theologians. In more traditional religious commentaries, this level
of interpretation involves using events from Scripture to illustrate
how biblical or fictional characters prefigured or imitated Christ in
their actions. In its broadest application, the allegorical level would
also be interpreted as referring to the church and its mission. In the
traditional religious sense, this level of interpretation was available
only to those with superior learning and advanced moral natures.
The third level that Dante describes is the moral or, as Hugh calls
it, the tropological level. At this stage, a work is read for the insights
it can give into everyday moral conduct. Tropological interpretations are designed to provide readers with sound morals to apply to
their own day-to-day existence. The final level of reading in
scriptual interpretation was the province of those who had reached a
very high level of moral perfection: The anagogical level Dante
defines as pertaining to "the supreme things belonging to eternal
glory. . . ." [28] This level provided revelations of God's glory and
His ultimate plan for man and the universe.

This method of interpretation can be illustrated by the story of
Job. Read at the literal level, it is simply the tale of the misfortunes

of an ancient chieftain. But typological interpretation shows that Job prefigures Christ: Just as Satan was given power over Christ in the wilderness, he had power over Job. Job resisted the temptations of pride and despair just as Christ resisted the temptations of food and political power that Satan set in his way. At the tropological level, we find that Job's patience and trust in the face of adversity may be interpreted as qualities that every man should emulate in his own life. Finally, an anagogical reading of this tale will reveal God's grace and glory. Job is redeemed by God's love for all of his creations. At the fourth level, the story of Job is to be read as a tale of love and forgiveness.

This approach to literary and philosophical analysis was not new either to Christianity or the Middle Ages. In a more general form, it dates from the sixth century B.C.[29] and is to be found in the works of Plato, who may have intended that the *Republic* be read at different levels by those with different abilities. Its careful systematization, however, Robertson considers characteristic of the Gothic period.[30] The spread of this multilevel reading was encouraged by rhetoricians such as Geoffrey de Vinsauf who suggested that *sententia* "may lend splendor to the work." [31] Robertson believes that its influence on literary and social thinking was pervasive in the Middle Ages.[32] He attempts to show that this type of analysis is valid not just for biblical tales or obviously didactic works but that it may be fruitfully applied to the *Roman de la Rose* and *The Canterbury Tales*. He views the Canterbury pilgrimage as a journey to the Celestial City, and he argues that Chaucer's pilgrims expound the nature of Christian charity. He concedes that all four levels of interpretation may not appear in a given work, and that it may not be necessary to insist on identifying separate anagogical or typological levels. However, Robertson argues that for medieval people general techniques of secular verse were seen as similar to those of Scripture: the teaching of a specific lesson through an appeal to the intellect against a background of commonly accepted dogma. Although Robertson's analyses have produced some curious readings of certain of *The Canterbury Tales*, in particular some of the *fabliaux*, broader applications of exegetical method have important implications for anyone who would understand the art of Robert Henryson.

Whether allegory is to be considered simply an artistic figure or the basis of a whole pattern of thought, there is no doubt that it profoundly influenced Henryson's aesthetic. Henryson's use of

allegory has been so extensively analyzed that it has adversely
affected his reputation. Henryson's insistence on affixing a "Moralitas" to the *Fabillis* and *Orpheus and Eurydice*, his position as
schoolmaster, and the preaching tone of some of his poems have led
critics to talk about his "stern morality," "serious character, and
steadiness of purpose." [33]

Henryson's own preference for allegorical interpretations is
supported by his theory on the nature of teaching in poetry. He is
always concerned about drawing the "morall sueit sentence / Out of
the scitell dyt of poetre" (prologue to the *Fabillis*, ll. 12–13).
Without proper "sentence," poetry is valueless or even pernicious.
Henryson may even express doubt through one of his characters
about the possibility that poetry can have the desired moral effect.
The prologue of "The Lion and the Mouse" is a dream vision in
which the poet sees Aesop. After welcoming him and addressing
him as "fader" and "maistir venerable," the poet asks him to "tell a
pretty feble / Concludand with a gude moralitie." Aesop's response
is startling. He is unwilling to tell a fable "For quhat is worth to tell
a fenyeit taill / Quhen haill preiching may no thing now availl" (ll.
69–70), but eventually he is persuaded to relate the fable of the lion
and the mouse. It would be fallacious to conclude that his opinion
on the value of fables accurately reflects Henryson's merely on the
basis of this line. Yet, other proof of Henryson's commitment to
morality in art is available. Besides his constant general emphasis on
"gud Moralitie" in *The Morall Fabillis*, he uses a dramatized
sermon in "The Preaching of the Swallow." Moreover, in some of
his poems he handles themes that were the standard subject matter
of medieval preaching and exegesis. [34] The legend of Orpheus and
Eurydice was a vital part of Christian thought in the commentaries
on Boethius written by William of Conches and Nicholas Trivet,
whom Henryson follows in the "Moralitas" of his poem. He uses a
prayer as the basis for "Ane Prayer for the Pest." "The Thre Deid
Pollis" and "The Ressoning betuix Aige and Yowth" employ the
memento mori motif of medieval religious lyrics, such as "Penitence
for Wasted Life." The logic of "The Prais of Aige" is obviously
theological: the poet counts himself lucky to be growing old because
he is that much nearer to heaven. "The Thre Deid Pollis" and "The
Ressoning betuix Deth and Man" are firmly grounded in the earlier
didactic tradition that produced "A Disputation Bitwene God a Man
and the Deuel" and "The Debate Between the Body and the Soul."
"The Want of Wyse Men" is a theme treated in numerous

fourteenth century sermons in John Bromyard's *Summa praedican-tium.* Henryson's use of allegory throughout his poetry and his concomitant belief in the essentially didactic nature of poetry show that he is within the mainstream of medieval thought and may possibly demonstrate yet another debt to the Ricardian poets.

Henryson might have been influenced by other Chaucerian conventions as well. In his list of characteristics of later Chaucerian poets, H. S. Bennett suggests that the prologue and dream-vision conventions were often borrowed by Chaucer's followers.[35] G. Gregory Smith and Stearns have shown that certain aspects of the portraits of the gods in *The Testament of Cresseid* may show Chaucer's influence, and it seems likely that Henryson may have known both *The Romaunt of the Rose* and "L'envoy a Scogan." [36] Of course, Henryson himself tells us that he was inspired in *The Testament* by Chaucer's *Troilus and Criseyde.* But generalizations about Chaucer's influence that extend beyond Henryson's own comments or direct verbal parallels must be made cautiously, if at all. Henryson's broad knowledge of medieval and even ancient literature makes it difficult to assert that Chaucer could have been his only source for any literary technique or body of ideas.

The influence of Chaucer on Henryson can best be evaluated by emphasizing the tradition that had earlier influenced Chaucer himself. Although Chaucer contributed substantially to the mainstream of English literature, he did not completely change it. The same literary forces that influenced Chaucer were at work on Henryson. As modified after Chaucer, the Ricardian tradition remained the major force in literary expression. As Speirs suggests, "Chaucer and Henryson wrote in general in traditions which were common to both; it is therefore not always easy to estimate the indebtedness of the latter to the former." [37]

II   *The Scottish Tradition*

Though strongly influenced by the Chaucerian English tradition, Henryson was equally affected by the native Scots literary tradition. Scottish literature in the fifteenth century was highly developed, and the language itself reflects this degree of sophistication. A proper understanding of Henryson's poetry must take account of its oral nature, and understanding the aural appeal of Henryson's poetry demands a brief explanation of the salient characteristics of Middle Scots. Excluding Gaelic, fifteenth-century Middle Scots had developed from the Northumbrian dialect of Old English. While numerous differences existed between it and Chaucerian Middle English, the spoken language was still very close to the speech of Northern England.[38]

Although numerous dialects of Middle Scots existed, two major branches of the language affect the literature. On the one hand, there was spoken Middle Scots, the composite of dialects of Highland and Lowland speakers, subject to the change and regional variation that affect all living languages. On the other hand, there was literary Middle Scots. Firmly grounded in the spoken tongue, literary Middle Scots also contained aureate terms and neologisms which would likely not have appeared in the spoken dialects. The following passage from Dunbar illustrates this aspect of the literary language:

> Hale, sterne superne, hale in eterne
>   In Godis sicht to schyne:
> Lucerne in derne for to discerne
>   Be glory and grace devyne:
> Hodiern, modern, sempitern,
>   Angelicall regyne,
> Our tern inferne for to dispern,
>   Helpe, rialest rosyne.

It is obvious that this and other passages from Dunbar are too ornate and Latinate in their vocabulary to reflect the patterns of everyday speech, except under the most restricted and artificial circumstances. The extravagant nature of such poetry has led to speculation that literary Middle Scots was a dialect created expressly for literary use.[39]

While the language of Dunbar and Douglas differed significantly from spoken Middle Scots, Henryson's lauguage draws extensively on the more common rhythms and diction of speech.[40] More than any other Makar, he uses the language of the countryside. But for a modern reader to gain access to Henryson's language he must gain an understanding of the characteristics of Middle Scots orthography and pronunciation.

Recent studies, particularly those by Adam J. Aitken, have helped to dispel some of the confusion surrounding attempts to reconstruct the pronunciation of Middle Scots.[41] Although it will not be possible to explore in detail the impressive discoveries by modern linguists, a brief sketch of the Middle Scots system of pronunciation can provide helpful insights. The vowel structure of Middle Scots has been complicated by both the general shift in English and Scottish vowels that was occurring during the fifteenth century and by earlier attempts to pronounce Middle Scots with reference to the vowel system of Chaucerian Middle English. Aitken has analyzed nineteen distinct vowel sounds for Middle Scots around 1450: [42]

	Spelling	Pronunciation
Long vowels	yi, y	ei
	ei, ey,	
	e, ee	i:
	ai, ay, e, a	e:
	oi, oy, o	o:
	ou, ow, ull	
	ul, ol	u:
	ui, uy, wi,	
	wy, o	∅
Diphthongs	ay, ai	ɛi
	a-e, a	e:
	oi, oy	oi
	ui, uy, wi	
	wy	ui
	ie	i:
	a, al, all	a:
	ou, ow, ol	
	oll	ou
	ew	iu
Short vowels	i, y	ɪ
	e	ɛ
	a	a
	o	o
	u,	u
	(sometimes o)	

In addition to these vowel equivalencies, a reader of Henryson must be aware of the consonant system. For the most part, consonants are pronounced as they are in Chaucerian Middle English; detailed information is available from a variety of sources. But there are some significant differences between Henryson's consonant structure and Chaucer's. Some of the most important are as follow: [43] (1) ch is often substituted for gh; (2) mb is often represented by m or mm; (3) th is represented by d or dd; (4) initial h is frequently dropped; (5) ng is often represented by m; (6) quh is equivalent to wh; (7) initial and final sh appears as s in stressed syllables; (8) final d appears as t.

A reader of Henryson's poetry can expect to find unfamiliar spellings of the plural endings ("is" or "ys"), Northern forms of the present participle (ending in "and") and unfamiliar endings on strong verbs in second-person plural. He may also expect to meet postnoun modifiers and more extensive examples of functional shift. Any reader familiar with Chaucer's syntax, however, will find little that is insurmountable in the grammar of Henryson.

There are major differences in metric and stanzaic techniques between the Scottish verse traditions and the tradition of Chaucer. Alliterative verse conventions flourished in the North and exercised a major influence on the poetry of Henryson. Even though we have already seen that he borrows certain of his metric and stanzaic patterns from Chaucer and the Southern tradition, he employs techniques of alliteration in all of his verse, no matter how Southern the surface structure seems. Perhaps his use of alliterative devices is most evident in "Sum Practysis of Medecyne": [44]

> Guk, guk, gud day, ser, gaip quhill ye get it,
> Sic greting may gane weill gud laik in your hude
> ye wald deir me, I trow, becauss I am dottit,
> To ruffill me with a ryme; na, ser, be the rude,
> your saying I haif a sene. . . .

>   (ll. 1–5)

Although "Sum Practysis" is unique in the Henryson canon for many aspects of its structure, tone, and diction, its use of alliteration only emphasizes a technique that appears in other Henryson poems. Alliterative patterns are an important part of the ornamentation of *The Morall Fabillis*, as these lines from "The Trial of the Fox" illustrate:

> The Bull, the Beir, the Bugill, and the Bair,
> The Woodwyss, Wildcat, and the Wild Wolfyne,
> The Hard Bak Hutchoun and the Hyrpilland Hair,
> Bayth Ottour, Aip, and Pennytt Porcapyne. . . .

>   (ll. 106–9)

The alliterating *b*'s, *w*'s, *h*'s, and *p*'s in the stressed syllables reveal Henryson's debt to the older Scottish verse tradition despite the influences of Chaucerian poetry in *The Testament of Cresseid.*

Henryson's lack of aureation in his style gives a key to the structure of his poetic vocabulary. He excludes neither French nor Latin elements, and words such as "similitude," "celsitude," "armony," and "fenyeit" appear in his vocabulary particularly in tales that use the jargon of Scots law or ecclesiastical affairs. But the effect of this element of Henryson's vocabulary is sharply reduced when his poetry is compared with that of Dunbar or Douglas. His Latin vocabulary is probably based on earlier church Latin or even the living Latin of Scottish commerce.[44] His French lexicon is derived in good part from the Central French that had permeated the Scottish vocabulary in the fourteenth century. The third element of Henryson's diction is the native Northumbrian lexicon that makes up the grammatical and lexical framework of Middle Scots.

The mixing of these three elements of the Middle Scots vocabulary results in a less "poetic" diction. While Henryson's vocabulary is less mannered than Dunbar's and is more nearly similar to what we believe to have been the popular speech, he is capable of varying style to meet the demands of his art. He employs the rhetoric of the law courts in "The Sheep and the Dog"; the rhetoric of the pulpit in "The Swallow"; and the hortatory tone of medieval exegesis in the *Orpheus.* His diction is appropriate to his variation of style. If Henryson thinks like a countryman, he is even more likely to speak like one. Although his poetry lacks interest for the virtuosity of word choice that we find in the work of Dunbar, his use of plain style has made his poetry more generally comprehensible and, as a result, more widely accessible.

The influence of the native Scots linguistic forms and meters was complemented by major Scottish influences on technique and philosophy. Ironically, two of his most "Chaucerian" characteristics, his literary realism and his sense of humor, show the influence of native Scots traditions. Henryson's realism has already been illustrated in *The Morall Fabillis* and *The Testament of Cresseid.* His interest in realistic character portrayal does indeed show the strong influence of Southern literary forces. But his excellence in seasonal descriptions is apparently due to native influences. Most often praised are passages in the "Preaching of the Swallow" and in *The Testament of Cresseid.* Even though much of his language is

conventional, Henryson takes great pains to describe the seasons in
the prologue to "The Preaching." He talks about Summer depicted
"with his jolye mantill grene," Harvest, represented by Ceres and
Bacchus, and Winter portrayed as Austern Eolus. But intermingled
with the conventional descriptions of seasonal figures and seasonal
change are concrete elements such as the description of sleet and
frost in winter. The growth and processing of hemp in July are
described in detail.

Henryson's masterpiece among seasonal descriptions, however,
is found in the prologue to *The Testament of Cresseid*. In the first
line he comments on the appropriateness of "Ane doolie sessoun to
ane cairful dyte." He then proceeds to describe in masterful detail
exactly the "doolie sessoun" that is his setting. The time is early
April, the poet "within myne oratour," when "Titan had his bemis
bright / Withdrawin doun, and sylit inder cure . . ." (ll. 9–10). The
night is cold:

> The northin wind had purifyit the air
> And sched the mistie cloudis fra the sky;
> The froist freisit, the blastis bitterly
> Fra Pole Artick come quhisling loud and schill. . . .
>
> (ll. 17–20)

Just the opposite of Chaucer's beautiful spring day for the
pilgrimage, Henryson's cold Scottish April is just as vividly drawn.

T. F. Henderson has suggested that the influence of the Scottish
tradition of realistic seasonal description helped Henryson "at least
intermittently, to escape from the old hackneyed classical imagery." [45] Earlier Scottish literature indeed shows the effects of a
strong interest in accurately describing weather and seasonal
change. Like Henryson, Barbour emphasizes details relating to
climate. In book 9 of *The Bruce*, he describes a battle fought at
Martinmas, "Quhen snaw had helit all the land" (l. 127). His
description of spring in book 16 shows his ability to mix conventional images with realistic detail (ll. 63–70). The fifteenth-century
mock-romance *Rauf Coilyear* provides a masterful depiction of a
"Scottish storm": [46]

> The wind blew out of the east stiflie and sture,
> the drift durandlie draif in mony deep dell.
> Sa fiercely fra the firmament, sa fellounlie it fure
> there micht na folk hald na fure on the heich fell.
> In point they war to perish, they proudest men and pure,

> in thae wichit wedderis there wist nane to dwell,
> Amang thae mirk mountains sa madlie they mer,
>> be it was prime of the day
>> sa wonder hard fure they
>> that ilk ane tuik ane seir way
>> and sperpellit full fer.
>
> Ithand wedderis of the east draif on sa fast
> it all to blaisterit and blew that thairin baid.
> Be they disserverit, sindrie midmorn was past.
>
> (ll. 16–29)

Equally striking seasonal portrayals are found in *The Forray of Gadderis* and in some of the ballads. Henryson's interest in visually concrete descriptions of seasonal settings is closely related to this tradition.

There are precedents in Scottish literature for Henryson's realism in character portrayal as well. Blind Harry's characterization of the dignified chivalry of William Wallace is tempered by his description of Wallace's grief over the death of his compatriot, John Graham. Although Barbour portrays Robert Bruce in terms of chivalric idealism, *The Bruce* contains other, more realistic depictions, such as that of Sir James Douglas:

> . . . he was nocht sa fair, that we
> Suld spek greatly of his beauty:
> In visage was he somedeal gray,
> And had blak hair, as I hear say;
> But of limbs he was weil made,
> With banes great and schuldoys braid.
> His body was weil made and large,
> As they that saw him said to me.
> When he was blyth, he was lufly,
> And meek and sweet in company:
> But wha in battle micht him see,
> All other countenance had he.
> And in spek lispit he some deal;
> But that sat him richt wonder weil;
> Til gude Ector of Troy micht he
> In many thingis likit be.
>
> (I, ll. 381–96)

Although firmly set in heroic grandeur, many of these traditional heroic figures share qualities with Henryson's animals. *The Antwyrs of Arthur, Rauf Coilyear,* and even some of the ballads also show the development of character in modern and realistic terms. Although Henryson's general techniques of characterication are the result of Ricardian influence, this native tradition may be crucial in individual instances.

There is no doubt that Henryson's use of ironic humor is indebted to the surpassing wit of *The Canterbury Tales*. But it is equally clear that he has a taste for hyperbolic and litotical lines "recognisable in Scottish humour to this day." [47] Rauf Coilyear's rough treatment of Charlemagne when the king visits his home and his own subsequent anxiety when he is thrown into the milieu of the court are a part of this tradition. Henryson's sense of humor is also related to the ironic twists and contrasts of *The Colkelbie Sow*, a fifteenth-century work containing three comic tales. One of the best examples of Henryson's use of this tradition appears in *The Morall Fabillis*. In "The Two Mice" the city mouse has invited her cousin to dinner after sampling the latter's stark country fare. In their meal they are interrupted by the spenser. Henryson's comment on their hasty leave-taking, "They tareit not to wesche, as I suppois . . ." (l. 134), is a masterpiece of litotes. The same sort of Scottish humor is evident in "The Cock and the Fox" when Sprowtok tries to stop Partlot's lamenting after Lawrence has taken Chantecleir. Not only does she suggest that Partlot leave off her lamenting, but she offers good reasons for giving no more thought to Chantecleir's plight: she accuses him of lust, pride, and sloth. The contrast between her accusation and Partlot's mourning is jolting indeed. This tone is most often associated with Henryson's satirical attack on undue pride, both in the *Fabillis* and other poems. This tone also appears in "The Ressoning betuix Aige and Yowth." A debate constructed around traditional rhetorical devices, the poem relates a confrontation between two allegorical characters. Yowth represents vitality, trust in the world, and pride. Aige who, like the Swallow, poses a warning, represents debilitation, skepticism, and wisdom. To Aige's advice "O yowth, thy flowris fedis fellone sone" (l. 5), Yowth can only answer with a vainglorious self-assurance:

> My Curage is of clene complexioun,
> My hairt is haill, my levar, & my splene;
> Thairfoir to reid this roll I haif no ressoun:
> O yowth be glaid in to thy flowris grene.

> (ll. 53–56)

There is no doubt that this ironic tone is in part developed from traditional Scottish humor.

Henryson shares an important bias of Scots poetry in favor of the rustic and the peasant. In the wars that marred the face of Scotland, it was the peasant who suffered most. When the barons warred on each other or the king, the peasants were the fodder for war's maw. It was their blood that stained the countryside and their farms and huts that were destroyed in the violent civil quarrels that broke the country's peace.

As Stearns suggests, Henryson's "warmth, tenderness, and compassion are reserved for the peasants." [48] He demonstrates a sympathy for the plight of the peasant, and he shows his respect for the peasant's humility, patience, and wisdom. His most impressive comments in praise of the peasantry are to be found in *The Morall Fabillis*. Henryson's awareness of the peasant's plight appears most strikingly in "The Wolf and the Lamb," where he singles out the Scottish nobility as the peasant's worst enemy. The tale concerns a wolf and a lamb who arrive at a well at the same time to get a drink. The wolf is angered by the lamb's presumption in being so bold as to drink at the same well and to pollute the wolf's drink with his "fowll slavering." Abashed, the lamb grants the wolf's superior force and asks the wolf to use "ressoun" in understanding the lamb's offense. Angered, the wolf refers to an old quarrel between himself and the lamb's father and uses that as an excuse to devour the lamb. Henryson's "Moralitas" clearly directs the reader's attention to the social implications of his tale. The lamb, he says, is "maill men, merchandis, and pure lauboureris." The wolf represents three kinds of men, "fals pervertaris of the lawis," "mychty men," and "men of heretege," all of whom pose major threats to the lower classes. He closes the poem with two prayers, one to the great lords to be less avaricious, and the other to God to "keip the lame, that is the Innocent, / fra wolffis byt, I mene extorteneiris . . ." (ll. 155–56).

Another traditional Scottish influence on Henryson appears in his theology. Long before the Reformation, Scottish literature had adopted a bluntness and independence in theological matters that foreshadowed Protestant attitudes. John Barbour is one of the earlier writers in Scotland who seem to be on terms of "informal intimacy with God (or the Devil)" [49] and are occasionally bold enough to argue with Him. Although Barbour does not mention angels or saints, he concludes that everything is firmly in God's hands:

> For in this warld, that is sa wyde
> Is nane determynat that sall
> Knaw thingis that ar for to fall:

> But God is off maist poweste,
> Reservyt till his majeste
> For to knaw, in his prescience
> Off alkyn tyme the mowence.
>
> *(The Bruce,* I, 128–34)

But his confidence in God's ways does not keep him or his hero from questioning God's actions. In several scenes, Bruce seeks God's help and immediate intervention almost in hortatory tones: Bruce directly invokes God's assistance before battle and, in book 5, makes vows to Him to return. This approach on the part of the protagonists serves to emphasize the lack of liturgical formality.

After Barbour, the most pronounced example of this theological directness is to be found in Henryson. In his characters' complaints to God, Henryson's straightforwardness foreshadows Presbyterian intimacy with God.[50] In Henryson's verse, there are two remarkable examples of direct address to God, the first of them in "The Sheep and the Dog." After the sheep has been robbed of his wool and has made a complaint that extends into the "Moralitas," Henryson concludes the poem with the sheep's direct plea to God for relief:

> . . . O Lord quhy slypis thow so lang
> Walk and descerne my caus groundit in richt
> ....
> Se thow nocht, Lord, this warld ourturnit is,
> As quha wald chenge gud gold in leid or tyn;
> The pure is pelit, the lord may do no miss;
> Now symony is haldin for no syn.
> ....
> Allace, Lord God, quhy tholis thow it so?
>
> (ll. 150–51, 162–65, 168)

The sheep's address to God is bold and disregards theological hierarchy. But even more striking is the way in which the lines question the purposes of divine Providence. Certainly orthodox theology would regard such a complaint with repugnance. It smacks of the first of the Seven Deadly Sins, Pride. To question divine Providence is to question God's purpose, and questions about God's wisdom or His purpose for the world often imply greater understanding on the part of the questioner. Since no human being can have greater knowledge than God, and since God is under no obligation to make His purpose known simply to satisfy man's intellectual curiosity, this questioning implies heretical intimacy and egotism.

This attitude extends into yet another poem. In "Ane Prayer for the Pest," Henryson's speaker again takes it upon himself to address God in the most direct manner. The prayer begins conventionally enough with an acknowledgment of God's power and might and the speaker's admission of his own guilt. In stanza 6, however, Henryson feels obliged to remind God of man's importance in His scheme of things: "Remmember, Lord, how deir thow hes us bocht, / That for us synnaris sched they pretius blude" (ll. 41–42). The speaker's further admission of his own ingratitude and sin is hardly a convincing melioration of the direct reminder to God about man's importance. The very mention of such a reminder implies that God is fallible, that He forgets like ordinary mortal men. This too seems direct and presumptuous in terms of late medieval theology.

Perhaps Henryson's respect for the peasant and his bluntness in theological matters may be due to what Wittig calls his "rustic philosophy." Although his *Fabillis* show a profound learning, Henryson seems to advocate common sense over abstruse philosophy, just as his language is the language of the countryside, direct and plain. But his rustic philosophy also includes the Scottish peasant's belief in his own importance and dignity when he confronts nobles or even God.

III *The Continent*

In addition to the Scots and Chaucerian strands, threads of French and Italian influence are woven into Henryson's poetry. French elements play a larger role. The close political ties between Scotland and France throughout the fourteenth century resulted in a marked French bent in the Scottish literary tradition. Some Scottish nobles held French titles and French lands as well as their Scottish honors and fiefs. The regular commerce between Scotland and France led to both linguistic and literary influences.

The language of Scotland was permeated with French elements long before the influence of Chaucer was ever felt in the North.[51] Although many of these French elements are not so obvious in Henryson's language, they certainly appear in the poetry of both Barbour and Dunbar. The appearance of French derivatives such as

"plesande," "auentur," "doutand," "heritage," "veriour," "per-
sauit," and "lecture" before the influence of Chaucer certainly
indicates the strong French influence on the vocabulary of Middle
Scots.

French influence also extended to literary forms. Whether the
romance came to Scotland from England or directly from France,
there is no doubt about its existence in early Scottish literature. The
lost Northern "Sir Tristrem," attributed by Sir Walter Scott to
Thomas the Rhymer, is most assuredly based on French models.
Barbour's *Bruce* reflects the same tone of patriotism that is to be
found in Froissart's *Chronicles*. If the generic characteristics of
Barbour's poem are not derived from French models, much in its
tone and language reflects marked French attitudes and techniques.
The most direct French influence on Henryson appears in his use of
the French *pastourelle*. Although Henryson makes extensive use of
other forms that he might have derived directly from French
literature, there may be concrete proof of his use of a French model
for "Robene and Makyne." Gregory Smith suggested that Henryson's poem was at least analogous with if not derived from Adam de
la Halle's *Li Gieus de Robin et de Marion* because of similarities in
structure and tone. W. Powell Jones suggests another Old French
pastourelle as a direct source for Henryson's poem.[52] He points to
the same general parallels in structure and tone that Smith notices,
but he also analyzes exact parallels between the two poems.
Particularly noteworthy are the parallels in the description of
Makyne and the language of the girl's refusal. Henryson's possible
use of French models is indicative of his general interest in the
structural conventions of French literature. Janet Smith has shown
how influential the *ballade* stanza was on Henryson's verse; she
points out that he employs it in "Robene and Makyne" and "The
Bludy Serk." She also suggests, "the Old French lyric, directly and
indirectly, formed a large part of the poetic background of the
Scottish poets."[53]

Most controversial, perhaps, is the influence of *amour courtois* on
Scottish literature. The debate over the very existence of courtly
love indicates the intensity of the arguments about its influence.[54]
Henryson's acquaintance with the concepts and the "rules" of
courtly love is demonstrated by a passage from "Robene and
Makyne." In response to Robene's assertion that he knows nothing
about the nature of love, Makyne says:

At luvis lair gife thow will leir,
Tak thair ane a b c:
be heynd, courtass, and fair of feir,
Wyse, hardy, and fre;
So that no denger do the deir,
quhat dule in dern thow dre;
preiss the with pane at all poweir,
be patient and previe.

(ll. 17–24)

He also explores the nature of love in *Orpheus and Eurydice* and *The Testament of Cresseid*.

The term *amour courtois* was reintroduced by Gaston Paris in 1883, although there is a long history of scholarship on the subject prior to Paris' work.[55] Numerous theories have been developed to explain the origins of courtly love, but, in the West, it is primarily associated with twelfth-century France.[56] The rules for courtly love are codified in the *Art of Courtly Love* by Andreas Capellanus, who, with a full realization of the potential harm that such love could cause, provided a set of maxims for potential lovers. In one form or another, courtly love was a major subject of the lyric and then the romance even through the fifteenth century.

The number of attempts to define courtly love is a partial indication of the complexity of the concept. Andreas provided a code for courtly lovers which in turn has become a touchstone for much modern scholarship. However, Paris, Tom Peete Cross and William Nitze, C. S. Lewis, A. J. Denomy, Denis de Rougement, Moshé Lazar, Peter Dronke, F. X. Newman, George Economou, and Joan M. Ferrante, among others,[57] have attempted to explore the nature of courtly love in Western literature, but each codification of courtly love is somewhat different from the others. The intense scholarly effort on this subject is sufficient to prove that "the concept is not a simple one but rather a cluster of personal feelings and social values."[58]

However, a body of common concepts emerges. Ferrante and Economou suggest that the basic assumptions of courtly love are: "the nobility of the lover, the sometimes insuperable distance between him and the lady, the exalting nature of his devotion, and the social context of his love."[59] The first premise, involving the lover's nobility, has two implications. First, it must be understood with reference to the social class of the lovers—courtly love was a

game for nobles, not *vilains* who had neither the resources or the
nobility of character to participate. This criterion also has implications for the lover's nobility of character. He attempts to show
himself worthy of the lady's love by emphasizing his exalted
character and often tells her that she herself is the source of his
nobility, as indicated in these lines from Peire Vidal:

> And anything I do or ever say
> I owe to her, for she's the one who imparts
> The knowledge and the skill to guide my way,
> And therefore I am gay, and so songs start.
> And anything I do that finds good end
> Is inspired by the sweet body of my friend,
> Including all reflections of good heart.[60]

This passage also shows how closely the lover's innate nobility is
related to the third characteristic, his exaltation. The lover must
prove both that he is already sufficiently noble to merit the lady's
love and that he will continue to improve himself in her service.

The second characteristic of courtly love has been treated
differently by different scholars. Andreas approaches the notion of
distance between the lovers in terms of adultery, when he states
flatly that "love cannot exert its powers between two people who are
married to each other" [61] because of the nature of marital
obligation. Paris suggested that the first characteristic of courtly
love was that it was "illégitime, furtif," while C. S. Lewis notes that
adultery is to be considered one of four salient characteristics of the
concept.[62] In these senses, courtly love may later lead to tragedy, as
in Malory's works, when love creates a conflict with social
obligations. However, if the distance between the lover and the
beloved is understood in terms of personal ethical development,
this aspect of courtly love need not necessarily be harmful. In some
ways, it is associated with two of the most positive characteristics of
courtly love: humility and the adoration of the beloved. Humility is
the male partner's abasement of his own will to the female's. Like
Amans in the *Roman de la Rose*, the lover had to be prepared to
suffer the *daunger* of his lady without complaining. Andreas touches
on this characteristic when he says that "Love . . . leaves it to the
woman's choice." [63] This quality is exemplified by Lancelot in *The
Knight of the Cart* when, in Meleagant's tournament, he is
alternately required to charge ferociously or retreat timidly at

Guinevere's bidding. The concept of the religion of love demanded that a lover worship his beloved as a major means to his own ennoblement. It follows quite naturally from the concept of benevolent Venus, *Venus caelestis*, whom Alanus de Insulis and Bernardus Silvestris portray as Natura's "subvicar in procreation." [64] Devout adoration of the lady is a standard subject of earlier lyrics, for example, "When the Nightengale Singes" and "Blow, Northerne Wind" in English. Lewis attempts to show how closely this sentiment parallels principles of religious adoration by examining the twelfth-century *Concilium in Monte Romarici*, which purports to describe a confession and debate about love arranged by a chapter of nuns. [65] Much more has been written about the relationship between courtly love and Mariolatry; whatever the social causes, it is clear that religious feeling and love were closely connected in the twelfth century. [66] Both humility and the adoration of the beloved could have very important personal and public benefits, contrasting with some of the interpretations of love in terms of adultery. If the beloved is considered a goal which the lover can only attain through his commitment to constant moral improvement, then the distance between the lovers may be viewed as directly related to love's ennobling effects, and, indeed, it was precisely so considered by Renaissance Platonists who emphasized this aspect of social or physical distance in their lyrics.

The exalting nature of courtly love must be understood with reference to the nobility of character that it might inspire. Insofar as courtly love was an ideal, a given individual might not be able to attain the levels of excellence to which it might inspire lyric poets or the heroes of romance. But, under the auspices of *Venus caelestis*, the beneficent aspect of love which led to universal harmony, a lover could aspire to levels of excellence in both his personal and public conduct. Andreas clearly emphasizes this concept of love when he admonishes lovers to avoid jealousy (II), to avoid avarice (X), and to avoid presumption (XXVIII). This same emphasis on the ennobling aspects of love appears in the *De planctu naturae* of Alanus de Insulis and Jean de Meun's portion of the *Roman de la Rose*, and it became a standard subject of romance. As a powerful force for exaltation, love could inspire the romance hero to deeds of valor and bravery or to acts of charity and piety. Andreas summarizes this element with the paean: "O what a wonderful thing is love, which makes a man shine with so many virtues and teaches everyone, no matter who he is, so many good traits of character." [67]

The social context of courtly love is closely related to the ennobling features. Denomy sees love as "the fount and origin of virtue," [68] a concept clearly having social implications. Although a lover cannot flaunt his love simply to achieve renown and the major joy it affords may be primarily private and personal, it can be a powerful force in motivating him to deeds of public importance. Chretien's Yvain performs deeds of bravery that affect his society because of his love for Laudine. And Lancelot, in *The Knight of the Cart*, is motivated by his love for Guinevere to answer a major challenge to Arthurian society. For the most part, later romances tend to emphasize the crisis between love and duty that may contribute to the tragic decline of a society, but in its benevolent aspects, love could play an important role in establishing both personal and public ideals.[69]

Chaucer was certainly familiar with the doctrines of courtly love, and Henryson's interest in the subject might well have been derived from the poetry of the South. But the most powerful source of the courtly love tradition in England and Scotland is French. As Charles Muscatine has shown, Chaucer derived not only the philosophy but also the rhetoric of courtly love from French sources.[70] Whether it is said to descend into Scottish poetry in a direct line or via English movements, Scottish courtly love was derived from French models.

Henryson seems to be aware of the ambiguous nature of love as exemplified in the two natures of Venus, one benevolent and the other malevolent. He deals most directly with the nature of love in the *Orpheus*, where he seems to explore both aspects. As MacQueen has shown, the love between Orpheus and Eurydice, representing the marriage of reason and emotion, can have great benefits and can result in harmony and moral rectitude.[71] On the other hand, when emotion becomes appetite, the harmony of love may be destroyed. In the *Orpheus*, Henryson borrows a standard allegorical interpretation of the legend from Nicolas Trivet and William of Conches to explore the impact of passion on man's rational behavior. He also treats the subject in *The Testament of Cresseid*. Cresseid's passion is responsible for her ultimate plight, and it is not until her benevolent love and reason at last overcome the forces of passion that she achieves true contrition and is able to attain true repentance.

Besides these major influences on Henryson's poetry, other French elements circulated in medieval Scotland. Thematic and structural influences descended to the Scots from their own direct relationships with France as well as from English sources. Henryson would have found his literary milieu permeated with French borrowings.

The French strain is not the only major foreign influence on Scots literature. R. D. S. Jack has demonstrated a strong case for Italian influence on Scottish poetry. He identifies three main ways in which Scotsmen were benefited by their Italian mentors who served "as purveyors of classical literature, as Latin stylists, and as providers of books for their formularies." [72] In explaining the general nature of this influence on Middle Scots literature, he points to the numerous visits to Italy by churchmen such as William Turnbull and Donald McNaughton, and the visits to the Scottish and English courts of prominent humanists such as Aeneas Sylvius, who visited the court of James I in 1435.

Italian humanism became a powerful influence in fifteenth-century Scotland as witnessed by the great poetic outpouring of Dunbar, Henryson, and others, representing in the words of John Durkan, "the popular version of a revival of classical learning already assimilated by an *elite*." [73] Henryson assuredly was influenced by classical models. *The Morall Fabillis* are based both on the vernacular Reynardine tales and on the fables of Aesop, his "maister venerable." His interest in Greek history appears in *The Testament of Cresseid* even though it also reflects typically medieval influences. Even more impressive is his interest in the mythology of the tale of Orpheus. John MacQueen has shown that *Orpheus and Eurydice* shows extensive influence of Italian humanism of the Quattrocento. [74]

Henryson's tales are influenced by the growth of classical humanism both in his choice of subject matter and his treatment of his subjects. Henryson's use of the "Moralitas" is, after all, in keeping with the principles of classical aesthetics. It is an ideal of the classical as well as the medieval mind that art should serve a higher purpose, that of moral instruction. Henryson's use of a moral at the end of each fable and the *Orpheus* may have much in common with medieval exegesis, but it also shares the emphasis of classical and humanistic thinking.

The influence of classical humanism on Henryson's style may be somewhat more difficult to detect. Jack draws a detailed comparison between Henryson's *Orpheus* and Il Poliziano's *Orfeo*. [75] He explains that Henryson's possible use of Il Poliziano is substantiated not only by verbal parallels but also by Henryson's hitherto puzzling references to music. Jack's explanation of Henryson's debt to Il Poliziano suggests that much of his artistic control and restraint might well be due to the influence of his wide reading in the classics, a natural part of his task as schoolmaster.

The precise extent of the Italian influence on Henryson's reading is difficult to assess. Although Jack argues convincingly that Henryson's access to the Latin fables of Gualterus Anglicus might have been through a copy purchased in Italy,[77] too little is known with certainty about the poet's life to permit any generalization about where he might have acquired his books. MacQueen is on safer ground when he demonstrates how the *Orpheus* reflects the symbolic and philosophic structure of fifteenth-century Italian Neoplatonism. Basing his conclusion on the best established aspect of the poet's biography, he suggests that Henryson would have had access to the work of Italian humanists through the library at Glasgow cathedral.[78] Henryson apparently used some Italian sources, perhaps even Il Poliziano, but any more specific suggestions must be made with great caution.

Both the French and Italian influences permeated English literature of the fourteenth and fifteenth centuries and may have entered the poetry of the Makars from their reading of Southern literature. But each tradition had also had an independent influence on Scottish literature. At the same time that French and Italian elements were influencing Scottish poets through their transmission in the literature of England, they were also exercising a more direct power over the Scottish literary imagination by the direct importation of manuscripts and the political and educational connections established between Scotland and the Continent.

These major influences all contributed to the development of a literary renaissance in Scotland. Scottish poets blended some of the best elements of their native literary tradition with the Southern heritage and the literatures of France and Italy to produce distinctive and important verse. Henryson's role in this new movement was central.

CHAPTER 3

The Morall Fabillis

I Major Critical Problems

NONE of Henryson's' major works has suffered as much neglect as *The Morall Fabillis.* In the overall appraisal of his poems, they have often been overshadowed by *The Testament of Cresseid.* Written relatively late in Henryson's career, the fables are comparable with Chaucer's *Canterbury Tales* in their scope, because they include a variety of characters representing all levels of society in medieval Scotland. Like *The Canterbury Tales,* they demonstrate a thematic richness which includes many of the major social and philosophical questions of the Middle Ages. Moreover, as Wood notes, in *The Morall Fabillis* Henryson's "independence and originality" are most evident.[1] They also illustrate the finest literary techniques of both the allegorist and the realist.

Their neglect is especially remarkable when the variety in characterization is considered even against standards set by Chaucer, Dante, and Boccaccio. Through animal characters, Henryson explores the social pretensions of vicious lords and aspiring burgesses, while he also examines the humility and sturdy honesty of the peasants. He exposes the social hypocrisy of the ignoble barons and egotistical clergymen. Henryson was all too familiar with pride, avarice, sensuality, poverty, injustice, and the lack of pity which permeated his society. He could hardly avoid transforming the fables into vehicles for social and political comment.[2]

His social concerns are pervasive in the poems. In "The Trial of the Fox" he attacks the sham justice of consistory courts. Even the monarchy does not escape his criticism in "The Lion and the Mouse." His themes, however, are not just related to social institutions. Although Henryson is essentially optimistic, his works raise questions about the efficacy of moral instruction and, in such fables as "The Cock and the Jasp," even about the nature of man.

Yet Henryson is not nihilistic. At least one of the fables reflects an
optimism similar to that in the more hopeful passages of *Piers
Plowman*. Others assert the essential capacity of man for good,
despite the temptations and problems that stand in his way. The
major questions of human purpose are raised and examined in all of
their complexity. As George Clark suggests, the fables "aim at fairly
representing rather than harshly reproving mankind." [3] Henryson
resists the temptation to dismiss questions of ultimate purpose on
grounds of either blind faith or exaggerated rationalism. His
exploration of the problems is based on a sound understanding of
the shortcomings and virtues of mankind. The *Fabillis* also
exemplify medieval literary techniques at their best. They incorporate basic principles of Patristic exegesis, but the tales are "at least
as entertaining as they are instructive." [4]

The comparative lack of attention to the fables has resulted in
inadequate discussion of many important questions. One of the
major problems is establishing the best text. Most likely, they were
all written in the last quarter of the fifteenth century. David Crowne
has argued that the prologue and seven of the fables were written
prior to 1481, [5] three fables after June 6, 1481, and two after March
24, 1484. Unfortunately, no fifteenth-century text of the fables has
survived.

The early texts are clearly divided into two basic groups: printed
editions and manuscripts. The earliest printed text is that published
by Robert Lekpreuik for Henry Charteris in 1570, but probably the
most reliable is that published in 1571 by Thomas Bassandyne. The
Bassandyne text was chosen by Harvey Wood for his edition of the
fables in 1933, and was reprinted by Charles Elliott in 1958. Its
authority among printed versions remains unchallenged. Two other
printed texts, the Smith version of 1577 and the Hart version of
1621, are of less importance.

Perhaps more important are the manuscripts. Of major signifi-
cance is the Bannatyne manuscript, dating from 1568. Although it
includes Henryson's works in a general collection with poems by
Dunbar and Holland, it seems to be the best text available for the
ten fables it includes. [6] The second most important manuscript is
Harleian MS 3865, copied in 1571. Other texts are incomplete.
Although the Makculloch manuscript in the National Library of
Scotland is possibly quite early, it includes only the prologue and
"The Cock and the Jasp." The Asloan manuscript contains only a
text of "The Two Mice."

MacQueen has solved many of the problems in the text of the fables, but some questions remain about the dating and the sources of the tales. Gregory Smith identifies four sources: the Latin fables of Gualterus Anglicus, the *Fabules* of John Lydgate, Caxton's editions of *Reynard* and *Aesop*, and Petrus Alfonsus' *Disciplina clericalis.*[7] MacQueen accepts Diebler's argument for a debt to the *Roman de Renart.*[8] Because of the lack of external evidence, Henryson's use of these sources has been the key to dating the fables.

Crowne believes that they are clearly divisible into four groups based on the poet's use of his source material.[9] The first group consists of those tales probably written between roughly 1470 and June 6, 1481, when Caxton's *Reynard* was published. In this group he includes the prologue, "The Cock and the Jasp," "The Two Mice," "The Sheep and the Dog," "The Lion and the Mouse," "The Preaching of the Swallow," "The Wolf and the Lamb," and "The Paddock and the Mouse." These fables are largely derived from the Latin-verse *Romulus* of Gualterus Anglicus and show the influence of Lydgate's *Fabules*. Because they do not indicate the influence of Caxton's *Aesop* or *Reynard*, Crowne speculates that they were written before the appearance of these two works.

Later and possibly more precise dating, however, is available for one of the tales, "The Lion and the Mouse," through its reference to the Lauder rebellion. In July, 1482, James III was seized by his nobles at the Lauder church, and the government of Scotland fell by default to the king's brother, the Duke of Albany, who had received help from Edward IV. In a rescue contrived to deliver James from the conspiratorial nobles and place him in the hands of his brother, he was released to the burgesses of Edinburgh, who staged a mock siege of Edinburgh castle. The incidents in "The Lion and the Mouse" may refer to James' imprisonment and his subsequent release to the burgesses of Edinburgh. Nicholson suggests that the head mouse is the leader of the burgess troops, Walter Bertram.[10] For the fable to refer to these events, it must have been written after September 29, 1482, the date of James' release. This date would place it in the second group of Crowne's classification or even later.

Besides "The Lion and the Mouse," the next group includes other tales written after June 6, 1481. In this collection Crowne includes "The Fox and the Wolf," "The Trial of the Fox," and, possibly, "The Fox, the Wolf, and the Cadger." All of these tales, he believes, show the influence of Caxton's *Reynard* in plot structure and characterization. MacQueen argues, however, that "The Fox, the Wolf, and the Cadger" is not based on Caxton's *Reynard* but instead directly on the *Roman de Renart*. He also suggests another method for dating the tales. In attempting to prove that the Bannatyne manuscript is the most authoritative source of the fables it includes, he tries to show that it is a copy of a manuscript dating from 1482 or 1483. The ten fables in Bannatyne were, he believes, the only ones completed at the time the source of Bannatyne was copied. MacQueen's case is somewhat supported by a study of the Bannatyne omissions. The only fables not included are "The Fox, the Wolf, and the Cadger," "The Fox, the Wolf, and the Husbandman," and "The Wolf and the Wether." Since the latter two are clearly based on the Caxton *Aesop*, they could not have been written before 1484. MacQueen's theory about the Bannatyne mansucript is borne out by some pre-Reformation textual references as well. If MacQueen's theory is correct, then "The Fox, the Wolf, and the Cadger" must surely have been written after 1482–1483, when the Bannatyne source was copied.[11]

Crowne's third group is dated after March 24, 1484, the date of publication of Caxton's *Aesop*, and includes "The Fox, the Wolf, and the Husbandman" and "The Wolf and the Wether." There is no reason to doubt the dating Crowne suggests. He lists as a last category a tale for which there is no indication of date, "The Cock and the Fox." Since this fable is based on Chaucer's "Nun's Priest's Tale," in Crowne's view there now seems to be no evidence for placing it in one of the other classes.[12] MacQueen's argument, however, has implications for this tale as well. Since it is included in Bannatyne, it must have been completed by no later than 1482–1483, and, in any case, before Henryson turned his attention to the *Roman de Renart* and Caxton's *Aesop*.

It now seems that a new ordering of the fables is necessary. Their chronology should be as follows: (1) Sections based on Gualterus Anglicus' *Romulus*, the French *Isopet*, or the *Fabulae* of Odo of Cheriton, and completed by 1482–1483: The Prologue; "The Cock and the Jasp"; "The Two Mice"; "The Sheep and the Dog"; "The Preaching of the Swallow"; "The Wolf and the Lamb"; "The Paddock and the Mouse"; (2) fables showing the influence of Caxton's *Reynard* (published June 6, 1481) or later political events and completed by 1482–1483, when the source of Bannatyne was copied: "The Fox and the Wolf"; "The Trial of the Fox"; "The Lion and the Mouse"; (3) fable based on "The Nun's Priest's Tale" and completed by 1482–1483: "The Cock and the Fox"; (4) fables showing the influence of Caxton's *Aesop* (published March 24, 1484): "The Fox, the Wolf, and the Husbandman"; "The Wolf and the Wether"; (5) fable showing the influence of the *Roman de Renart* and completed after 1482–1483: "The Fox, the Wolf, and the Cadger."

The dates specified for the composition of the fables are still not precise. However, when even general periods of composition such as these are available, topical allusions may help provide more exact dates of composition.

Vital as Henryson's sources are in dating the fables, they are even more significant in helping us to understand the nature of his art. Indeed, Henryson makes use of "the mass of popular medieval literature," [13] but he also draws on many of the learned beast fables of the Middle Ages.

Seven sources have been clearly identified:[14] (1) the Latin *Romulus* of Gualterus Anglicus and the French *Isopet de Lyon* derived from it; (2) Chaucer's "Nun's Priest's Tale"; (3) the *Roman de Renart*; (4) the *Fabulae* of Odo of Cheriton; (5) Caxton's *Historye of Reynard the Fox*; (6) Caxton's *Aesop*; and (7) Lydgate's *Isopes fabules*. Although all of these tales draw on the folk traditions of the beast fable, a substantial element of learning is present in each.

Possibly the most important in terms of its proportionate influence is the verse *Romulus*, attributed to Gualterus Anglicus, who was chaplain to Henry II. His Latin text is an ultimate medieval source for Henryson's prologue, "The Cock and the Jasp," "The Wolf and the Lamb," "The Paddock and the Mouse," "The Sheep and the Dog," "The Two Mice," "The Lion and the Mouse," and "The Preaching of the Swallow." There are even direct verbal parallels between Gualterus' text and Henryson's, as for instance in line 28 of Henryson's prologue. The Latin text, however, is in many ways a less rewarding subject of study than the *Isopet de Lyon*. MacQueen has shown that the author of the French text which Henryson probably used was as much "a creator as a translator," [15] and that Henryson learned much by studying his work. The French poet's technique is similar to Henryson's discriminating expansion of his source material. Yet Gualterus contributed many of the basic elements of plot and characterization, and his influence on both Henryson and the *Isopet* poet is pervasive. Even "The Fox and the Wolf," which shows significant influence of Caxton's *Reynard*, is apparently based on fable 67 by Gualterus. Gualterus provided the basic structure of the tales, but the *Isopet* furnished Henryson an example of superb narrative style.

Henryson uses Chaucer's "Nun's Priest's Tale" as his source for "The Cock and the Fox." Donald MacDonald, who has thoroughly analyzed Henryson's use of Chaucer in this fable, finds much in the Scottish poet's work to praise.[16] Henryson's remarkable "economy" in his borrowing from Chaucer here is similar to the poetic compression found in *The Testament of Cresseid*. He has adapted Chaucer's characters to his own purpose with no loss in their development or appeal. He also introduces elements from the Scottish tradition by using names from *The Colkelbie Sow*. Very specific comparisons with Chaucer can be made in this fable, and Henryson stands up well under the test.

There is strong evidence that Henryson made use of the fourteenth branch of the *Roman de Renart* in "The Fox, the Wolf, and the Cadger." [17] The poem uses narrative details and structural patterns that are closer to the *Roman* than to Caxton's *Reynard*, including the fact that Reynard, not Isegrim, is the hero. This modification changes the focus of the tale. Additional correspondences between the fable and the *Roman* appear in the specific identification of a fish in the plot as a herring and in the fox's playing dead, neither of which appears in Caxton. There is no doubt that Henryson would have known French and become familiar with French literature; in fact, the strong ties between Scotland and France might have made it inevitable. Although Henryson could have made all of the changes for himself, MacQueen is probably correct in asserting that "when the *Roman de Renart* preserves another version of the story, in a language known to Henryson, and in a form closer than Caxton's to that given by Henryson, it is reasonable to assume that Henryson based his work primarily on the *Roman*." [18] There is one other explanation, however, that we shall consider when we evaluate Henryson's total debt to Caxton.

I. W. A. Jamieson has suggested that two of Henryson's fables show that Henryson used tales from the *Fabulae* of Odo of Cheriton, a fourteenth-century English priest.[19] He believes that Odo's tales are at least partial sources for "The Two Mice" and "The Trial of the Fox." He argues that the prolonged conclusion and the appearance of the cat in "The Two Mice" are distinctive to the versions of the tale by Henryson and Odo. More obvious, Jamieson believes, is the influence of the *Fabulae* on Henryson's "The Trial of the Fox." In particular, the summons to the mare to appear at court seems to Jamieson to reflect more of Odo's influence than Caxton's. Jamieson's arguments, however, are subject to a general objection raised by Denton Fox.[20] It may be that in this tale and others, Henryson is relying on a more general tradition of beast fables than usually believed.

Critical debate has developed about the extent of Caxton's influence on Henryson. It has been traditionally accepted that four of the fables were influenced by Caxton, including "The Fox and the Wolf," "The Trial of the Fox," "The Fox, the Wolf, and the Husbandman," and "The Wolf and the Wether." [21]

"The Fox and the Wolf" and "The Trial of the Fox" apparently show the influence of Caxton's *Reynard,* perhaps most significantly in the latter fable. There are four significant parallels between the *Reynard* and "The Trial of the Fox." First, the name of the lion who rules the other animals is "Nobill" in both. There is also a similiarity in the designation of the assembly of animals as a parliament. Moreover, the term "Doctor of Divinity" is used as an ironic title for an animal who acts foolishly. Finally, the same animal character who has been kicked by the mare for his efforts is chided by the other characters in similar fashion in both works. In reviewing the case for Caxton's influence, MacQueen also argues for the influence of *The Kingis Quair* on this tale.[22]

Caxton's influence is apparently strong in "The Fox and the Wolf," as well. The fox's confession closely parallels chapters 12 and 27 in *Reynard.* Most significant, perhaps, is the name "Waitskaith" which is provided for the wolf.[23] Since this name appears in Reynardine tales only in Henryson and Caxton, it is strong proof that Henryson was indeed using the *Reynard.* However, the name also appears in *The Colkelbie Sow,* which Henryson had surely read.[24]

"The Fox, the Wolf, and the Husbandman" and "The Wolf and the Wether" show the influence of Caxton's *Aesop.* Three details are significant: Henryson's use of the term "wether" instead of "aries," the omission of the removal of the wether's horns which is present in other versions, and the wolf's defecation from fear. All of these elements are common to Henryson and Caxton. Henryson's sharpening of the narrative focus of Caxton's tale has been carefully explored by MacDonald. He believes that the tale shows the influence of Petrus Alphonsus' *Disciplina clericalis,* as Smith argued, but that Petrus' influence descends through Caxton's

Aesop. MacDonald's analysis emphasizes Henryson's ability to expand Caxton's tale.[25]

"The Fox, the Wolf, and the Husbandman" contains verbal echoes of Caxton. One proverbial expression appears in the fable and also in both of Caxton's works. The lines from Henryson are "thus fairis it off Fortoun: / As ane cummis up, scho quheillis ane uther doun." The phrasing is directly parallel to lines in both the *Aesop* and the *Reynard*. Other proof of Henryson's use of Caxton is to be found in the diction of the fable, especially in the use of the word "shadow," the exchange in the well, and in the wolf's anger.[26]

Denton Fox objects to the argument that Henryson made extensive use of the *Reynard*. He attempts to evaluate all of the evidence and concludes that the *Reynard* cannot be considered to provide the closest analogue to any of Henryson's tales. He believes that parallels can be explained entirely "by the fact that both men are following the same tradition." [27] He goes on to argue that it is the general Aesopic tradition, not Henryson's specific use of Caxton's *Aesop* or *Reynard*, that shapes *The Morall Fabillis*. This theory would have implications not only for our understanding of Henryson's use of his sources but also for the chronology of the fables as well. Although Fox presents strong proof that some of the structural similarities between Henryson's poems and the works of Caxton may be explained by reference to the general tradition, the verbal parallels noted by MacQueen cannot be so easily dismissed. Surely the Aesopic tradition exercised major influence on any specific fables written in the Middle Ages, but the evidence for Henryson's reliance on Caxton seems too strong at this point to discount.

Another important influence is Lydgate's *Isopes fabules*. There are direct verbal parallels with Lydgate in Henryson's humble comments on his lack of rhetorical abilities, although this certainly was a general rhetorical figure in the Middle Ages. There are other minor verbal echoes, but more substantial borrowings appear in "The Cock and the Jasp" and "The Paddock in the Mouse," where numerous similarities in both language and structure may be detected. "The Two Mice" also shows proof of structural borrowing from Lydgate. While hardly a major source, Lydgate's fables had a significant effect on Henryson's work.

The numerous unanswered questions about the text and social background of the fables do not greatly interfere with modern appreciation of their artistry. Although they may be based on the most general tradition of beast fables, the perfection of Henryson's technique is almost unmatched in fifteenth-century British literature. His ability to develop plot structure shows a keen awareness of the balance between the need for organic unity and the demands of moral didacticism. Henryson's own incisive examination of human nature appears in the portrayal of animal characters who transcend both stereotypes and historical allegory to achieve the universality and appeal of Chaucer's pilgrims. The fables are strongest in their realism, humor, and broadly tolerant morality.

II *The Prologue*

The prologue contains many of the keys to all of the fables. In its concern for morality or "a morall sueit sentence," [28] it explains Henryson's approach to all of the succeeding tales. Although Henryson's commitment to moral didacticism in poetry appears in the "Moralitas," it also appears in the plot of each of the tales. The poet investigates problems in ethics and morality for the purpose of understanding man and his position in the universe, not for the egotistical satisfaction of scornfully describing a depraved world. Moreover, his training in exegetical techniques would have led him to search out the meaning in all aspects of experience. Not only would such hidden meaning reflect God's plan for the world, but it would also provide a means of understanding the basic principles of human conduct. Of course, the fables are in a long tradition of Aesopic moral instruction, but, as Clark notes, even in the prologue, "Henryson maintains a clear distinction between Aesop and the narrator." [29]

Henryson realized that understanding the moral lessons to be drawn from experience was not always easy. He uses a common figure to explain the effort demanded to extract the "sentence" from the literal level of interpretation:

Thir nutis schellis, thocht thai be hard and tuich,
Thay hald the cirnall sueit and delectable;
So lyis thair a doctryne wyse anewch,
And full of fruct, undir a fenyeit fable.

(ll. 15–18)

Henryson never doubts what "clerkis sayis" when they advise him to seek out what is profitable and neglect the dross in poetry. For

him this is the main task of the more advanced and thoughtful
reader who mines surface interpretations for deeper meanings.

However, Henryson does not see the only goal of the fables as
instruction. He is concerned that they prove interesting and
delightful as well:

> Thocht fenyeit fables of auld poetre
> Be nocht grundit all upoun trewth, yit than
> Thair poleit termis of sueit retory
> Ar rycht plesand unto the heir of man;
> And als the caus quhi thay first began
> Was to repreife the vyce of mysdoing. . . .
>
> (ll. 1–6)

His desire that his fables provide "sum mirriness" is of course
ultimately in harmony with his belief that art should be studied for
its moral sense. The major purpose of the pleasure he describes is to
prepare the mind to receive the moral of art. But these lines reflect
his awareness that morality and merriment are not always at odds.

Henryson's interest in the artistry of his fables is treated in other
passages in the prologue. The "poleit termis of sueit retory" are of
vital importance to him, an emphasis evident in the lines on their
value and on his own lack of ability. He interprets rhetoric to mean
arrangement and style, and he sees it as a major factor contributing
to the moral sense of art. It is rhetoric after all that makes the
message palatable:

> For as we se the bow that ay is bent
> Wordis unsmart, and dullis on the string,
> So dois the mynd, that is ay diligent
> In ernyst thocht and in studdeing.
> With sad materis sum mirriness to myng
> Accordis weill. . . .
>
> (ll. 22–27)

For Henryson, a delightful style that corrects man's folly through
symbolism and figurative language is a vital element of poetry.

Despite his modest disclaimers of rhetorical ability, Henryson is a
skilled craftsman. His craft, however, cannot be compared in its
goals with the aureation of Dunbar and some of the other Makars.
The Morall Fabillis are even less ornate than *The Testament of
Cresseid* and *Orpheus and Eurydice*. Henryson has chosen a low or

middle style for most of the tales, with diction and sentence structure that reflect folktale backgrounds.[30] These stylistic elements do not preclude the substantial learning which permeates the tales or the use of consciously literary sources. Very likely the poet's use of such plain style does not express his intent to be "folksy"; instead it may indicate his reverence of Aesop, whom he may have venerated on the same level as Virgil.[31] This level of style is also in keeping with the suggestions of rhetoric manuals for instructive writing. Despite his "termes rud," Henryson is not a mere translator or recorder of folktales; he is a skilled and well-educated rhetorician.

Much of the rest of the prologue is devoted to another recurrent theme in Henryson, the opposition between reason and passion. In explaining the nature of the beast fable, Henryson is drawn naturally to compare and contrast the nature of man and the nature of beasts which take on human characteristics. He explains first that Aesop in his fables tells how brutal beasts speak, argue, and even use syllogisms. He goes on to suggest that Aesop has allowed beasts to take on the best characteristic of man, his ability to reason and to understand reason. Although such understanding is not part of their natural endowment, the beasts must possess it in the fables to make the genre possible. If beasts have been given the foremost quality of man, man also occasionally takes on the characteristics of beasts:

> No mervell is a man be lyk a beist,
> Quhilk leivis ay in carnall fowll delyte,
> That schame can nocht derenye nor arreist,
> Bot takis all thair lust and appetyt. . . .

> (ll. 50–53)

Carnality and foul delight, the essential characteristics of the beast, are at the root of tragedy and woe not only in the fables but in *Orpheus and Eurydice* and *The Testament of Cresseid* as well. As Matthew McDiarmid argues, "the theme that haunts and oppresses the imagination of Robert Henryson is the tragedy of sin, that men made in the image of God should become 'beistis Irrational,' reason signifying the state of Christian charity, intelligent and practicing love for God and man." [32] Henryson is committed to the ascendancy of reason. When man errs, it is because he abandons his rationality and acts like a beast governed by carnality. This battle between reason and passion is a constant theme in the fables and is one of the unifying ethical concerns in all of Henryson's works.

III *"The Taill of the Cok and the Jasp"*

This tale has been called "the slightest of the fables," [33] but it is nevertheless one of the most puzzling. It contains some apparent contradictions, both in theme and style, which illustrate some of the major critical problems of the fables.

In many respects, it is the least narratively interesting of the whole collection. There is almost no action. In stanza 1, the cock "with fethreme fresch and gray" flies upon a dunghill in his search for food and discovers the jewel. In stanza 8 he leaves the jewel to be about his business. The balance of the poem records the cock's reactions to and comments about the jewel he has discovered. The main interest of the tale is in his comments on the jewel.

The apparent ethical contradictions in the tale appear in the putative lack of agreement between the cock's comments when he finds the jewel and Henryson's "Moralitas". When the cock discovers the jewel he immediately recognizes what it is:

> O gentill gem, O riche and noble thing,
> Thocht I the fynd, thow ganis nocht for me;
> Thow art a Iowall for ony warldly king.
>
> (ll. 79–81)

He takes note of its great monetary worth and further marvels that he has found it instead of someone else. The great virtue of the jewel, he sighs, will make him but little cheer. The jewel's beauty will avail him nothing. Instead he should have found "corne, or drase small worme, or [s]naillis" (l. 94). Finally the cock bids the jasp rise and make its habitation in a royal tower, and, with that, he leaves. Henryson insists that he does not know what happened to the stone and is instead more interested in the moral of the tale. His "Moralitas" lists seven wonderful properties of the jewel, including the ability to make man "in honour ay to ring" (l. 131).

The straightforward narrative seems easy enough to comprehend. There are subtle suggestions that the perspective on the cock is favorable.[34] His recognition of the nature and position of the jewel seems appropriately medieval in its acceptance of a completely ordered universe in which structure cannot be questioned. Moreover, the cock seems to have common sense on his side. He needs food, not jewels. He even incorporates the traditional wisdom of the proverbs into his arguments when he says that "hungry men may nocht weill leis on loikis" (l. 104). It does indeed seem that he is a "knowledgeable, modest, and sympathetic creature," [35] whose wisdom should be vindicated. It has been a shock to many to find that, in the "Moralitas," Henryson disapproves of his conduct.

Yet disapprove he does, comparing the cock's conduct to that of the ignorant who scorn science. In the "Moralitas" he informs us that the jewel has seven properties, including the ability to make man hardy, strong, gracious, and wise. The jewel represents "perfyt prudens and cunnyng" (l. 128) which helps man to eschew all vices and vanquish the spiritual enemy. He believes it to represent the riches that shall endure forever. The foolish cock, he says, is "Makand at science bot a knak and skorne" (l. 143), because he wanted food instead. He is one of the "ignorantis" who scorn science and despise what they do not understand. Because of the cock's actions, the jewel is now lost forever. Fox suggests that there is a major discrepancy between the tale and the "Moralitas." The tale, he believes, throws the weight of medieval theology and common sense behind the cock's reasoning, but Henryson contradicts it in his search for the inward sense. [36]

This issue goes right to the heart of the question about the function of the "Moralitas" in the fables. MacQueen suggests that the various forms of the "Moralitas" display a variety which reflects Henryson's broad understanding of the meaning of poetic allegory and his interest in the thematic structure of a particular tale. Fox believes that discrepancies between a tale and its "Moralitas" can be explained by Henryson's use of "figurative technique." Both Kinsley and Wittig suggest that the "Moralitas" is often artificial, appended merely because the author somehow felt obliged to provide it. Wood believes it is boring, while Speirs thinks it is to be viewed only as a potential source of interference with the poet's humor. McDiarmid argues that the allegorical meanings of the fables "are not all, or indeed the most important thing, that they have to say." The major question is whether the "Moralitas" is an artificial addition or whether it develops organically from the inception of a given tale. [37]

Although the variety of critical opinion is understandable, Henryson is not forcibly imposing a "Moralitas" on his tales, even in the case of "The Cock and the Jasp." As MacQueen has shown, the whole fable is permeated with biblical allusions from Proverbs, Matthew, Luke, Job, John, and Revelations. All of these allusions show that Henryson intended the cock to be understood as a type of "false intellectual pride." [38] Also established by biblical allusions is the equation between the jewel and wisdom or even the City of God. This foreshadowing of the theme explicitly stated in the "Moralitas" shows that the tale and Henryson's moral are not contradictory. The discrepancy between the tale and its "Moralitas" is partially caused by the lack of biblical knowledge on the part of modern readers.

The allusive foreshadowing is supplemented by narrative elements. The jewel is swept out in the first place through the neglect of "madynis wantoun, and insolent" (l. 71), an indication of the moral nature of others who have neglected to observe the powers of the stone. Moreover, the desires of the cock must be weighed against the marvelous powers the jewel possesses. All he is interested in is the immediate need of his stomach. Henryson attempts to make the desires seem even more base by listing the worms, grain, and snails which are suitable for a real cock's diet, but which seem genuinely contemptible when compared with the powers of the jewel.

A third major consideration is the style of the cock's comments. He often uses low style in his address to the jewel. This is appropriate not only to his position in the scale of animals but to the sense of his response as well. His rejection of the jewel is the general equivalent of the antiintellectual or antitheological reaction of the peasants or the burgesses to science or religion: if the result cannot be measured in concrete terms, why pursue it? This shortsightedness is logical in one manner of speaking, but it is not an attitude for which Henryson has much sympathy. The cock, in fact, is a kind of comic figure. Even his attempts to use florid style in certain sections of the tale seem bathetic. The cock is a type of individual common to all societies and all times.

There are also implications in this fable for the social structure of medieval Scotland. Rowlands has suggested that Henryson was distressed by the displacement of traditional medieval values with the blatant materialism of the developing Scottish middle class. [39] She suggests that the "science" of the "Moralitas" is knowledge in general which was being pushed aside in favor of the values of middle-class materialism. She views Henryson's response as that of the disaffected intellectual who finds his society, or at least one of the most influential segments of it, casting aside intellectual and moral concerns for the pursuit of wealth. Henryson's distress with the burgesses and their values is documented in at least one other fable, "The Two Mice." But his satisfaction with the political activity of the burgesses is possibly documented as well in "The Lion and the Mouse." While it is possible that Henryson is specifically criticizing materialism in the middle class, his criticism is probably of a more general kind. His comments could equally likely be directed at political turmoil and uncertainty; he might well be suggesting that all of the people of Scotland change their priorities. Since his social satire most often uses mice as symbols of the middle class, it is quite likely that the cock is a more inclusive symbol of the nation. The inconsistency between the jewel and what it represents to the cock is yet another possible objection to the suggestion that only the middle class is being attacked, although Henryson could have been using the symbolism suggested by medieval lapidaries with an ironic touch. General societal myopia was very likely his target.

Even if Henryson is concerned about the displacement of a value system, it is not absolutely certain that it was the medieval value structure he was defending. The cock, as already demonstrated, uses many of the basic principles of medieval reasoning in his rejection of the jewel. It is the medieval world view that would compel him to recognize his place in the universe and those things that are appropriate to it. Nor is this to say that medieval values are not a part of what the jewel represents. Certainly the jewel represents biblical wisdom, but it also represents wisdom in general and is associated with the dichotomy that Henryson drew between man and beast. The cock, it must be remembered, is standing on a dunghill which is one of his sources of food while addressing the jewel. While food is a necessity for life, it is also a carnal need, like sex, because it satisfies man's physical appetites. Henryson reinforces this interpretation by comparisons between the cock and a sow, the traditional symbol of gluttony. If the cock stands for carnality, the jewel must stand for both spirituality and reason. We must take Henryson at his word when he tells us that the jewel represents prudence and knowledge. Part of the poet's greatness is that his value system in this fable, as in others, is too broadly humanistic and pluralistic to be narrowly categorized.

There is no question that Henryson is railing against the ignorant who foil the purposes of knowledge. But his wrath is likely not aroused by the rejection of a value system by just one class, nor is he simply an intellectual snob. He is concerned about those general

values that make life human. There may indeed be an implication
that man, "the prisoner of his inescapable limitations, has no plain
and easy choice of wisdom and folly." [40] Neither can we conclude
that apparent discrepancies between a tale and the "Moralitas"
represent shallow thinking or poor art on the part of the poet. As we
shall see, all of the tales are closely linked to the "Moralitas," and
both tale and moral are necessary to convey Henryson's complete
meaning. [41]

IV   "The Taill of the Paddok & the Mous"

After the prologue and "The Cock and the Jasp," the next tale in
Bassandyne is "The Two Mice." In the Bannatyne manuscript,
however, the second tale is "The Paddock and the Mouse," which
like "The Cock and the Jasp" is credited by Henryson to Aesop.

In this fable, tale and moral are very closely related, primarily
through the methods of Patristic exegesis. The plot concerns a
mouse who wishes to cross a river. She is deceived by a frog and
finally she and the frog are both carried off by a bird of prey.
Henryson likens the mouse, who is hungry and wishes to cross the
river to find food, to the soul of man "Bundin, and fra the body may
nocht twin" (l. 174). Its desire to cross the river is inspired by carnal
"lust" which always draws the soul toward earthly things. The false
paddock, who offers to carry the mouse and even swears to protect
her, is similar to man's body. Henryson also explains the jumping
and swimming of the two after the mouse has agreed to tie herself to
the paddock. He interprets their motions as the cares and
vicissitudes of the world which often seem to overwhelm men.

The water in which they swim is the world, constantly changing
and full of tribulation. This use of water is directly in the Patristic
tradition and hearkens back to symbolism employed by Boethius,
Langland, and even the Pearl Poet. The binding of the mouse to the
paddock has a two-fold meaning. It represents the false snares
which are used by the evil to entrap the innocent, but it also
represents the relationship between the soul and the body. The
attempts of the paddock to drown the mouse he interprets as being
the result of the natural inclination of the corporeal part of man:

> The spreit upwart, the body preissis doun;
> The natur of the saule wald our be borne
> Out of this warld unto the hevinly trone.

(ll. 183–85)

Just as the two animals struggle in the water, so the soul of man must fight carnal desires to overcome the flesh. When the two thrash about, sometimes moving up and sometimes down, they imitate the progress of the soul toward God.

Henryson still follows the tradition of tropological exegesis when he interprets the gled that ends their struggle and carries them both off. He can be only one thing, death, and death is the enemy of both body and soul. It is particularly distressing, however, to the man who, like the unwise mouse, binds himself to the pleasures of the body. Henryson concludes his tale with a medieval preacher's moral. He advises his readers to make a strong castle of faith in Christ so that they will be prepared for death. This moral is common in sermons such as those in the collection of the fourteenth-century Dominican John Bromyard. That Henryson had such works in mind is proved by his comment, "I left the laif unto the freiris" (1. 195). Bromyard and other biblical exegetes certainly provided the basis for the "sample or similitud" which Henryson draws from his tale.

Like "The Cock and the Jasp" this fable deals with man's attempt to overcome carnal desires, specifically for food. The mouse emphasizes that she must cross the river because she has only an unacceptable diet of hard nuts on her side. She acts just as foolishly as the cock in attaching herself to the paddock, who represents demands of the flesh. Yet there is a major difference between the two fables. The jewel which the cock rejects represents science or secular wisdom, while the mouse loses her temporal life which symbolizes eternal life. The cock relinquishes wisdom, which could help him fulfill his basic needs in this life. The mouse loses life in this world and apparently salvation in the next.

Another tradition behind this fable is closely related to Patristic exegesis. Many medieval religious poems remind man of his mortality and caution him to prepare for the last judgment. In this poem, as in some of his shorter poems such as "The Thre Deid Pollis," Henryson reflects the tradition of mortality poems such as "Ubi sunt qui ante nos fuerunt" and "Timor mortis conturbat me." In particular he uses the debate form of poems such as "The Debate Between the Body and the Soul." Such debates are usually arranged to determine dramatically the responsibility for the condition of man after death. The best-known English version is developed through a dialogue between the body and the soul after death, when both must face the consequences of their life. Although this fable does not contain the passages of blame and complaint that appear in

"The Debate," it explores some of the same themes. In "The
Debate" the soul charges the body with more concern about carnal
delight than salvation, but the body responds that the soul too must
bear part of the blame for the fate they both face. In Henryson's
fable, the paddock deceives the mouse in the same way that the
body deceives the soul, but such deceit does not eliminate the
responsibility of the mouse or soul.

Other forms of medieval religious literature exercised a strong
influence on the fable. Particularly important is the bestiary.
Although similar in technique to the beast fables that were
Henryson's sources, the bestiary gave concentrated attention to the
allegorical significance of every animal. Much of the tone of the
"Moralitas" is drawn not only from the sermon but from a specific
figure of liturgical rhetoric, the *exemplum*. Like Chaucer's "Pardoner's Tale," these moral stories provided examples of conduct to be
emulated or avoided. Each *exemplum* developed a single theme,
just as Henryson's fable advocates distrust of carnality.

The extensive use of exegetical techniques and religious traditions must be understood for a proper reading of the fable. If the
tale sometimes seems excessively didactic, it is because of Henryson's desire to reinforce his theme and the generic standards of the
exemplum. Poetic vehicles for religious instruction always gave
more attention to theme than narrative pace. Therefore, the
mouse's long hesitation in trusting the paddock and her digression
on physiognomy, which slow the speed of the action, are designed
to stress the theme. Instead of digressions, these lines contribute to
an investigation of the relationship between appearance and reality
or between carnality and spirituality, when tropologically interpreted. The suspension of the narrative can also be explained by the
nature of allegory, which characteristically distorts time.[42]

The prolongation of the narrative serves yet another purpose, the
development of character. Henryson's keen eye for animal conduct
has made it possible for him to apply human psychology to beasts
without destroying the nature of the beast fable.[43] His animals have
the characteristics of common humanity, and the poet carefully
probes their reactions. The passages about the mouse's distrust of
the paddock and her hesitation to bind herself to his leg show
realistic frustration and hesitation. It is this sympathetic understanding of human nature that helps to lift Henryson's fable above
Gualterus' tale or the preacher's *exemplum*. While Henryson wishes
to give proper attention to his doctrinal point, he possesses the

genius to base his teaching squarely on a sound understanding of and sympathy for his fellow humans.

V *"The Taill of the Uponlandis Mous and the Burges Mous"*

This fable, the third in the Bannatyne text, is also attributed to Aesop. Its social references have garnered considerable critical attention. If we accept the social interpretations of "The Cock and the Jasp," it is not "the first fable to have a particular reference to fifteenth century Scotland." [44] However, references to political and social structures are unequivocal in this fable. The fable does not concern merely a wealthy mouse and a poor one, nor is it simply about any city mouse and country mouse; the characters instead are specifically Scottish, a country mouse from the lower classes and a city mouse who is a burgess. It too relies on allegory, but the allegorical interest is social as well as tropological.

Henryson gives elaborate attention to the class markers and social backgrounds of the two mice. The younger lives "up on land" outside the city in which the elder dwells. She lives a solitary life, hiding "As outlawis dois," supporting herself by her wits and often enduring great hunger and cold. Her movements are secret, and she seldom uses a candle. She seems to live outside the law, but she is also a symbol of a larger class. She is specifically called a "rurall Mous" and is a general representative of the rural classes. Indeed, many aspects of her life-style fit peasant life perfectly. The hunger, cold, and great distress she faces were doubtless characteristic of Scottish peasant life in the winter. Moreover, even peasants who were entirely within the law led solitary lives and did not use candles because they could not afford them. The implications of outlawry may certainly be present, but the fable loses part of its effect if the "uponlandis mous" is considered only an outlaw.

Contrasted with the solitary life of the country mouse, the life of the burgess mouse embodies the virtues and luxuries of the urban middle class. She is first of all a guild brother and a free burgess. She has permission to come and go as she pleases. Her position as a guild brother indicates her commercial importance, and she shares in the perquisites of the increasingly important group of prosperous commoners who helped shape fifteenth-century Scottish cities. She is "toll-free" which means that she has been relieved of both the greater and lesser customs by virtue of her status as a member of the Merchant Guild. Despite her handsome social position, however, the burgess mouse is in one sense an "outlaw" too.[45] She robs the public purse, since her freedom from contributing to the customs increases the tax burden on other segments of the public. This and other aspects of her character lead inevitably to the conclusion that Henryson's sympathies lie with the country mouse.

He is not completely hostile to the burgess mouse, however, as illustrated in the early scenes in which, dressed as a "pure" pilgrim, she searches for her sister. This manner of dress and travel reflect her common sense about how to make a journey into dangerous territory. Her first words to her sister are not, as Stearns suggests, the indignant rejection of food but a salutation: "Cum furth to me, myne sueit sister deir; / Cry peip anis" (ll. 25–26).[46] She is also genuinely glad to see her sister. When the country mouse finally comes out of hiding and they meet, the narrator exclaims:

The hairtly cheir, Lord God, gife ye had sene
Was kyid quhen thir sisteris twa wer met;
Quhilk that oft syis was schawin thame betuene.
For quhyle thai luche, and quhyle for joy thay gret. . . .

(ll. 29–32)

The burgess mouse is treated with some sympathy, but her snobbery soon becomes apparent.

The country mouse sets a feast which reflects both her possible status as an outlaw and the cruel realities of peasant fare in Scotland. Out of her pantry she brings nuts instead of spices, and the two eat without a fire or candle. She tries to treat her sister to the finest food she has available and launches into a discussion of family matters. The burgess mouse rudely interrupts with an exclamation that she cannot eat her sister's food. She goes on to assert that "My Gud Fryday is bettir nor your Pase" (l. 87), implying that her worst meal is better than her sister's finest. These comments help to polarize a reader's sympathies in favor of the country mouse. They also prepare for the ironic perspective on the burgess mouse's life that is to follow. By her haughtiness and excessive bragging she is daring the fates, a dangerous action for medieval people.

The country mouse is in some ways the perfect foil for her snobbery. She is innocent and generous. Hardly taking offense at her sister's insults, she replies charitably. One should not be too committed to the pleasures of town, she asserts, especially if they are purchased with trouble and worry. Far better, she believes, to live a simple life without care.

At the insistence of her sister, the country mouse goes to the city. The two depart quietly like thieves, possibly another ironic comment on the true morality of the burgess mouse, and arrive at a "spens with vitall of grit plentie" (l. 102). At the level of political and social allegory, this great pantry represents the milieu of a fifteenth-century Scottish town, particularly in its commerce. The burgess mouse is certain it will always be hers. The country mouse asks her how long such delights will last; the burgess mouse confidently replies "For evirmoir, I wait, and langir to" (l. 118). Their feast is interrupted, however, by both the spenser and the cat. They both avoid the spenser by hiding, but the country mouse is not so fortunate when Gib the cat appears. She is bounced to and fro and barely escapes with her life.

The intrusions of the spenser and the cat probably stand for the constant hazards which plagued Scottish merchants. English invasions, royal tariffs, and even royal loans all cut into their profits and made life perilous.[47] More specifically, Gib might even represent James III. The poem could then be interpreted as an expression of dissatisfaction with a monarch who toyed with his subjects the way Gib toys with the country mouse. Gib's attack suggests the economic havoc wrought by James' heavy tariffs, the country's debased coinage, and large grants to the king's familiars. The argument that James is symbolized by Gib is supported by both general literary tradition and historical fact. The use of the cat as a symbol for an unreasonable monarch has a long history in political poetry. One of the best-known examples in medieval literature is to be found in *Piers Plowman* (B, Prologue, 146–207), in which timorous rats discuss who will be daring enough to try to "bell the cat," or apply political controls to the monarch. Historical justification for Henryson's use of the cat symbol for James is to be found in the language of the conspirators who attacked the king at Lauder church. They apparently thought of their actions in terms of this traditional metaphor, for the chief conspirator, the Earl of Angus, became known as "Archibald Bell-the-Cat" after the rebellion. Henryson certainly became more sympathetic to James after the rebels captured him, but he would have also been distressed by James' ineptitude on the throne. Before the 1482 rebellion, James' popularity reached its nadir around 1480, the approximate time Henryson would have been writing this fable. Despite recent attempts to vindicate James' policies, his shirking of political responsibility and inability to control the nobility made him unpopular. He became a favorite target of political satirists, who attacked him in poems such as *The Thre Preistis of Peblis* and *The Harp*:

> Bot of a thing al gude men mervalis mair:
> Quhen grete consale, with thine own consent,
> Has ordanit strate justice na man to spair,
> Within schort tym thou changis thine entent. . . .[48]

As we shall see, Henryson's change of sympathy in favor of the king in "The Lion and the Mouse" is not contradictory to the attitude expressed in this poem. After James' imprisonment, public sentiment changed. That Albany was a puppet of the English must have been evident to all and deeply resented by many. Even if James was considered by some to be a "poor thing," at least he was Scotland's own.

Once the country mouse has escaped from Gib, she hurriedly leaves, swearing that her sister's prosperity is "mynglit all with cair" (l. 183). She vows that if she can ever return to her home she will never leave again. Henryson leaves her in her den with her simple fare. Despite her relative poverty, she is able to live a life "withouttin dreid," a far better state than her sister's.

The larger tropological meaning is developed around the same theme which Henryson had treated in "The Paddock and the Mouse." The burgess mouse represents those who trust in the delights and pleasures of this world. In the typically myopic fashion of the carnally rapt, she believes that her delights will never cease. Her answer to her sister's question, "How long will this last?" is not only politically optimistic but also philosophically naive. The country mouse's humble meal is far more secure than her own, but she is so blind to the realities of life that she believes the delights of the world are hers permanently.

The interruptions of their feast by the spenser and the cat are to be interpreted tropologically as the uncertain forces of life which threaten worldly pleasure. Certain of these forces are more powerful in the world of influential burgesses than in the lives of the peasants. Their substantial danger is reflected in the country mouse's oath after her encounter with Gib: "Almychty God keip me fra sic a feist" (l. 189). After her narrow escape, we can well understand Henryson's comment that she raced merrily back to her home.

It is this interpretation that Henryson most fully develops in his "Moralitas." He directs his "gud moralitie" to his readers and begins an attack on carnality as found in the conduct of the burgess mouse. As in "The Cock and the Jasp," the primary form of carnality he attacks is gluttony, for he decries wanton men who make a god of their bellies. He reinforces the country mouse's advocacy of the simple life in his own series of beatitudes: "Blissit be symple lyfe withouttin dreid, / Blissit be sobir feist in quiete . . . " (ll. 212–13). The "Moralitas" is concluded with a quotation from Solomon on the advisability of cultivating virtue and an exhortation to his readers to strive for happiness at heart and few possessions.

This fable is one of Henryson's richest. It combines the psychological interest and humanitarian sympathy of Henryson's tropological allegory with his perceptive observation of political events. While it is in some respects the most dated, it is also the most timeless of his tales.

VI "*The Taill of the Scheip and the Doig*"

Also an Aesopic fable, this tale has the same blend of social and tropological implications as that in "The Two Mice." While the latter fable focuses on economic problems, this tale examines the legal problems of the peasantry. From the beginning Henryson is on the side of the poor.[49] The plot concerns the misfortunes of a sheep called to appear before a "frawdfull" wolf who, as judge, demands that he answer charges raised by a dog. Legal forms are observed throughout, even in the formal summons issued to the sheep. He is compelled under pain of "suspentioun, / And gret cursing, and interdictioun" (ll. 11–12) to compear and answer the dog. The penalties to be levied against him were the traditional arsenal of church courts. The court also has all the officers who would appear in a human court. Besides the wolf as judge, there are the raven as apparitour, the fox as clerk and notary, and the kite and crow as lawyers who could plead at the bar.

In pleading his defense, the sheep requests a change of venue because of prejudice in the court. He asserts that the objectivity of the judge is open to question because he has slain many of the sheep's kinsmen. He goes on to attack the other officers of the court who, he declares, are his mortal enemies. Surprisingly, his appeal is taken under consideration by the court, although there is little chance for his plea to succeed. The bear and the badger deliberate a

long while about his case before they respond that he must stand
trial in the wolf's court. The sheep learns that there is no adequate
mechanism of appeal.

Once on trial, the sheep is trapped in a mass of legal snares which
have been prepared for him. The dog contends that the sheep owes
him "certane breid." The verdict is quick and clear. The wolf
charges the sheep to either deliver the goods or pay him in silver, a
judgment against "gud fayth, gud law, and conscience" (l. 97). As
happened all too often in legal proceedings in fifteenth-century
Scotland, the "innocent" is sacrificed to the avarice of bribed court
officials and greedy plaintiffs. The sheep must sell his wool to satisfy
the judgment and is left shivering "In middis now of wintir" (l. 142).
Henryson's accuracy in the depiction of the court, its officers, and
its penalties is remarkable.[50]

While the "Moralitas" of this tale emphasizes the tropological
interpretation, the tale itself contains obvious political allegory.
Henryson takes a stand clearly on the side of the peasants. The
sheep, he says, represents the "pure commownis, that daylie ar
opprest / Be tirrane men" (l. 114–15). The wolf is likened to a
"schires stout," typically a judge of Assizes of the Justice-Ayre, who
preys on all of the "pure men" of the land. He treats the other
officers of the court in similarly scornful fashion. The poet then
expounds on the oppression of the common men by the nobility as
set forth in the sheep's complaint. The sheep not only bemoans his
destitution in the face of a hard winter, but he is even brought to
question the ways of Providence. A legal system which sanctions
such covetousness generates Henryson's most desperate lament
about the ways of God:

> O Lord, quhy slypis thow so lang?
> Walk and descerne my caus, groundit in richt
> ....
> Se thow nocht, Lord, this warld ourturnit is. . . .
>   (ll. 150–51, 162)

In the theological directness of these lines Henryson approaches
blasphemy. His direct address to God, without the intermediaries
usually employed, is unusual in itself, but the almost impudent
questioning of God's ways is especially characteristic of Scottish
literature in the Middle Ages. In both poems and prayers, Scotsmen
were traditionally less humble in their attitudes toward God.[51]

The innocent sheep's complaint is not answered. Henryson concludes that man's lot is such that the only recourse for "pure" people is to pray God for good rest in heaven. The evils of social injustice are caused by man's "grit offens" and there will be no succor until men mend their ways. He thus brings political oppression into focus as a result of moral iniquity and develops the tropological implications of legal inequities. The close knitting of social and tropological allegory partially explains one of the most curious features of the relationship between the tale and its "Moralitas." The court in the tale is undoubtedly ecclesiastical; its structure, officers, and penalties are derived from religious judicature. Yet, the "Moralitas" attacks justice in civil courts, specifically the consistory court. Lord Hailes suggested that Henryson probably "stood more in awe of the court spiritual than of the temporal" and his feelings account for the emphasis on ecclesiastical justice in the tale.[52] MacQueen suggests that the inconsistency between tale and moral can be explained by the goal of Henryson's satire. While the tale is satirical of ecclesiastical courts, the moral tries to expand the attack to all types of courts.[53]

Generalizing his satire is another way of developing the tropological implications of the fable. In the moral vision of this tale, Henryson is most similar to Langland. By attacking all courts Henryson stresses that man should not put his trust in temporal institutions, especially for the administration of justice. Henryson sustains this interpretation through biblical references, which appear in the possible reference to Doeg in the word "Doig" and the reflections of Psalm 44:23 in the complaint of the sheep. In one sense, the ultimate message of the fable is found at this level. The "grit offens" which man gives God is responsible not only for legal injustices, but for all "truble and plaigis soir." It is not just the plight of the sheep which is brought on by man's depravity.

VII *"The Taill of the Wolf and the Lamb"*

This fable also blends political and tropological interpretations. Like "The Sheep and the Dog," it is devoted to championing the peasantry. The wolf and the lamb meet at a drinking spot. The wolf asserts that the lamb has affronted him by beslobbering the water. The defense offered by the lamb is similar to that of the sheep in the immediately preceding fable. The lamb falls to his knees and begs for mercy, but he makes the same mistake as the sheep in basing his plea on law and formal logic. The wolf's accusation, he contends, is "contrair till ressoun." He goes on to prove his argument in syllogistic form. His position was far beneath the wolf's when he drank, so he concludes "Ergo, for me your drink is nevir the war" (l. 35).

The wolf, however, disregards reason in his indifference to the lamb's plight. Seizing on any grounds for a dispute, he accuses the lamb's father of offenses and asserts his right to vindicate himself on the lamb. The lamb objects to the injustice of the wolf's attitude, but he is greeted with an argument based on the highly selective use of Scripture. Still ignorant of the wolf's full intent, the lamb makes one last appeal. He argues that the law forbids one man to punish another without due process. This assumption is grounded on the belief in reason and justice, and the sheep voices it in the mistaken assumption that his adversary is fair and reasonable. The wolf dispels his illusions when he answers with the argument that the lamb has misjudged the means of settling their dispute: "Ha, quod the Wolf, wald thow intrus ressoun, / Quhair wrang and reif suld dwell in properte?" (ll. 78–79). Obviously the wolf has no hesitation about shifting or ignoring moral values.[54] This passage also contains the most explicit statement of the moral viewpoint of Henryson's oppressors, who refuse to harken to reason when they have made up their minds. The tale concludes with the wolf's murder of the lamb.

The "Moralitas" contains verbal echoes of "The Sheep and the Dog" and explores the social implications of the tale. Again, the sheep signifies "pure" people, including merchants and laborers, but the wolf is more broadly interpreted. He represents three types of oppressors of pure men.[55] The first type has already been encountered in the previous fable, the clever judge or lawyer. These "fals pervertaris of the lawis" (l. 100) make false accusations and prosecute false quarrels without regard for God or common morality. They stretch the limits of justice and victimize the common people. Joining them in the persecution of the poor and innocent are the mighty men who are so greedy and so covetous that they will not leave the poor alone. These mighty lords are so callous that they have no pity for a starving man or his family. They seize land with the sole object of satisfying their avarice. The third type is the man "of heretege," who milks his tenants dry. In this portrayal, Henryson attacks particularly the custom of demanding a grassum for rental property. The grassum had to be paid in advance to obtain rental lands. In fifteenth-century Scotland, many landlords developed the practice of evicting tenants immediately after they had paid the grassum. The landlords would then be free to rent the property again and collect another grassum. Henryson attacks this as an especially damnable practice, given the difficult nature of life in rural Scotland during the fifteenth century. He concludes the "Moralitas" with an appeal to the rich to mend their ways and a request to God for good deliverance from the power of the wolves.

The political commentary in this fable is similar to that in *The Thre Prestis of Peblis*.[56] Henryson's poem is quite specific in its attack on the unjust practices of appropriation and eviction in his society. Less obvious are the tropological elements in the fable. Although it is hardly as prominent as that in "The Paddock and the Mouse," there is still a moral lesson to be gleaned from this tale, specifically a warning against excessive pride and avarice.

Pride, the first of the Seven Deadly Sins, was also attacked in the snobbish conduct of the burgess mouse. In "The Two Mice," however, pride is used for comic effect, as the burgess mouse's snobbish pride in her own life is ironically undercut by the dangers that are revealed during her feast. In "The Wolf and the Lamb" pride is a source not of comedy but of tragedy. It is pride that moves the wolf to assert himself over the lamb, despite his victim's appeal to law, reason, and nature. The pride of power and social position frames the wolf's decision, despite his own awareness that he is wrong, and it is this pride which makes him a force uncontrollable by the intellectual and religious restraints governing good men.

As in "The Sheep and the Dog," the tropological interpretation develops from the poet's treatment of social and political themes. Henryson's conclusion employs a device typical of complaints, such as "On the Evil Times of Edward II," which blends his ethical and social concerns. Since the ravenous barons and lawyers are not capable of self-restraint, some kind of external check on their conduct must be imposed. Henryson asks God for help, but the form of the help he requests is practical and political. The solution, he believes, is for God to give the king "hairt and hand" (l. 159) to drive the wolves out of the land. That the king needs the heart for the task indicates that he is not entirely blameless for the state of affairs described in the fable. This attitude toward James III coincides with possible references in "The Two Mice" and "The Lion and the Mouse." Despite James' vices, he was far and away the best hope of the Scottish commons. If the nobles could not check

their own avarice and pride, then there was only one earthly power
that could control them. Unfortunately, the king did not heed
Henryson's pleas.

VIII   *"The Taill of Schir Chantecleir and the Foxe"*

The most Chaucerian of Henryson's fables, "The Cock and the
Fox" borrows extensively from "The Nun's Priest's Tale." It affords
an excellent opportunity to appraise the extent of Henryson's debt
to Chaucer. Eight major common elements demonstrate Henryson's borrowings from Chaucer's tale: (1) the names of the animal
characters; (2) the designation of the cock's owner as a poor widow;
(3) the emphasis on Chantecleir's beauty; (4) the praise of the cock's
singing by the fox; (5) the fox's attempt to disguise his tricks; (6) the
attempt to trick the cock a second time; (7) the reversal of the final
speeches; and (8) the structure of the digression in the debate. After
having examined the evidence, MacDonald concludes that there
can be no doubt that Henryson used Chaucer's tale and modified it
in ways that suit his thematic concerns.[57]

The subject is one that Henryson has treated in previous fables,
"Nobility, with its obverse Pride." [58] The problems of pride and
nobility are linked in this fable with another of Henryson's favorite
themes, the contrast between rationality and passion. The difference between reason and passion as exemplified in the difference
between man and beast is examined in the first lines of the poem:

> Thoucht brutale bestis be irrationale,
> That is to say, lakking discretion,
> Yit ilkane in thair kyndis naturale
> Hes monye divers inclinatioun. . . .
>
> (ll. 1–4)

These lines echo the prologue and reflect one of his major concerns
in "The Cock and the Jasp," "The Sheep and the Dog," and "The
Wolf and the Lamb." Yet each of the four fables treats the theme in
a different way. In "The Cock and the Jasp," irrationality is caused
by hunger and results in the cock's disregarding the jewel of
science. In "The Sheep and the Dog," irrationality appears in the
form of a prejudiced legal system, while in "The Wolf and the
Lamb" it takes the form of an ethic which advocates power over
justice. In "The Cock and the Fox," irrationality appears in the
effects of flattery and fear on both of the major animal characters.

It is irrational vanity that makes the cock such easy prey to the unctuous greeting of the crafty fox Lawrence. Falling on his knees the fox affirms, "Wald I nocht serve yow, ser, I wer to blame, / As I hawe done to youre progenitouris . . ." (ll. 43–44). There is dangerous ambiguity in the word "serve," but superficially the fox's language is filled with words of worship and subservience. Lawrence makes a series of appeals to Chantecleir, one of which would have had special meaning in Scottish culture. He especially emphasizes his service to Chantecleir's ancestors and even affirms that when the cock's father died "I held his hede" (l. 51). Again there is ambiguity in Lawrence's words, but Chantecleir is so taken with his compliments that he loses his scruples. Family background is treated more seriously in *Orpheus and Eurydice*. Henryson must have witnessed the arrogance of numerous late medieval barons, particularly in Scotland, who had only family histories or clan traditions to keep up their pretense to nobility. Such pride was a particularly prevalent form of superficial nobility, which was often coupled with ignoble deeds.

The fox's second appeal is directed more specifically to the cock's pride of person. He blinds Chantecleir with praise of his appearance. Lawrence extols his fair feathers, beautiful beak and breast, and comb. Such exaggerated acclaim is typical of the courtier's flattery of a noble lord. Like the commendation of the cock's family line, it has nothing to do with true nobility. It is instead more of the fox's magnificent rhetoric which inflames the cock's pride to such heights that he neglects due precautions.

Having preened the cock's ego with a hyperbolic appraisal of his family line and personal beauty, the fox suddenly challenges both Chantecleir's birthright and his identity. He accuses the cock of being changed and degenerate because he is probably unable to crow like his father. The key point in this challenge is that it is based on the superficial definition of nobility that Lawrence has been constructing in his praise of the cock. If, indeed, true nobility consists of a beautiful appearance and other surface characteristics, then Chantecleir must try to allay the fox's doubts to meet the test of nobility. The cock is "inflate with the wind of fals vaine gloir" (l. 78). He is wanting in discretion for he does not discern the difference between true nobility and the false definition Lawrence has created. His desire to "win a grit worschip" (l. 80) is the cause of his being seized and nearly killed.

The irony of Chantecleir's desire to win Lawrence's good opinion is accentuated by the speeches of the hens after his capture. The widow faints because of her sorrow for the loss of the cock. Chantecleir might certainly have expected her grief to be general, but his hens are not uniformly bereaved. Partlot begins a lament over the loss of the hens' "darling," but her grief is motivated by self-interest, as becomes evident when she asks "Quha sall our lemmane be?" (l. 106). Sprowtok, however, interrupts with an exhortation to "Seiss, sister, of your sorrow" (l. 113), because she believes Chantecleir's loss was not a great one. She reminds them all that he was guilty of anger, lust, and pride. Coppok elaborates the theme of pride in his character and avows that Chantecleir was "ane verrye veangeance fra the hevin" (l. 135). The irony of their comments confirms the moral perspective on Chantecleir created in his conversations with the fox.[59]

There is a double irony in the tale as Lawrence is duped with some of the same techniques he has used on Chantecleir. When he realizes that he is being pursued, he is so in fear of his life that he is willing to heed the cock's advice to turn around and tell his pursuers that he and Chantecleir have become friends. Lawrence's terror makes him act just as irrationally as Chantecleir had in earlier scenes. Chantecleir, of course, manages to escape and ignores the fox's second attempt to capture him with flattery.

Despite the numerous similarities, Henryson has made departures from "The Nun's Priest's Tale." The cock's dream, for instance, is omitted. It is no longer necessary because Henryson's theme is the danger not of imprudence but of excessive vanity.[60] The cast of supporting characters has been reduced in number to emphasize the importance of the two protagonists. Secondary plot elements have also been deleted to focus attention on the central theme. These and other changes designed to make the fable more credible are implemented to stress the folly of Chantecleir's pride and to provide a forceful lesson.

Henryson's "Moralitas" dwells on the tropological meaning of the tale, including a unique panorama of character types. The tale's prologue includes an examination of the several different character classes of the animal kingdom. At the start of the "Moralitas," he explains that Lawrence and Chantecleir must be considered "typis figurall" from whose conduct our lesson is to be drawn. Yet he applies tropological methods to social types. The cock, for example, represents "A nyce proud man, void and vaneglorious" (l. 195) whose arrogance is usually based on kin or goods. Having defined the social type, he returns to moral considerations in a tirade against pride, which caused the fall of the angels and which will cause the fall of any man who gives in to it. Henryson next interprets the fox who may "wele be figurate / To flatteraris" (ll. 204–5), who do whatever is necessary to please their lords. Once again he expands the analysis of the type into a general attack on the desire for adulation which is also poisonous. Both of these types must have been common in fifteenth-century Scotland. Many of the old feudal nobles who victimized the peasants and resisted the centralization of authority were doubtless as vainglorious as the cock. If the cock represents one real social type, the fox is another. As a type of courtier he symbolizes the new system of government and political power by intrigue and innuendo. His characteristics are close to the popular impression of the courtiers surrounding James III.[61] In this fable, Henryson is providing an eyewitness account, though veiled in allegory, of the conflict between the value systems of the knight and the courtier. As in previous fables, Henryson blended these political concerns into a skillful tropological framework.

As much as any of Henryson's poems, this fable illustrates his relationship to "Chaucer glorious." It also exemplifies the very selective method by which Henryson expands crucial elements "to intensify the humorous incongruity of the fable." [62] He applies this discriminating technique to "The Nun's Priest's Tale" as much as any other source. While Henryson revered Chaucer, he was not overpowered by him.

IX *"The Taill how this forsaid Tod maid his Confessioun to Freir Wolf Waitskaith"*

A substantially different type of social satire appears in this fable. Although it has received less critical attention than "The Two Mice" or "The Cock and the Fox," it is very likely the best illustration of the "strengths and weaknesses of Henryson's didactic style." [63]

The first stanza provides a clear point of transition between this fable and "The Cock and the Fox." The poet tells us that he is now prepared to leave the widow in her happiness and turn to the further adventures that befell "this Fox." This reference establishes both the probable sequence of composition and continuity in characterization. "The Fox and the Wolf" is the second in a series of three tales dealing with the misadventures of first Lawrence and then his son. Each of the fables treats abuses in one of the major

social institutions of Scotland. While "The Cock and the Fox"
satirizes two different kinds of nobles and their typical vices, this
fable satirizes members of the clergy.

Henryson makes extensive use of the tradition of estates satire in
his attack on the friars. The fox, terrified by astrological suggestions
that his death is near, hurries to a friar to make his confession. Friar
Wolf Waitskaith, "A worthy doctour of divinite" (1. 53), gives
Lawrence solace. The wolf is identified as a Franciscan by his gray
apparel, and his surface appearance is that befitting a fifteenth-
century contemplative. Yet his appearance does not reveal his
personality, and as in traditional satires his holy demeanor is belied
by his actions. The very fact that the author chooses a wolf to
represent the friar alerts the reader to his irony. Most often in the
fables, the wolves are oppressors and naturally arouse suspicion.
This wolf's name, "Waitskaith," proves that he is no different from
the others.

Despite his apparent holiness, this friar does not observe the
three parts of the sacrament of confession.[64] He administers
confessio, when he hears Lawrence's confession, and neglects
contritio, true contrition on the part of the penitent. The *satisfactio*
or penance he administers may strike modern readers as trivial, but
when the fox's carnivorous nature is considered, it may be
appropriate. Nor can there be any possibility that he is duped by the
fox. Waitskaith openly tells Lawrence that he is wanting in two parts
of confession, perhaps contrition and forbearance, but that even so
they may pass along to the third part, penance. Lawrence agrees to
take penance only if it is light, short, and not contrary to his
"tendirness." The fox acts as if he expects easier penance from the
friar than he would be granted by a parish priest, a common
situation often criticized in estates satire. The fox's expectations are
met. Friar Wolf Waitskaith demands that the fox eat no meat until
Easter but qualifies the penance by allowing him two exemptions a
week if the need arises for "neid may haif no law" (1. 118). Lindsay
calls this confession "a masterpiece of good-humored satire." [65]

The dissembling of friars is criticized in numerous medieval
poems, including "The Isle of Cokayne," *Vox clamantis*, and *Le
Roman de la Rose*. The ease with which confessions may be
obtained from friars is the subject of special comment in *Le Roman
de la Rose*, in which Faus Semblant even boasts of his superiority to
the parish priest while asserting "J'ai de tout le monde la cure." [66]

Langland's Frere Flatere is similar to Chaucer's Friar Hubert in his interference with the work of the parish priest by easing the penance of the congregation. Similar passages in numerous other poems suggest that Henryson's use of estates satire would be widely recognized by his readers.[67]

Henryson's satire is not directed only against wolfish friars who provide easy confessions. He is also criticizing the unrepentant sinner who makes the whole sacrament a mockery by his insincerity. John B. Friedman has shown that Lawrence's confession is motivated by the worst of reasons, zodiacal warnings.[68] After having found that Saturn has ascendancy over his fate, Lawrence fears that "With mischeif mynget is my mortall fait" (l. 38). His anguish is well-founded if considered solely on astrological principles.[69] But in *Orpheus and Eurydice*, Henryson inveighs against putting trust in the planets, and he must have been aware of medieval manuals of penance which "give specific injunctions against the practice of judicial astrology because of its emphasis on the created rather than the Creator, as well as because of its denial of free will."[70] Lawrence's motive in seeking penance is wrong, and that motive affects the validity of the act.

Henryson also attacks the unrepentant in his use of the fox symbol. In the fable tradition, foxes are even less trustworthy than wolves. In both the Reynardine and Aesopic traditions, foxes are usually crafty and insincere, sometimes specifically in religious matters.[71] Jacques de Vitry emphasizes the association between the fox and religious hypocrisy when he defines the *confessio Reynardi* as the confession of men who observe the form of religion but not the spirit. As Friedman suggests, this is the kind of confession Lawrence makes to the wolf.[72]

If any further proof of Lawrence's unregenerate nature were needed, it is supplied in the way he carries out his penance. When he leaves the wolf, his intentions are good; he plans to live entirely on fish. Yet his good intentions are ineffective. When he approaches the water, he rues his penance and vows that he will be unsuccessful in his fishing, for he has neither boat nor bait. The opportune appearance of a goat herd completely destroys what resolution he has left. He steals a kid and drowns him while simultaneously rechristening him to preserve the forms of his penance: "Ga doun ser Kid, cum up ser Salmound agane" (l. 138). MacQueen believes that this is the comic incident around which the whole fable is

structured.[73] It is certainly the center of the narrative structure in
that it both climaxes the fox's false confession and leads to his later
downfall.

The end which Lawrence meets is the type generally reserved for
the unrepentant sinner. As soon as he has feasted on his "new made
Salmound," he stretches out in the sun and recklessly comments
"Upoun this bellye ware sett a bolt full mete" (l. 147). No sooner has
he spoken than his observation becomes reality. The irate goatherd
sees Lawrence and pins him fast to the earth with an arrow. Since
the fox has robbed the goatherd of his kid and done other wrongs,
he takes the fox's pelt as compensation. The nature of Lawrence's
death is directly related to his sin; a similar example is seen in
Chaucer's "Pardoner's Tale." As in Chaucer's tale, the sinner's
refusal to give up his sin—be it theft, violation of the sacrament of
penance, avarice, or pride—results in his death. Ironically, all of the
factors surrounding Lawrence's death coincide with the prediction
of his horoscope. Saturn is in control of Lawrence's fortune because
he is in Capricorn and Aquarius is ascendant. Capricorn is the goat,
and a kid leads Lawrence to his death. Jupiter is in Sagittarius, the
archer, who does indeed have good luck when he kills Lawrence
and gets his skin. MacQueen even suggests that there is significance
in Mercury's being in exaltation over Virgo, who controls the lower
bowels through which Lawrence is shot.[74] But Lawrence's fortune
comes true precisely because he is not willing to take the advice of
the friar. He neglects to carry out the elementary and superficial
penance which might have saved his life.

In this fable Henryson builds on the traditional attack on friars in
estates satire, but he blends his satire of the demagoguery of lax
holy men with an attack on insincere penitents. Stearns, believing
the fox to be a well-meaning penitent, finds it difficult to explain
why Henryson would have made such abrupt departures from the
traditional characterization of the fox.[75] In fact, Henryson has made
no such departures; he has used the traditional craftiness of the fox
to create an unregenerate sinner who is a match for his hypocritical
friar. As vividly demonstrated in "The Paddock and the Mouse" and
"The Cock and the Jasp," Henryson's fables do not have to have a
hero who gains our sympathy. Instead of being concerned with a
sympathetic or heroic protagonist in this tale, he is instead
determined to explore the roles of penitent and priest in a religious
rite.

X *"The Taill of the*
Sone & Air of the forsaid Foxe callit Father wer: Alswa the
Parliament of fourfuttit Beistis, haldin be the Lyoun"

This fable is the third in the Lawrence series. Unfortunately,
problems of textual corruption make it difficult to discern clearly
Henryson's political commentary, but the poet was apparently
examining the Scottish monarchy, particularly in its relations with
the church and clerical advisors. The opening of the tale explains
that Lawrence had no legal heirs but that he had one bastard son.
The story line begins where "The Fox and the Wolf" leaves off.
Lawrence's son goes to the scene of his father's death and carries off
the body for burial, all the while thanking God that he will inherit
his father's possessions. He throws Lawrence's body into a peat bog
full of water and commends his bones to the devil. This lengthy
introduction establishes that the younger fox is indeed "his father's
son," while also providing narrative continuity between this fable
and "The Fox and the Wolf." Given the fox's ultimate fate, it is
important that the reader know from the start that he is a bad
character.

Immediately after Lowrye has buried his father, he is called to a
parliament of animals, organized by King Nobill the lion. As
MacQueen has demonstrated, Nobill's court is distinctively Scottish. The animals are summoned to the lion's presence by a unicorn
pursuivant, while the court itself is fenced by the panther, a
relationship that exists between the two animals on the royal seal
of Scotland.[76] All of the estates of Scottish society are represented
by the various types of animals that crowd the setting. The listing is
not simply a casual embellishment. Near the top are:

> The Menataur, a monstour mervelous,
> Bellorophant, that beist of bastarde,
> The Warwolf and the Pegasus perolus,
> Transformit be assent of socerre:
> The Lynx, the Tegir, full of tyrane. . . .

> (ll. 92–96)

Although this catalog includes the most regal of beasts, it also
includes monsters. The minotaur, in particular, is traditionally
associated with sensuality. Henryson might have been subtly

attacking James' associates by describing such creatures at the pinnacle of the animal kingdom. The list continues, describing all classes of animals from the leopard through the sheep and the swine.

There are certainly echoes of the Scottish monarch in Nobill. His tone reflects the haughtiness associated with James, and there is even an adaptation of the motto of the Scottish kings, *Parcere prostratis scit nobilis ira leonis*, in one of his speeches:

> I lat you wit, my mycht is merceabill,
> And steris none that ar to me prostrat;
> Angrye, austerne, and als unameabill,
> To all that standis aganis myne estait. . . .

> (ll. 134–37)

Henryson has certainly been as explicit in this characterization as prudence would dictate.

Lowrye first appears at the parliament in disguise, partly because of his father's sins. He is eventually revealed, and, surprisingly, is asked to be the king's ambassador to a mare who has failed to compear. That he should be chosen for such a task implies questionable judgment on the part of the king but it also provides a clue to his real-life equivalents. He might very well represent Thomas Cochrane or Thomas Preston, unpopular courtiers who were entrusted with important missions by James.[77]

Nobill, however, insists on having his way. The fox at first refuses to go:

> A lord, mercye, lo I have bot ane e.
> Hurt in the hanch, and crukit ye may se;
> The Wolf is bettir in ambassadry,
> And mair cunning in clergye than I.

> (ll. 186–89)

His attempt to shift the responsibility makes Nobill even more adamant, and he declares that both the fox and the wolf must go to summon the mare. His insistence gives additional proof of the initial bad judgment which resulted in the selection of the fox for the mission.

Although this fable employs a tradition of medieval political commentary, much of the tale seems to focus on historical events in Scotland. Throughout the reign of James III there was controversy between the church and the king about the appointment of clergy to benefices. The crown had attempted to extend its power over the filling of vacancies, sometimes leaving them empty simply to benefit the royal treasury. In a series of papal decrees, however, the king's authority had been undercut by the church, which firmly asserted its own control. The quarrels reached a climax in 1472, when Patrick Graham was made archbishop of St. Andrews without James' approval. In an attempt to check the church's authority, James managed to secure the appointment of William Scheves as Graham's successor. Even in objective contemporary accounts, Scheves was described as undistinguished as a clergyman or scholar. It is quite possible that the Scheves appointment is at least partially the subject of this fable.

In the "Moralitas" of the tale only in the Bannatyne manuscript Henryson tells us that the mare is representative of "monkis and othir men of religioun," who are forced by the crown to become involved in politics. She could indeed be a symbol for the whole class of men of contemplation, but she could also more specifically represent Patrick Graham, whom James resented and similarly antagonized. She is reluctant to go. When she is first approached by Lowrye and the wolf, she informs them she is not forced to compear since she has a year's respite from state duties written on her hoof. The fox, perhaps suspecting a trick, refuses to investigate. The wolf, "autentik and a man of aige" (l. 204), decides to inspect her evidence. In his power and gullibility, the wolf resembles William Scheves, James' appointee to the see. When he bends down to look at the mare's hoof she kicks him in the head, seriously wounding him. Lowrye declines to pursue the matter further, and he and the wolf return to the court. When the lion demands to know why the mare did not come with them, the fox replies:

> . . . My lord spere nocht at me;
> This new maid doctour of divinitee,
> With his rede cap, can tell yow wele yneuch.
>
> (ll. 242–44)

The red cap is a covering of blood on the wolf's head and cheeks, but it again calls attention to the wolf's ecclesiatical background, as does the lion's reply. Still chiding the wolf's lack of wisdom, he concedes that "The grettest clerkis ar nocht the wyssest men" (l. 255). The proverb probably originally meant that men rich in learning are not necessarily wise, but the word "greatest" can be interpreted as "highest in position." Scheves' political position would certainly place him among the "greatest" clergymen in the land; unhappily for him the rest of the proverb would certainly apply as well. The attempt to persuade the mare to come to court could well be interpreted as efforts to bring more ecclesiastical benefices under the auspices of the crown.[78]

The attack on court life is climaxed by the downfall of Lowrye. Just after his return from the mare, a ewe approaches the lion to ask justice for the fox's killing of her lamb. Her accusation is twofold: Not only has the fox committed murder, but in so doing he has also broken the king's peace, proclaimed at the beginning of the parliament. The latter act is treasonous. Her accusations and the fox's conviction throw even more doubt on the lion's judgment in sending him on a mission to the mare. His death is strikingly similar to that of the king's favorites at Lauder bridge. When James was captured, the court favorites with him were hanged from the bridge at Lauder. After a trial, the fox is shriven and summarily hanged. The reference seems quite pointed, and the tone of the poem's conclusion seems to bear out this argument. The death of the fox seems to be a hopeful sign for improvement at the lion's court just as the death of the king's favorites inspired hope in many Scotsmen. Yet the court still remains a gathering place for such as the wolf and the fox.

As in the best of his fables, Henryson supplements his political interpretation with a more general tropological interpretation. Some difficulties in the text make it difficult to assess how successfully the tale and "Moralitas" are blended, but the moral focuses on the tropological elements in this "fable figurall," an excellent means of diverting attention from his potentially explosive political allegory. The lion, he asserts, represents

> . . . this warld be liklynace,
> To quhom lowtis bayth emperour and king,   [bow down
> And thinkis of this warld to get mare grace. . . .
>
> (ll. 295–97)

While this explanation is more cautious than a bare analysis of the political allegory would be, it still establishes a connection between the political and tropological themes. He is implying that emperors and kings are foolish in their pursuit of earthly possessions. The

lion's oppression of the mare, who represents men of contemplation, suggests tropologically the world's tendency to force religious
men into the pomp and pride of secular life. This situation as well is
critical of James' attempt to politicize the church.

The wolf is sensuality, which overwhelms man, when, like a
beast, he gives himself over to the vanity of this world. If man flees
this worldly vanity, then "sall reasoun ris," and for man's soul there
is nothing better. As in earlier fables, Henryson is counseling his
reader to avoid carnality and sensuality and to follow the rule of
reason. Most significant for his political allegory is that the lion is
the source of sensuality, possibly a veiled comment on the conduct
of James' court. The mare's hoof is the thought of death which "may
brek sensualiteis hede" (l. 317) and free man from the power of the
lion and the wolf. Henryson quotes Solomon and reminds man to
think on his end, not sin. The fox represents temptations, including
vain thoughts and sweet persuasions. His withdrawal is the result of
seeing sensuality almost slain.

Henryson has forged some strong links between the two themes
of his tale. The moral lesson explains the political situation. It is
after all the lack of reason among the members of the parliament of
animals that keeps the mare away, just as the irrationality of political
affairs alienates men of contemplation. He also relates this
irrationality to pride. Pride is the dominant characteristic of the
lion's personality as shown in his haughty declarations about his own
might. It is also significant that the cause of the wolf's downfall is
that he was blinded with pride. This pride is both an effect of
irrationality and a cause of further error. In his analysis of the
morality of political life, Henryson has attempted to impart a lesson
particularly appropriate to the Scottish court.

XI *"The Preiching of the Swallow"*

One of the richest of the fables in thematic and narrative texture,
this tale is "in some ways the most rewarding of the *Fabillis*." [79] It
offers further exploration of the opposition between reason and
sensuality, some of Henryson's most effective descriptive passages,
and numerous insights into Henryson's theology. It also shows
Henryson's ability to blend the traditions of medieval science and
theology with the burgeoning humanism of the fifteenth century.

Henryson's view of the universe is carefully explained in the prologue of the fable.[80] He first touches on the nature of God, emphasizing His omnipotence:

> The he prudence, and wirking mervellus,
> The profound wit of God omnipotent,
> Is so perfyt and so ingenis,
> Excelland fer all manis argument. . . .

(ll. 1–4)

In addition to His omnipotence, God may also be defined by His excellent reason. Henryson views God as perfect intellect working itself out in ways too complicated for the feeble understanding of man. There are parallels in this passage with *The Kingis Quair*,[81] and many modern readers may find similarities with Milton's God in book 3 of *Paradise Lost*.

God's perfect reason and omnipotence also result in His ability to see all time as the present. This explains the specific nature of God's foreknowledge, and it provides a pattern for man's own behavior. Man can best fulfill the goals of his life by seeking to emulate God in developing his reason and achieving a transcendent view of the universe. Nevertheless, there are certain things that must remain beyond man's ken. He is bound in a "presoun corporale", and, as a result, he may not see or clearly understand God or celestial things. Although Henryson makes use of proverbs and biblical sources in this fable, he also uses contemporary works and ancient philosophy. In this instance, he quotes Aristotle in explaining that man's soul is like a bat's eye which may not be able to see daylight. As the bat cannot see light, so man's soul, "with phantesye opprest" is unable to discern complete truth.

Even if man is unable to plumb the depths of God's wisdom, there are still numerous opportunities for the exercise of his limited faculties. Though natural reason is not sufficient to search out the secrets of the Trinity, it may provide some knowledge of God through his creatures. This is one of the most humanistic, almost empirical, tenets of his philosophy. The redemption of nature and its study was the very task that Francis Bacon felt impelled to undertake over a hundred years later, when he was attempting to dispel Christian notions about the inherent evil of nature after the sin of Adam. Henryson foreshadows Bacon by suggesting that from our knowledge of nature, we may infer that God is "guid, fair, wyis, and bening" (l. 31). Henryson then lists the evidence for his view of

God, including the flowers, the firmament (clearly ordered according to the laws of medieval astronomy and considerably different from the astrological theories in "The Fox and the Wolf" and *Orpheus and Eurydice*), the fish, the fowl, the beasts, and even man himself, the latter described as God's "ymage and his similitude." Henryson concludes that from this evidence man knows that God is fair and good. Henryson's humanistic view of nature also appears in his ruminations about the role of man in the universe. All other creatures, he asserts, were "maid for the behuisse / Off man" (ll. 50–51), a comment that has important implications for his use of the beast fable. Despite the basic optimism of his outlook, Henryson is not blindly naive. The world is not without peril; it is full of snares and nets which man must work to avoid.

This philosophy is dramatically exemplified in the tale itself. The plot concerns the attempts of a churl to catch the swallow and other birds who are eating his seed. Despite the swallow's warnings, the other birds take no heed and are captured and killed by the churl. The fable shows man, as represented by the swallow and the birds she tries to warn, confronted with the problem of evil, and as Burrow notes, the "unifying principle" of the tale is prudence, one possible solution to man's dilemma.[82] The forces that trap men are represented by the churl who sows his seed and sets the snares. Henryson believes that the snares can be avoided, a faith he explores in the swallow's sermons to the other, duller birds. From the very beginning of the growing season, when the narrator first comes upon the birds, the swallow is aware of the danger posed by the hemp crop. She utters three increasingly passionate warnings in her attempt to keep the birds from their fate. As she watches the planting of the hemp crop, she becomes aware of the churl's intention: to make nets with which to trap the birds. She therefore advises a course of action to abort his scheme. She counsels the other birds to wait until he is gone and then to dig up and eat the seed. In his tropological "Moralitas" Henryson compares the swallow to a preacher, who is always alert to the dangers of the "nettis of our wickit ennemye." He assists his fellowman to avoid the devil's snares by "Extortand men to walk, and ay be war" (l. 304). Despite his attempts to help, he is often ignored, as shown in ·the birds' reaction to the swallow's warnings.

The birds who berate the swallow and ignore her advice represent "wretchis . . . / Ay scraipand in this wardlis vaine plesaunce" (ll. 296–97). In their portrayal, Henryson returns to his

favorite theme, the dangers of irrationality and carnality. He
specifically states that in their error their "Reasoun is blindit with
affectioun" (l. 285) and they are overcome with carnal appetite. As
in "The Cock and the Jasp" and "The Paddock and the Mouse," this
appetite takes the particular form of hunger, but in the "Moralitas"
of this fable that hunger is generalized into the hunger for worldly
goods and is coupled with an ill-founded complacency. The birds
and the men they represent do not know that everything in this
world is mutable and that all prosperity is only fleeting. To stress
this point, Henryson goes to the traditional language of the pulpit in
lines that may also contain a reference to "The Debate Between the
Body and the Soul":

> Alace, quhat cair, quhat weping is and wo,
> Quhen saull and bodye pairtit ar in twane,
> The bodye to the wirmis kitching go,
> The saull to fyre and evirlasting paine. . . .

(ll. 309–12)

By sounding the same warning that appears in lyrics such as
Dunbar's "Timor mortis conturbat me," he is trying to turn man's
mind from the petty concerns of temporal affairs to thoughts of
eternal life.

The foolish birds ignore not only the swallow's first warning but
two succeeding warnings as well. Each of the three warnings marks
an important structural division in the poem and a stage in the life of
man.[83] The first sermon comes during the spring, tropologically
symbolizing the youth of man. The second is placed in the midst of
the growing season, after the middle of June, a time period that
suggests middle age. The swallow continues to be alarmed at the
growth of the hemp crop and the inaction of the birds. She once
again tries to make them understand the danger around them:

> O blind birdis, and full of negligence,
> Unmyndfull of your prosperitie,
> Cast up your sycht, and take guid advertence,
> Luik to the lynt that growis on yone lye. . . .

(ll. 169–72)

She again foretells the churl's plan and advises the birds to pull the
seed out of the ground, thereby avoiding potential catastrophe. The
birds disregard her advice.

Henryson then provides an explanation of the hemp industry in Scotland with so much detail that he has been credited with presenting the most complete early description in Britain.[84] Immediately after the depiction of the hemp harvesting and processing, the poem moves to a description of winter, representing old age in the life of man. The churl, angry because the birds have taken up residence in his barn and stolen his grain, sets traps for them with nets made from the hemp in his field. His bait is food, which the birds desperately need, but, despite their need, the swallow utters yet a third warning:

> Thair is na corne, ye laubour all in vaine;
> Trow ye yone churll for pietie will you feid?
> Na, na, he hes it lyit heir for a traine. . . .
>
> (ll. 233–35)

The other birds, however, give in to their hunger and rush into the churl's trap. When they are captured, the churl kills them with a cudgel. The moral of their plight is reflected in the swallow's own meditations on the death of her companions:

> Lo, quod scho, thus it happin oftin syis
> Off thame that will nocht tak counsale nor reid
> Off prudent men, or clerkis that ar wyis.
>
> (ll. 261–63)

There is a touch of the exasperation here that is also found in the "Moralitas" of "The Cock and the Jasp." If Henryson was indeed disappointed that men would not take advantage of the opportunities offered by the science he loved, he was more distressed that they would not follow the paths of salvation.

In his narrative structure and his use of seasonal and landscape allegory, Henryson is quite similar to Langland. One of the major narrative similarities is the use of a narrator who also participates, even if only indirectly, in the action. Just as Langland wanders out in the Malvern Hills on a summer day and has a vision of a fair field of folk performing all of the world's tasks, Henryson wanders out in the spring "Off lawboraris to see the besynace" (l. 100). Although they may not be engaged in all the tasks of the world, they illustrate a wide variety: some are making dikes, some plowing, and some sowing seed.[85] While Henryson does not fall asleep as Langland does, there is no doubt that he is transported to a visionary world where he begins to hear birds speak and listens in on their conversations. Langland's poem is developed over the span of his entire life; at one point he spends as much as twenty years away from his dream in the business of the world. In Henryson's poem, the dream is interrupted by diversions of the poet's attention through the seasons that span a year and tropologically represent the lifetime of a man. The transitions between the visionary world and the external world are treated in the same casual and homely fashion in both poems.

Henryson's seasonal descriptions deserve special attention. Not only do they align his narrative structure more closely with that of Langland, but they also have considerable independent artistry. The seasonal pageant that precedes the narrative action is, as MacQueen has shown, "an organic part of the argument of the prologue" [86] and it also forms a vital allegorical link between the philosophical exposition of the prologue and the narrative action of the tale. Henryson starts with "somer with his Iolye mantill grene" (l. 57) and proceeds through a conventional description of fall, ". . . quhen seres that goddes / Hir barnis benit hes with abundance" (ll. 65–66). His description of winter is particularly biting:

> Thir dailis deip with dubbis drownit is
> Baith hill and holt heilit with frostis hair
> And bewis bene ar bethit bare of bliss
> Be wikkit windis of the wintare wair. . . .
>
> (ll. 78–81)

He then concludes with a portrayal of spring, "the secretare of Somer," who regenerates plant and animal life. The descriptions combine remarkably realistic elements, apparently drawn from the Scottish countryside,[87] and traditional elements including the listing of seasonal gods and goddesses such as Flora, Phoebus, Ceres, Bacchus, and Eolus. Because of the transitional nature of this passage and its relationship with the realistic seasonal descriptions in the tale, it needs realistic details; but because the seasonal pageant is also intended to help the poet explore the traditional associations between the seasons of the year and the seasons of man's life, his use of conventional descriptive elements is also necessary. The tale and the "Moralitas" are closely integrated in this fable. George Clark, in fact, believes that the use of time in this fable helps to establish "competing impulses toward an Aesopian or moralistic reading based on philosophical optimism and a tragic interpretation rooted in philosophical pessimism." [88] Henryson's philosophical prologue, biblical allusions, and narrative structure all support his moral teaching. All of the borrowings from the tradition of religious allegory lend this fable a fiery indignation and sad disappointment common to the preachings of humanistic moralists.

In no other fable does Henryson offer as much explicit information on his view of the universe. Like *The Testament of Cresseid*, this fable illustrates Henryson's best use of a narrative persona and the techniques of allegory. Despite his pessimism about changing human behavior, the poet's love and concern for his fellowman are clearly evident. We can indeed agree that this fable "deserves to be counted as one of the minor masterpieces of English poetry." [89]

XII "The Taill of the Lyon & the Mous"

Although this fable is obviously more political in its implications, it is closely related to "The Preaching of the Swallow." Both fables use the dream-vision technique, even though the latter does not include a dream as such. Both incorporate a first-person narrator who observes the action of the fable and reports it to the reader. In both fables, the narrator is near or under a hawthorne tree in spring when he has his vision. Moreover, besides its political overtones, the "Moralitas" of this fable carries a message similar to that in "The Preaching."

In this fable, Henryson's narrator goes out into the countryside in the middle of June and arrives at the hawthorne tree where he lies down, closes his eyes, goes to sleep and dreams. Through his use of the dream-vision convention, Henryson attempts, in Spearing's words, "to provide authority and authenticity for the whole work," by relating it to the larger tradition. [90] The content of this dream, however, is significantly different from that in *Piers Plowman* or "The Preaching." Instead of seeing talking animals or a fair field of folk, Henryson's narrator beholds "The fairest man befoir that evir I saw" (l. 28). The figure proves to be none other than Aesop, and Henryson's vision becomes a literary event. Aesop proves to be a perfect medieval blend of Christian and pagan, both in thought and appearance. [91] Even though Aesop comes from Rome and has studied civil law, he says that his dwelling is in Heaven forever. The combination of the classical and medieval, the pagan and Christian,

in this character reflects a similar balance in the nature of
Henryson's poetry, and Henryson acknowledges a close relationship
between himself and his literary progenitor. Aesop greets him with
a familiar "God speid, my sone," to which Henryson responds
"Welcum fader." Henryson immediately identifies Aesop with his
fables and requests a tale. He makes a point of asking that Aesop
conclude his tale with "a gud moralitie." At first Aesop denies his
request with a comment that reminds the reader of "The Preaching
of the Swallow":

> . . . My sone, lat be,
> For quhat is worth to tell a fenyeit taill,
> Quhen haill preiching may no thing now availl?
>
> (ll. 68–70)

MacQueen suggests that this possible reference to "The Preaching"
indicates that it was already well known before the composition of
this tale.[92] It is more likely that Henryson is making a more general
reference to preaching in the generic sense, particularly since the
major thrust of the dialogue is to develop further the parallel
between preaching and the art of the poet. Moreover, the reference
can be explained as an element of narrative transition, valuable even
if no one but Henryson had seen the earlier fable.

Aesop goes on to complain that the world is so bad that
comparatively few men approach God's word in a spirit of true
devotion. Instead, he laments, men give themselves over to the
satisfaction of earthly desires. Even so, after Henryson makes a
second request, Aesop gives in and begins the fable about the lion
and the mouse. Henryson retains the basic story line about a lion
who captures a mouse and lets him go, only to be later helped by
the mouse when he has been captured by hunters, but he may also
have attempted to relate the action to the Lauder rebellion.

The lion seems to be James III, and the ambivalence of his
portrayal is to be expected after the portraits in "The Two Mice" and
"The Trial of the Fox." Although James has retained his regal
proportions from the latter tale, once again his noble stature is
diminished by numerous vices. At the opening of the tale, he is
found "Bekand his breist and belly at the son" (l. 87). While there is
no harm in the lion's enjoying his leisure, he is so still that the mice
are not afraid to run back and forth over him as part of their common
pathway. These references to the lion's inactivity are likely a veiled

description of James' withdrawal from the affairs of government to
his courtiers, art objects, and mistress. When the affairs of state go
untended, such sloth is hardly laudable. Even more despicable is
the lion's capricious cruelty. He awakens and captures one of the
mice who have been walking over him. After having fiercely
threatened the mouse, the lion releases him and goes on a rampage:

> . . . the Lyone yeid to hunt,
> For he had nocht, bot levit on his pray,
> And slew baith tame and wyld, as he wes wunt,
> And in the cuntre maid a grit dirray. . . .
>
> (ll. 190–93)

The phrase "For he had nocht" probably refers to the fact that the
Scottish monarch had a pitifully small independent income and was
forced to rely on his barons and burgesses for support. His lack of
income, however, still does not justify his slaying both "tame and
wyld" or innocent and guilty, and the habitual nature of his action
makes it even more vicious. If there were any doubt remaining
about the object of Henryson's attack, it is dispelled by the
"Moralitas" in which he interprets the lion as "a prince or empriour,
/ A potestat, or yit a king with croun" (ll. 254–55). He further
comments that the ruler he describes

> . . . takis no lawbour
> To rewll nor steir the land, nor justice keip,
> Bot lyis still in lustis, slewth and sleip.
>
> (ll. 257–59)

James III was accused of this very indolence in contemporary
chronicles and satires.[93]

The mice who affront the lion by ignoring his power stand for "the
commonte." Although Stearns believes the first mouse is a symbol
for "the sturdily independent peasant," he is more likely a
representative of the middle classes.[94] All of the mice are guilty of
thoughtlessness in their trespass against the lion, but his sloth has
encouraged their error, and their fault is unwitting. In fact, their
chagrin at having angered him is expressed by the first mouse when
she is captured:

> Se als [h]ow thingis done by negligence,
> Nocht of malys nor of promissioun,

Ever suld haif grace and remissioun.
....
Ye lay so still and law upone the erd,
That, be my saule, we wend ye had bene deid,
Ellis wald we nocht dansit our your heid.

(ll. 117–19, 124–26)

Though the mice's actions constitute a kind of treason, Henryson carefully differentiates them from the treasonous acts of the hunters. Moreover, this speech even contains a hint of righteous indignation, particularly in its description of the essential attributes of a monarch. The qualities the poet emphasizes are those that were most lacking in James III: active concern, restraint, justice, and mercy.

The lion's capture results in some soul-searching on his part and an expression of his distress at his own foolish trust in his power and worldly position. In the midst of his lamenting, a solution to his predicament appears in the form of the mice who had been walking and dancing over him before. The leader of the mice recognizes the lion and, grateful for his earlier mercy, organizes the others to chew through his bonds. The lion is freed to go on his way "becaus he had pete" (l. 249).

Vital to an understanding of the political allegory of this fable is the role of the hunters. In the "Moralitas" Henryson describes them as "crewall men" who "Waitit alway amendis for till get" (l. 290).[95] Stearns points out a parallel between the capture of the lion and the kidnapping of James by Sir Alexander Boyd in 1466,[96] suggesting that the hunters would be Boyd and his companions. More likely, the subject of the fable is the Lauder rebellion, and the hunters of the lion represent the Earl of Angus, Sir Robert Douglas, and even members of the king's own family. Doubtless the power of the conspirators, as well as the kinship some of them shared with the king, accounts for Henryson's reluctance to identify the hunters more specifically. He states only that they are men seeking revenge and adds cryptically, "king and lord may weill wit quhat I mene" (l. 293).

The rescue is parallel to other political events that followed James' capture by Angus and the others. The Duke of Albany, James' brother, had fled to England to escape persecution after the execution of the Earl of Mar, another brother. Albany aided England in her war against Scotland, and, at the time of the king's capture, he was besieging Berwick in company with the Duke of

Gloucester. When he found that James had been captured, he hurried further into Scotland to assume the reins of government. Once Albany took over the government, he effected a truce with England and began to plan to gain permanent control of the crown. Apparently, his mother recommended that James be released from prison as prologue to his abdication in favor of Albany. The duke then had to find a way to release James from his captivity without arousing the ire of the Lauder conspirators, who were still powerful even though they had disbanded. It seems likely that he encouraged Walter Bertram to organize the Edinbrugh burgesses to lay siege to Atholl castle so Albany could privately arrange for James' release. Free of his obligations to the conspirators by virtue of the state of siege, the Earl of Atholl let the castle fall into the burgesses' hands and James was released. Henryson's praise of the valor of the mice is not praise of the peasantry but of the Edinburgh burgesses, and his serious attitude toward the action proves that "Albany's exercise in propaganda was not in vain." [97]

Henryson has been very cautious in this fable by placing the tale in the mouth of Aesop and by refusing to provide specifics about the hunters, and he has also protected himself by exploration of the tropological allegory. The forest, a generalized setting, is not specifically Scotland but is to be understood as the world and its prosperity, subject to rapid change. He also introduces the general theme about the fall of princes when he bemoans how quickly a lord of great renown can fall from his position through lust and vanity. The major tropological themes of the poem, he asserts, are pity and the effects of good deeds. Henryson does not examine these tropological elements simply as a smokescreen, for as we know from other fables they were subjects close to his heart. Yet the tropological interpretation is a safe diversion from the political considerations which permeate the tale.

Henryson's attitude toward James in this fable is ambivalent at best, but the poet is quite evidently speaking as "the representative of ordinary people who suffer under the conduct of their superiors." [98] The poet expresses monarchist attitudes in his use of the lion symbol and his sympathy for the lion instead of the hunters, but he has little admiration for the sloth and lust which limited James' effectiveness in his position. It seems in many ways that James is praiseworthy only because his captors are so much worse than he. Henryson hopes for better things as he utters a prayer through Aesop:

> . . . My fair chyld,
> Perswaid the kirkmen ythandly to pray,
> That tressone of this cuntre be exyld,
> And justice ring, and lordis keip thair fey
> Unto thair soverane lord both nycht and day.
>
> (ll. 295–99)

Henryson does indeed see a solution: he believes that for James "salvation from the power of the nobility depended on the equity with which his justice was administered; that so long as the commons felt no resentment against him, the nobility would be powerless to unseat him." [99] Unfortunately James did not recognize his situation, and lasting peace and internal tranquillity were still in the distant future for Scotland.

XIII   "The Taill of the Foxe, that begylit the Wolf, in the schadow of the Mone"

While this fable is based on the same plot as "The Vox and the Wolf," the oldest Reynardine fable in English, it also shows some plot similarities with Chaucer's "Friar's Tale." The influences of the two poems appear in two separate sections of the tale. The first section, which shows the most similarities with Chaucer's tale, concerns the efforts of the wolf to swindle a farmer out of a team of oxen. In both Henryson's tale and Chaucer's, a character makes a foolish vow, conveying in one case his oxen and in the other his soul to an agent of evil. In both cases, the evil protagonist has overheard the vow and comes to collect what has been assigned to him. In the second section, the plot is derived from "The Vox and the Wolf," in which the fox, stranded in a well, persuades the wolf to lower himself into the well too so that the fox is able to escape. Henryson's blending of these two plot lines creates new opportunities for both social and political satire, along with a chance to explore some of his favorite tropological themes.

The political and social satire in the tale again attacks the conduct of the proud lords who seize property of the commons without due process, a subject Henryson treated in "The Wolf and the Lamb" and "The Sheep and the Dog." The wolf happens by a farmer whose oxen are not working as they should, much to the farmer's distress. In a fit of anger, the farmer cries out that he wishes the wolf might take his oxen, and, when the team arrives at the end of the furrow, the wolf appears to demand what he has been given. The wolf's presumption in claiming the oxen is clearly parallel to that of the proud barons of the fifteenth century. Even his language echoes the haughtiness of the avaricious nobility:

> The Wolff said "quhether dryvis thou this Pray?
> I challenge it, ffor nane off thame ar thyne"
> ....
> . . . 'Carle, gaif thou not me this drift
> Airlie, quhen thou wes eirrand on yone bank? [100]

The wolf's demanding tone and his rude demeanor are both characteristics Henryson associates with the lawless nobles. As in "The Wolf and the Lamb," they are greeted meekly, for the husbandman answers the wolf soberly and addresses him as a social superior. Flabbergasted, he replies "Schir, be my Saull, thir oxin ar all myne" (l. 2263). Henryson leaves no doubt about the social relationships in this dialogue. The husbandman is a social inferior who becomes a victim of the wolf's greed, just as the Scottish peasant was often a victim of the rapacity of the Scottish lords.

Despite the peasant's denial that he has really given the oxen to the wolf, the wolf insists on his rights. To the wolf's legalistic demand for possession, the husbandman responds in kind. He again denies that the wolf has any claim to his animals and suggests that they take the matter to court. The wolf remains adamant, and his response provides additional clues to the social hierarchy that divides the two:

> "Carll" (quod the Wolff), "ane Lord, and he be leill,
> That schrinkis for schame, or doutis to be repruvit,
> His saw is ay als sickker as his Seill."

> (ll. 2280–82)

Stearns believes that these lines are the very heart of Henryson's social satire; he points out that Henryson obviously approves the husbandman's assertion that their differences must be settled in court and scorns the wolf's false and selfish appeal to shallow standards of loyalty.[101] The husbandman's response is double-edged: he uses a proverbial argument: "I may say, and ganesay, I am na King" (l. 2289). On the one hand, this might be an ironic comment on James' conduct, but it could also be an attack on barons who tried to use the king's own pronouncements to bring the kingdom down around his ears.

The wolf has yet another means of deciding the issue. He proposes to offer a witness and calls Lawrence, the fox, to come forward and testify about what he has heard. Instead of merely giving evidence, the fox establishes himself as judge and offers to settle the case if both parties will be bound by his decision. At this point Henryson slightly changes the focus of his satire. He does not forget the ignoble conduct of the barons, but he turns to the theme he pursued in "The Sheep and the Dog," the inequities of the legal system. There is certainly suspicion raised about the fox's role as both witness and judge; his hatred of the light, carefully emphasized when he appears, brings at once to mind his stealthy nature. Moreover, his association with the wolf makes his objectivity suspect. Any suspicions about his lack of integrity are borne out by the fashion in which he makes his judgment. He wins from the husbandman a bribe of six or seven hens, and his rationalization for accepting the bribe is outrageous. He relies on pragmatic proverbial wisdom: he believes that "God is gane to sleip" (l. 2332) and therefore men should follow the advice that "Buddis beiris Bernis throw" and "With emptie hand na man suld Halkis lure" (ll. 2322, 2335). His use of such proverbs is an attempt to make the bribery seem to be a matter of common sense and common practice, but Henryson finds it scandalous.

The second part of the fable relates the conflict between two almost equally despicable oppressors. Having agreed to accept the husbandman's bribe, the fox finds himself forced to satisfy the wolf. He promises him a cheese if only he will drop his case against the husbandman. Grudgingly the wolf agrees, and both animals go quickly "to ane Manure place." When they come to a well with two buckets, the fox tricks the wolf into believing that the "shadow" of the moon is the cheese he has been promised. To reassure the wolf, the fox jumps into one bucket and descends to the bottom of the well. Once the wolf has been cajoled into coming down to claim his cheese, he grabs the other bucket, and, as he descends, the fox comes back to the top. Realizing he has been tricked, the wolf shouts his anger up to the fox, who calmly replies, "thus fairis it off Fortoun: / As ane cummis up, scho quheillis ane uther doun!" (ll. 2418–19). The social satire in this portion of the tale is less pointed, but Henryson may be showing that great lords as well as the commoners are enmeshed in the inequities of the legal system. The fable also generates a certain delight by showing two types of rogues at odds with one another.

Despite the social implications of the tale, Henryson's "Moralitas" stresses the tropological level of interpretation. The wolf, he explains, does not specifically represent evil lords but is any "wickit man" who is tempted to trespass on the rights of others and pick quarrels whenever he can. The fox is not just a corrupt judge but the devil, who goads men to commit unrighteous acts. Like the fowler in "The Preaching of the Swallow," the fox entraps men in his nets with the lure of riches. Ironically, these riches are the "wodds waist" wherein all of the action of the tale takes place. The cheese stands for covetousness through which the fox goads the wolf into unwise action.

There can be no doubt about the sincerity of Henryson's message. In this tale he treats once again a theme that was part of his inheritance from the medieval pulpit. The search for riches is simply another facet of the myopic carnality which is condemned in most of the fables. Henryson is not, however, concerned only with the temptations of the evil man; he is apparently more interested in showing the effects of evil on the good man, in this fable obviously the husbandman. The hens with which he bribes the fox are not evil deeds but are instead "warkis that fra ferme faith proceidis" (l. 2437). At the tropological level, it is the well-being of this good man that is Henryson's main interest, a concern he shares with Langland. His love of good men is the motivation for the benediction with which he concludes the fable: "Christ keip all Christianis from that wickit well!" (l. 2454).

As MacQueen argues, the outstanding feature of this tale is its balance, both in structural and symbolic complexity.[102] The result of this complexity is the most delicate interweaving of political and tropological allegory. While Henryson attacks pride in the characterization of the wolf, he also attacks false social ideals of nobility. While he examines the attempts of Satan to woo mankind away from God, he also explores the social exploitation of all classes by false judges. This balance of interests provides the tale its historical force and timeless appeal.

XIV *"The Taill of the Wolf that gat the Nekhering throw the wrikis of the Foxe that begylit the Cadgear"*

This fable explores the treachery often involved in feudal loyalties while again examining some of Henryson's favorite moral themes. The tale has received extensive attention for both its use of sources and its thematic texture. It concerns the relationship between a wolf and a fox that he impresses into his service, the efforts of both to rob a cadger, a dealer in fish, and the fox's attempts to regain his freedom. The theme of feudal loyalty is developed primarily in the relations between the wolf and the fox. Although the wolf comes across the fox quite by accident at the beginning of the tale, there is evidence of a long-standing relationship between them, one that is clearly structured in feudal terms. When he first sees the wolf, for instance, the fox kneels and rises only with the wolf's permission. The wolf chides him for not coming to court, a complaint James III often made about his nobles and other officials, and even assigns him new court duties: the wolf assigns the fox to bear office as his steward. The fox defers the honor in a passage containing pronounced political overtones. His "roib is reid," he objects, and, as a result, the other animals will have nothing to do with him, all of which may constitute a possible veiled allusion to his clerical status. During a series of lines in which the wolf argues the fox's suitability to serve him, the fox continues his denials. Their discussion reaches a climax when the wolf becomes angry with the fox's reluctance to serve; the fox then admits that he sees the folly in trying to play his master "fallis in ressoning" and takes an oath of fealty "to be leill attour all levand leid" (l. 2022).

The oath of loyalty is wrong from the start. The wolf is wrong for impressing the fox into his retinue, and the fox is wrong for using the oath of fealty to deceive his master. This aspect of the fox's personality, however, accords well with his tropological role. After the wolf has been betrayed, Henryson sums up his social and moral messages in his description of the fox "That had betraisit his master and the man" (l. 2200). That the fox is a "steward," the family name of the ruling family of Scotland, makes the social satire all the more pointed.

Another element of social satire may exist in the characterization of the cadger. Stearns sees affinities between this character and portrayals of the middle class in "The Two Mice." He believes the cadger, who is tricked by the fox but captures the wolf, is the "butt" of part of the fable as a representative of middle-class avarice. He points to the cadger's sense of business values and lack of charity which result in his anger at the loss of the fox's pelt and his frustration in his own lack of foresight in dealing with the fox when he tries to make his escape. All of these elements seem to be part of the business ethics of fifteenth-century Scotland. If the cadger represents the middle class, the fable may contain heavily veiled references to the relationships among the burgesses, the barons, and the king.[103]

The political interpretation of this tale exists primarily by implication from Henryson's discussion of loyalty in the prologue and in the last stanza of the tale, along with some possible references to social classes in the portrayal of the characters. That the moral and ethical considerations were closer to the center of the tale may be proved by the prominence accorded them in the "Moralitas," which was entirely Henryson's. The poet's interpretation of this tale is again fraught with symbols characteristic of the pulpit. The fox, like the lion in "The Lion and the Mouse," may be compared with the world, which is a kind of steward to man and helps him forget the ultimate fact of his death. The wolf too is generalized. He is not just a proud baron, but now he is "ane man but leis" who is deceived by the world. The herring which the fox steals and with which he tempts the wolf is gold, which often tempts man as he makes his way in the world. The cadger, the sole human character in the fable, is "Deith, quhome under all man preis" (l. 2207). Henryson then sets about to explain how the feudal relationship between the fox and the wolf and their actions with the cadger may represent traditional relationships among the world, Death, and man, as theologically conceived. The feudal bond between the fox and the wolf is reinterpreted as the relation between man and the world. Just as the wolf forces the fox to become his steward, so foolish men try to force the world to come under their control. The world, of course, contains gold and can cheat Death, but man cannot. He is led to believe that Death is a sham and that he will be able to obtain and keep permanently the riches to which the world leads him. The fox is false, explains Henryson, and so is the world.

As in previous fables, Henryson exploits the association between hunger and other types of carnality in his use of the herring as a symbol of greed for all types of earthly things. His tirade against the influence of gold and man's lust for it could have come directly from a contemporary sermon:

> The micht of gold makis mony men sa blind,
> That settis on Avarice thair felicitie,
> That thay forget the cadgear cummis behind. . . .
>
> (ll. 2224–26)

Man is deceived by his love of gold just as the wolf is deceived by the fox's promises of the herring. Man, who is betrayed by his own shortsightedness, thinks he will live forever and increases his trust in the value of worldly possessions. The tropological interpretation of the fable is reinforced by Henryson's use of proverbial sources and folk wisdom.

The single issue in this fable which has stimulated most comment is neither politics nor tropological allegory. It is instead Henryson's sources. Diebler suggested that portions of the *Roman de Renart* in conjunction with one chapter of Caxton's *Reynard* offer the most likely sources for the fable. Gregory Smith chose to ignore Diebler's arguments and concluded that no source for the fable had been positively identified. More recently, Gavin Bone has again examined the relationship between Henryson's tale and the *Roman de Renart*, while Anthony W. Jenkins has provided more detailed analysis of Henryson's debt to the *Roman*. Jenkins also points out that much of the confusion has been caused by the variations in the text of the *Roman* and that many of the parallels are to be found primarily between Henryson and the Meon version of the *Roman*.[104] Henryson's use of the French source now seems well attested.

Once the source of the fable has been identified, it becomes possible to evaluate Henryson's expansion of that source into the long fable we have now. One of his major areas of development is characterization. In every instance, Henryson has taken the opportunity to develop characters in more detail than his source offers. The cadger, for instance, has been developed into a single major character from a series of carters who appear in two branches of the *Roman*. The result is a figure so lively and human that Stearns sees him as a major focus for the social satire in the tale.[105] Jenkins argues that Henryson has contributed to the character's development by internalizing his monologue on the value of the fox's pelt.

Another change in characterization is the omission of the explanation of the motive for the fox's revenge on the wolf. In the *Roman de Renart*, this motive is explained as a quarrel over a goose. By deleting this trivial motivation, Henryson has expanded the social implications of the fable, making the wolf another tyrannical lord whose bullying of the fox is the sole cause of the fox's hatred. This development of characters through expansion reveals Henryson's very modern interest in personality and character motivation. Henryson's use of the *Roman* illustrates as clearly as any of his sources that he is not interested simply in animals as stereotypes. Instead, he uses animals to reveal the truths he has won by close observation of his fellowman.

XV   *"The Taill of the Wolf and the Wedder"*

Although this tale may have some very specific applications to the court of James III, the "Moralitas" explores its general tropological significance. Henryson takes considerable pain to examine the ill effects of pride and its concomitant presumption, particularly at the highest levels of society.

The action of the fable involves a sheep who tries to take the place of a faithful watchdog whose death puts the flock in great peril from a ravenous wolf. The sheep puts on the dog's skin, scares the wolf, and chases him away.[106] When the dog's hide catches on a briar, the sheep is exposed for what he is and is killed by the wolf. As MacQueen suggests, the opening of the tale provides a perfect setting for allegory. The forest in which the action takes place is a usual locale for allegorical tales. The effects of the allegory are heightened by the pastoral characters and the casual interaction between man and beast.[107] Henryson interprets the events in the most general way. The dog's skin is the "riches of array," which cause men to be presumptuous. The wether is "pure men" who are depraved by the love of wealth and fine clothing. They are deceived by the first of the Seven Deadly Sins, Pride.

In his tropological allegory, Henryson becomes very traditional in his criticism of this sin. He finds a certain kind of man particularly vulnerable to this kind of pride:

> Richt swa in service uther sum exceidis,
> And thay haif withgang, welth, and cherising,
> That thay will lychtlie Lordis in thair deidis,
> And lukis not to thair blude, nor thair offspring. . . .
>
> (ll. 2602–5)

The emphasis on blood lines and the suggestion that "blood will tell" make up the most traditional elements in Henryson's definition of nobility. He had criticized the view that nobility could be determined solely on the basis of inheritance in "The Cock and the Fox," but, in this fable, he seems to argue that proper ancestors are essential elements in personal nobility. He is especially angered by the presumption of men who lack proper breeding. He exhorts such men "To knaw thame self" (l. 2610), by which he means that they should know their own stations in life. Knowledge of their stations should prevent the wretched arrogance of which these men are often guilty. Henryson warns: "It settis na servand for to uphald weir, / Nor clym sa hie, quhill he fall of the ledder" (ll. 2613–14). He also cautions them that they should "fall not with thair better in debait" (l. 2611). Although he attempts to generalize the warning to "men of everilk stait," there is no question that he seems to have particular individuals in mind.

Henryson's conservatism in his arguments for the privilege of hereditary nobility may have been caused by political events related to the Lauder rebellion. Among the faults of which James III was believed guilty was unduly advancing the careers of some "unworthie persons" who were of humble origin, and his assistance to them seemed so unreasonable that Bishop Lesley even felt justified in suggesting the existence of homosexual relationships. Whether any such relationship existed or not, the Scottish barons were irritated by James' gifts of land and money to his favorites.[108] The hanging of James' courtiers at the time of the Lauder rebellion may be the subject of the political allegory in this fable.

The wolf might represent the rebellious barons, whom Henryson characterized as the hunters in "The Lion and the Mouse." He is ambivalent in his characterization of the wolf. As in previous fables, the wolf is a predator. After the death of his dog, the shepherd laments that he will lose everything "For with the Wolff weryit beis all my scheip" (l. 2467). As a predator, the wolf is hardly a hero, especially when the first point of view that a reader encounters is that of the shepherd and the wether. Yet, the wolf does have reason for his anger, as he shows in enumerating the offenses of the wether, just as the nobles in the Lauder rebellion had reasons for their revolt. Henryson's ambivalence about this character may be easily explained: even though his sympathies may have been ultimately with James, he must have found himself, along with many of his countrymen, approving the work of the nobles in relieving the country of a substantial financial burden in the support of James' courtiers.

The same ambivalence about the ethical standing of the protagonists is reflected in the characterization of the sheep. The traditional association of the sheep with the victimized lower classes as in "The Sheep and the Dog" and "The Wolf and the Lamb" would certainly establish sympathy for the animal in this fable. Moreover, the sheep is a representative of the shepherd, who has a legitimate grievance since his flock has been depleted by the wolf's raids. Jamieson has even shown that Henryson has deleted portions of Caxton's text that reflect unfavorably on the sheep in an effort to make him a more laudable figure.[109] Yet the sheep is certainly not without ethical blemish. Not only is he the major object of the attack in the "Moralitas," but he is also shown to be excessive in the ethical framework of the animal kingdom.

His suggestion that he take the dog's place is the beginning of a series of actions in his developing presumption. The forlorn shepherd greets the wether's offer with glee; "Quha sayis ane scheip is daft, thay lieit of it" (l. 2492) he exults and skins the hound's body. The sheep's well-intentioned offer, however, soon makes him irrational and incautious: " 'Now off the Wolff' (quod he) 'I have na dreid' " (l. 2496). This boast foreshadows all of his later folly. Although he imitates the dog in many praiseworthy ways, his pride will not permit balanced self-appraisal, and, as his vainglory grows, there is a developing "comic incongruity" about his new airs.[110]

The wolf is fooled by the sheep's disguise and believes him to be the watchdog. He is finally driven to an attack on the flock by his extreme hunger and steals a lamb. The wether follows fast on the wolf's trail, and the wolf is terrified, dropping his prey in the belief that the "dog" would give up the chase. Had the sheep remembered his identity, getting the lamb back should have been sufficient, for his master's interests would have been protected. He is so caught up in his role, however, that he forgets himself and continues to pursue the wolf, declaring "It is not the Lamb, bot the, that I desyre" (l. 2535). This presumption leads to his destruction, for his real identity is revealed when his disguise is ripped off on a briar in the pursuit.

At this point, Henryson structures the value system in the tale around the scale of animals in the hierarchy of creation. Up to this section, the sheep has been operating on ethical principles imposed by the shepherd who must deal with members of the animal kingdom but who is above them. In his pursuit of the wolf, the sheep has gone beyond the boundaries of the shepherd's protection, just as the king's "favorites" were outside his protection at Lauder. The sheep has entered a realm in which the shepherd's ethical standards do not apply, a world in which brute force reigns supreme. In this kingdom the sheep is subject to the power of the

wolf, and, indeed, the wolf's admonitions suggest that he is angered
not just by the fright of his recent escape but also by the effrontery
of the sheep in attempting to destroy the order of nature:

> Quhat wes the cause ye gaif me sic ane katche?"
> ....
> Quhether call ye this fair play, or nocht?
> To set your Maister in sa fell effray,
> Quhill he ffor feiritnes hes fylit up the way.
>
> (ll.2553, 2564–66)

Suddenly aware of his predicament, the sheep resorts to a stance
and form of address that show his awareness of the order of the state
of nature: " 'Maister' (quod he), 'bot to have playit with yow; / I yow
requyre that ye nane uther trow' " (ll. 2558–59). Further
confronted with the wolf's increasing anger over the treatment
accorded him and the damage to his dignity, the sheep can only
bleat out a halting and false excuse. His purpose, he asserts, was
"never to do your persoun ill," and he argues that often one fleeing
will acquire a follower in either play or earnest. Unconvinced by
these excuses, the wolf cannot be dissuaded from his revenge. In his
wrath, he breaks the wether's neck, a means of execution
particularly pertinent to the political allegory.

All of the circumstances of the narrative reflect the incidents of
the Lauder rebellion. In his presumption and arrogance, the sheep
certainly seems to represent James' courtiers. The depiction of
James III as the shepherd would certainly coincide with Henryson's
portrayals of the monarch in other tales. The shepherd is justified in
wishing to protect his flock, but he flies in the face of reason in the
means he chooses to gain his ends. He ignores proverbial wisdom
about the abilities of sheep in replacing his watchdog. It is just this
kind of proverbial wisdom about aristocratic breeding that Henryson reinforces in the "Moralitas." Just as the shepherd ignored
common sense in allowing the sheep to disguise himself as a dog,
James ignored common sense in governing the conduct of his
courtiers.

Like most of Henryson's later fables, this tale reflects the strong
influence of the pulpit. His views concerning human nature and
nobility in this fable are based on those of medieval exegetes and
even religious apologists for chivalry, such as Bernard of Clairvaux.

It is also clear from this fable and "The Lion and the Mouse" that Henryson was much concerned about the Lauder rebellion of 1482. His references to the events at Lauder are a natural result of his concern for the political and ethical well-being of his fellowman.

CHAPTER 4

The Testament of Cresseid

IF Henryson is known for any single work it is *The Testament of Cresseid*. Although it lacks the scope of *The Morall Fabillis* and the distinctly medieval flavor of *Orpheus and Eurydice*, *The Testament* has been both praised for its modernity and denigrated for its inability to compete with Chaucer's *Troilus and Criseyde*, the inspiration for Henryson's work. It has been suggested that Henryson's "stern morality" forces him to deal more harshly with Cresseid than most modern readers would prefer.[1] While no one doubts the excellence of the passages containing the planet portraits and Cresseid's complaint, Henryson is accused of being less consistent in structure than Chaucer. The poem's "morality" and its inconsistency, moreover, have been the cause of arguments about its theme, particularly as regards the role of Christianity in the poem's value system. Many critics who believe Henryson is charitable toward Cresseid suggest that he attempts to find ways of circumventing the theological penalties for her transgressions.

The Testament has proved its appeal to readers of subsequent generations. Spearing praises its modernity in style by suggesting that it is timeless, not limited to only the medieval view of poetry. Elliott praises its artistic unity, which he believes to be missing in *The Morall Fabillis*. Henryson's style and the characterization of Cresseid have both combined to make it, in Denton Fox's words, the "best poem, English or Scottish, of the fifteenth century— perhaps even the best poem ever written in Scotland."[2]

Although it is impossible to date the composition of the poem with certainty, B. J. Whiting has shown that it was very likely completed by 1492. The "uther quair," which Henryson identifies as the source for the tale of Cresseid's degradation, may have been Myll's *Spektakle of Lufe*, completed by July 10, 1492. The *Spektakle* is a series of tales about women of bad repute, putatively translated from a Latin source. If, however, as Whiting suggests, it is not the source, the author may have read Henryson's poem. Whiting concludes, in fact, that "G. Myll had read Henryson's *Testament* sometime before 10 July 1492." Fox believes that verbal parallels make Whiting's case certain.[3] Eleanor Long has challenged this theory by arguing that Henryson's "uther quair" was a Latin moral treatise which Myll also happened to read.[4]

There are five major versions of the text: two manuscripts and three printed editions. The manuscripts have comparatively little importance: One stanza of the poem is included in the Book of the Dean of Lismore, while three stanzas are to be found in the Ruthven manuscript. The earliest printed text is in Thynne's edition of Chaucer, published in 1532. Probably the most important is the Charteris printing of 1593, the basis of most editions, including Fox's and Wood's. The Anderson publication of 1663 is of somewhat less authority.[5] The texts are not without problems, such as the crux in line 48.

Throughout the sixteenth century, in England the poem was believed to be Chaucer's. Thynne included it as a "sixth book" of *Troilus and Criseyde* in his edition of Chaucer's works. Indeed, the technical aspects of the poem show possible Chaucerian influence. Of the eighty-six stanzas, seventy-nine stanzas are in rhyme royal, the form used in *The Kingis Quair* and used by Chaucer in *Troilus and Criseyde*. Henryson acknowledges that he builds on Chaucer in the narrative prologue to his poem.[6] The narrator states that on a day in a "doolie sessoun" he took down a book "Written be worthie Chaucer glorious / Of fair Cresseid and worthie Troylus" (ll. 41–42). Henryson then begins his poem by explaining that Cresseid has been deserted by Diomede and has passed through the common court. The poet tells of her illness and degeneration after her desertion by her lovers. Many of the characters are the same, at least in name; Cresseid and Troilus both appear as does Calchas. Diomede and the other members of the Greek camp are mentioned in the narrative prologue. In many respects the characterization is consistent. Cresseid is shortsighted and self-seeking in many of the same ways she is in Chaucer's poem. Troilus is generally the same noble knight, "gentil and fre," that he seems in Chaucer's poem. Diomede proves to be the same heartless wretch suggested by his taunting of Troilus in Chaucer.

Thematically, both poems emphasize transcending the values of this world and the snares and entrapments of love. Henryson has used Chaucer's plot and characters, and he shares the thematic

concerns of his predecessor along with something of his attitude
toward courtly love. Yet Henryson nowhere more vividly shows his
independence from Chaucer.

There is perhaps a warning that he intends to depart from
Chaucer's poem in significant ways when he asks in the prologue,
"Quha wait gif all that Chauceir wrait was trew?" [7] Henryson's
departures from *Troilus and Criseyde* are quite important. Spearing
suggests first that Henryson's style is generally not derivative from
Chaucer in the poem. Whereas Spearing believes Chaucer to be a
writer noteworthy for his "prolixity," he finds in Henryson a
remarkable "brevity." E. M. W. Tillyard admires the poem for its
tight unity of style and incident, and Edwin Muir praises the poem's
"high concise style," while Elliott emphasizes that there is no
prolixity in key passages. [8] Doubtless, the apparent brevity of
Henryson's style is partly traceable to the structure of his dialogue.
While *Troilus and Criseyde* is full of long, sometimes colloquial and
wandering speeches, such as the love complaints of Troilus and the
detailed reports of Pandarus, *The Testament of Cresseid* contains
proportionately fewer lines of dialogue, and any long monologues
that appear are often formally structured, as for instance Cresseid's
complaint. Even the introduction of Henryson's narrator prepares
the reader for a more formal and less colloquial poem than
Chaucer's. The reason for Henryson's brevity could be found in the
poem's didactic tone. Brevity in literature of instruction is a
rhetorical principle traceable back to Aristotle.

Other important changes have been made in characterization,
although Elliott says the characters "are not radically altered." [9]
Calchas, for instance, has been changed from a priest of Apollo to a
priest of Aphrodite, thereby making Cresseid's sin all the more
ironic. He has also been made more sympathetic. Chaucer's Calchas
leaves Troy at once when he discovers through his augury that the
city is to be destroyed. He shows little interest in the fate of his
daughter, even when she is confronted with the danger into which
his abrupt departure has placed her. There is evidence of strong
antipathy between them. Henryson's Calchas is much more kindly.
He takes his daughter in even after she has been guilty of sexual
excesses, and his reaction to the discovery that she has leprosy is an
expression of genuine concern:

> He luikit on hir uglye lipper face,
> The quhylk befor was quhite as lillie flour;

> Wringand his handis, oftymes said allace
> That he had levit to se that wofull hour;
> For he knew weill that thair was na succour
> To hir seiknes, and that dowblit his pane:
> Thus was thair cair aneuch betuix thame twane.
>
> (ll. 372–78)

Fox suggests that this more sympathetic portrayal of Calchas has the effect of making Cresseid's blame completely her own.[10]

The characterization of Cresseid too takes a different direction. Florence Ridley believes that this is a crucial difference between the *Troilus* and *The Testament*; she suggests that Henryson "found in Chaucer's poem a latent idea and the outline of a static character which he proceeded to develop fully."[11] While Chaucer's heroine seems to degenerate from a "goddess" of love into a creature who disappoints her lover, Henryson's Cresseid changes, as Stearns says, from "a weak, selfish and unfaithful, even lascivious woman"[12] into a pathetic and finally a noble character. Cresseid does not merely suffer and die to provide an object lesson to young girls. Her suffering brings out virtues in her character that would otherwise have remained hidden. Through her plight she works her way to self-knowledge and a kind of salvation.

Henryson has also introduced Cresseid's punishment. The suggestion that she becomes a leper seems to be found in no work before Henryson's *Testament of Cresseid*. There is a kind of remarkable appropriateness in the punishment Henryson constructs, for during the Middle Ages leprosy was often connected with venereal disease and sexual excess.[13] It is also an appropriate punishment for the sin of pride for which she is indicted. In its destruction of her physical beauty, the disease makes it unlikely that Cresseid will carry on the sexual excesses which have led her to betray her lovers and herself, and it makes pride impossible.

That Henryson intended the disease to be leprosy and nothing else is clear from the detailed description of her illness:

> Thy cristall ene mingit with blude I mak,
> Thy voice sa cleir, unplesand hoir and hace,
> Thy lustie lyre ouirspred with spottis blak,
> And lumpis haw appeirand in thy face. . . .
>
> (ll. 337–40)

Sir J. A. Y. Simpson diagnosed her disease as elephantiasis, and S. N. Brody has shown Henryson has a "demonstrable reliance upon

convention" in his portrayal of Cresseid's symptoms.[14] Henryson's
sure artistry has captured the repulsive details of Cresseid's
condition. Another striking difference between Henryson's Cresseid and Criseyde is the former's prostitution. Stearns notes the
contrast between Criseyde's resolve to be true to Diomede in
Chaucer and her characterization in *The Testament of Cresseid*.[15]
While Chaucer's Criseyde is not a prostitute, however, her attitude
toward love as a means of obtaining what she wanted certainly
suggests the development Henryson introduces. It is possible, in
fact, that Cresseid's prostitution might have been introduced into
the legend some time before and is not Henryson's innovation.

One other change in characterization is quite important. Henryson has apparently ignored Chaucer's report of Troilus' death. He
has also changed the nature of Troilus' attraction to Cresseid. By
displaying fewer and fewer of the symptoms specifically of courtly
love, he is more the "typical romantic lover." [16] Vital to Henryson's
plot line and his treatment of Cresseid's salvation is the revival of
Troilus for the major recognition scene near the end of the poem.
Just as no other disease would have so completely affected
Cresseid's thinking, no other character would have served for the
street meeting in lines 490–525.

There is also a difference between the two poems in the
introduction of the narrator. While Chaucer introduces his narrator
at the beginning of *Troilus and Criseyde*, the character is quite
distinct from Henryson's. Chaucer's narrator has indeed been
subservient to courtly love; in fact, he has been one "that God of
Loves servauntz serve." He says that he himself is in the torments of
love, but he is far from help and asserts that his work will be
worthwhile if it gives solace to any lover, even though his own case
offers no respite. He states his position on the events in the poem,
either unequivocally or ironically, when he says that he loves all of
love's servants "As though I were hir owene brother dere." For the
most part, Chaucer's narrator is initially less developed as a
character, appearing only occasionally until the conclusion when he
tells us that he might have written of Troilus' warlike deeds if he had
chosen and then dedicates the book to Strode and Gower. Chaucer's
authorial intrusions are doubtless important, but their importance is
not so much for the development of the narrator as to provide the
reader a perspective on the events of the poem in the most
economical fashion possible.

Henryson's narrator has also been in the service of love but is no longer.[17] His case, like his predecessor's, is hopeless, but now the problem is advanced age for, "Thocht lufe be hait, yit in ane man of age / It kendillis nocht sa sone as in youtheid" (ll. 29–30). Although he has some regrets about his state, he is resigned to his predicament. Like the Chaucerian narrator, Henryson's persona expresses his feelings on his protagonist. He introduces Cresseid as the "flour and A per se / Of Troy and Grece," and, after abhorring her sin, sighs "I have pietie thow suld fall sic mischance" (l. 84). He goes on to say that despite what others may write or say about her inconstancy, "I sall excuse, als far furth as I may / Thy womanheid, thy wisdome and fairnes" (ll. 87–8). In view of the prominence Henryson gives these lines and the lack of signals for irony, it is curious that so many critics have accused Henryson of being too stern with Cresseid. On the contrary, like Chaucer he has profound sympathy for his heroine.[18]

Yet Henryson's narrator differs remarkably from Chaucer's. He is a more central character and is more important in setting the tone and foreshadowing events in the major part of the poem. No anonymous "I" this figure, he is instead introduced to us as an older man in his study. He is a concrete character in a specific location doing specific things even at a specific time of the year, "Ane doolie Sessoun,"in Scotland. The narrator introduces himself as a some-time servant of Venus. Hoping for a restoration of his abilities, he begins to pray to her and then stops because of the "greit cald." He mends the fire and sits down to take up Chaucer's book. He makes several comments on the book and then relates that he picks up the famous "uther quair." He comments on Cresseid's fate, and, fourteen stanzas into the poem, finally starts the narrative. Nearly fifteen percent of the poem is occupied with the events of the narrator's prologue. Proportionate attention in Chaucer would have changed the *Troilus* considerably. But the number of lines itself is not the most significant aspect of this prologue. The narrator becomes a fully developed character whose physical state and wishes have a marked effect on the way we are to judge the events in Cresseid's life. Ironically, he is capable of just the kind of patience that she lacks and has the kind of understanding of life that she does not gain until the poem's conclusion.[19]

One final way in which the poem differs from Chaucer's is that Henryson's poem also contains literary criticism. From Henryson's introductory question about the truth of Chaucer's poem to the final events of Cresseid's encounter with Troilus and death, *The*

Testament is concerned with its source. Henryson is making a comment on both Chaucer's theme and technique. As Fox suggests, *The Testament* is "literary, witty, and sophisticated. . . . But *The Testament* is also *about* Chaucer's poem in the same sense that a critical essay is about a piece of literature." [20] The comments that Henryson makes on Chaucer's poem are best understood through an analysis of *The Testament*'s structure and theme.

The structure of *The Testament of Cresseid* is complex. The poem has been praised for its narrative brevity and attacked for its descriptive prolixity. Moreover, the relationship of the narrative prologue to the rest of the poem is not so easily explained as it might first appear, partially because of the thematic echoes of the narrator's personal comments throughout the poem. The narrative prologue contains Henryson's finest example of symbolic naturalism. His poem, he informs us in the first line, is "ane cairful dyte," and he chooses "Ane doolie sessoun" to be "equivalent." As Tillyard and Fox have shown, the season Henryson actually chooses is spring, the time of the year marked by the traditional renewal of nature and laden with symbols of fecundity. [21] Henryson's choice of spring is a possibly satiric use of a courtly love convention, for spring is the most popular setting for poems written in praise of *fin'amor*. Henryson's spring, however, is not the typical season of love and romance. In the midst of a period of "fervent" weather, "Schouris of haill gart fra the north discend, / That scantlie fra the cauld I micht defend" (ll. 6–7). When he looks out from his "oratour" he finds that

> The northin wind had purifyit the air
> And sched the mistie cloudis fra the sky;
> The froist freisit, the blastis bitterly
> Fra Pole Artick come quhisling loud and schill,
> And causit me remufe aganis my will.
>
> (ll. 17–21)

It is so cold that he is even unable to pray in his study. The striking nature of this weather is even more apparent if it is remembered that this is about the same time of year in which Chaucer's pilgrims set off toward Canterbury.

The unseasonable weather is symbolic of contrasts that exist in the characters in the poem. Fox believes that it is also a symbol for Cresseid's state, her beauty "blighted" by leprosy." [22] Fox, MacQueen, and Jane Adamson explore the allegorical significance of this prologue. [23] Spring is usually the season of love, and the weather conditions for spring usually bring fair days, light, warmth. and vernal beauty, all characteristics associated with sexual love. Henryson's spring has none of these characteristics. The contrast between what the season should be and what it is can be found in the characterization of the narrator himself. As one of love's servants and as a humble suppliant of Venus, he should have the warmth and passion of youth. Instead he is "ane man of age" (l. 29). In lieu of the natural warmth of the young, he finds the coldness of age. His weapons against age are precisely those he uses against the cold spring: the fire, a drink, and his patience. This contrast also appears in the characterization of Cresseid. As a lusty young widow, she should have and enjoy the passions of her life, but she is, through her own reckless actions, symbolized by the events in the parliament of gods, condemned to a fate that reflects the same dry and cold condition to be found in both the narrator and the season. After all, she is condemned by Saturn and Cynthia. Saturn, one of the most powerful gods, is portrayed in terms of age and cold:

> His face fronsit, his lyre was lyke the leid,
> His teith chatterit, and cheverit with the chin,
> His ene drowpit, how sonkin in his heid,
> Out of his nois the meldrop fast can rin. . . .
>
> (ll. 155–58)

Cynthia too is a cold symbol since "all hir licht scho borrowis at hir brother" (l. 258). These two gods of the cold and dry forces of the universe carry out a sentence on Cresseid that coincides with their natures and the contrast established in the prologue and in the narrator's character: among the other parts of Cresseid's fate, "Thy moisture and thy heit in [to] cald and dry" (l. 318) are changed. This is the main physical change in the theory of the humors that would account for all of Cresseid's other changes, including loss of beauty and her melancholy temper.[24] All of these elements in the characterization of the narrator and the heroine are foreshadowed by the weather in the prologue. The tension between cold and hot, dry and moist, is the major unifying force in the symbolism and imagery of the poem.

In the prologue, Henryson establishes a narrator whose own life and attitudes provide ethical standards against which we may judge the conduct of Cresseid. The narrator's acceptance of his lot is a major quality in the poem, a kind of "homage to the Venus of the *Testament*."[25] He does not offend against the physical nature of

things by trying to force his powers of lovemaking once they have
given in to old age, nor does he offend against morality. He is able to
accept change and to feel sympathy for his fellow human beings.
These are the same virtues—patience and charity—that Henryson
vindicates in the *Fabillis*.

The introduction of Cresseid establishes a picture of the heroine
which shows the depth of the narrator's pity. Physical and moral
excesses are indicated in the lines describing Diomede's desertion
of her:

> Quhen Diomeid had all his appetyte,
> And mair, fulfillit of this fair ladie,
> Upon ane uther he set his hail delyte,
> And send to hir ane lybell of repudie
> And hir excludit fra his companie.
>
> (ll. 72–75)

Fox comments particularly on the phrase "And mair" which he
believes suggests the sexual excesses to which Cresseid had
agreed.[26] Her affair with Diomede and her desertion of Troilus,
which the reader remembers from Chaucer, are preparation for
Henryson's announcement of her less discriminating sexual activities: "Than desolait scho walkit up and doun, / And sum men sayis,
into the court, commoun" (ll. 76–77). The phrase "sum men sayis"
establishes distance between Henryson's narrator and the reader.
For the purpose of his theme it is absolutely imperative that the
reader suspend his disbelief long enough to believe that the narrator
is reporting real events, just as Chaucer appeared to in *The
Canterbury Tales*. This moral distance places the narrator at the
observer's angle on Cresseid's misfortunes and makes his profes-
sions of sympathy more genuine.

Cresseid returns to her father, relates the tale of her woes, and
receives his sympathies. Calchas welcomes her with open arms into
his house: "Welcum to me; thow art full deir ane gest!" (l. 105).
Immediately hereafter, Calchas' position as a priest of Venus is
introduced along with a comment about Cresseid's former devotions
to the goddess. We are told Cresseid "Usit to pas" to Calchas'
temple to say her devotions. The designation of past habitual action
suggests that perhaps she has not been a proper votive since she left
Troilus or became a prostitute. Her conduct has reflected only the
influence of *Venus scelestis*, the destructive aspect of love. She has
neglected the devotion to *Venus caelestis* and the beneficent aspects

of love.[27] She has worshipped *Venus scelestis* only for the
satisfaction of her own appetite.

To keep from letting the people know she has been cast off by
Diomede, Cresseid now goes to worship in a secret "orature," the
same word by the way used to describe the narrator's study. Once
there she falls on her knees and begins her prayer, but it is not
pious. Instead of imploring the aid of Venus she accuses the goddess
of love and her son of disappointing and deliberately deceiving her:

> Ye gave me anis ane devine responsaill
> That I suld be the flour of luif in Troy. . . .
> ....
> O fals Cupide, is nane to wyte bot thow,
> And thy mother, of lufe the blind goddes!
> Ye causit me alwayis understand and trow
> The seid of lufe was sawin in my face,
> And ay grew grene throw your supplie and grace.
> Bot now, allace, that seid with froist is slane,
> And I fra luifferis left, and all forlane.

(ll. 127–28, 134–40)

Cresseid's prayer contains elements which directly contrast with the
attitude of resignation and patience found in the narrator. In every
way, her complaint is unfounded and her accusations are unjust.

First, she is impious. In addressing the planets which govern "all
thing genereabill," her tone is disrespectful and presumptuous.
Tillyard divides this aspect of her sin into three parts: infidelity to
Troilus, pride, and anger.[28] In affronting the powers of the
universe, she is also attacking a universal medieval principle of
order, the hierarchical structure of the cosmos. In the hierarchy of
creation, as described by a philosopher such as Pseudo-Dionysius,
man was placed directly under the ranks of supernatural creatures.
At the top was either the Christian God or the Graeco-Roman gods,
often symbolized by the planets. According to medieval thought,
this plan of order was designed to insure the best possible
organization and functioning of the various elements of the
universe. To attempt to question one's place in this scheme was the
worst kind of impiety. Such questioning was also philosophically
irrational. It implied that a creature on the lower rungs of creation
was capable of guiding forces at higher levels. Questions about
universal order implied possible chaos. It is precisely this kind of

questioning of principles of universal order which is implied in
Cresseid's blaming the gods for her fate.

Cresseid's impiety is closely connected with her immaturity and
her selfishness. She is unable to accept personal responsibility for
her fate. The gods, she contends, had given her to believe that she
would be the queen of love in Troy, as indeed she was. She
somehow interpreted Venus' promise to mean that the gods would
sustain her as queen of love, no matter how "gigotlike" she might
act. Refusing to assume whatever blame might be due her Cresseid
finds two scapegoats, Venus and Cupid. But they are not to blame
for her physical and moral excesses. At one level, Cresseid makes
herself vulnerable to the judgment of the gods by unjustly accusing
Venus and Cupid. At another level, Cresseid's refusal to understand
her own role in creating her unhappy state leads her to a state of
inertia. She takes no steps to improve her lot. She does not repent
her own fickleness, repudiate Diomede, beg Troilus's forgiveness,
or even resign herself to her fate. Any of these actions might have
saved Cresseid, but her inability to accept personal blame prevents
her from doing what she should. In this regard, she is similar to
Milton's Eve.

The magnitude of Cresseid's sin in affronting Cupid and Venus is
adequate preparation for the court of the gods which follows.
Henryson made extensive use of Lydgate's *Assembly of Gods* and
Boccaccio's *Genealogia deorum*. MacQueen regards the gods as
principles which govern the universe, while E. Duncan Aswell sees
them as the forces of fruition and decay.[29] There is in any case no
question of Henryson's originality in their portrayals. After her
bitter repudiation, Cresseid falls into an "extasie" in which "Cupide
the King" appears ringing a silver bell. Much controversy has been
generated about the precise nature of Cupid and the extent of
Cupid's power. It has seemed incongruous that Cupid should be
referred to as "the King" and that it should be he who summons the
gods to the council. H. S. Bennett, however, suggests that Cupid
was traditionally viewed as a majestic figure.[30] For Tillyard, there is
evidence that Cupid may be representative of the Judaeo-Christian
God.[31] Whether he is a representative of the supreme power of the
universe in Christian terms or whether he simply acts as chairman
of the court because he is the most offended male god, it is clear that
his power is not to be doubted.

In these portraits, Henryson makes use of a procession similar to
that of the Seven Deadly Sins in *Piers Plowman*. The first god to

appear is Saturn, whose extra power is indicated by the fact that he "gave to Cupide litill reverence" (l. 152). Traditionally, as the father of the gods, Saturn is regarded as the supreme power among them. In astrological terms, however, he is regarded as "the greater misfortune." [32] As has already been shown, Saturn appears to be possessed of qualities antithetical to those associated with love and youth. Besides his associations drawn with age and time, there are references to cold and grayness:

> Atouir his belt his lyart lokkis lay
> Felterit unfair, ouirfret with froistis hoir,
> His garmound and his gyte full gay of gray,
> His widderit weid fra him the wind out woir. . . .
>
> (ll. 162–65)

This unattractive portrait foreshadows Cresseid's fate in the court. It is also closely associated with time: Saturn may represent time, which brings with it decay and death. As a destructive force, his part in the judgment of Cresseid is inevitable, as is his power in the change wrought on anyone who expects youth and beauty forever. In his role as time, Saturn represents a malicious and inevitable force in the court, one with which Cresseid is unable to cope because of her immaturity.

The second god in the court is Jupiter, "richt fair and amiabill" (l. 169).[33] He is traditionally represented in astrology as "the greater fortune." Emphasizing a characteristic common to the other benevolent forces in the planet portraits, Henryson describes Jupiter's function as "Nureis." A source of nourishment and protection in the universe, Jupiter is clearly antithetical to Saturn. This is borne out in his whole description. Henryson tells us he is "Fra his father Saturne far different" (l. 172). He has a "burelie face and browis bricht and brent" (l. 173). His voice is clear, and "as cristall wer his ene." Both of these characteristics are associated with Cresseid prior to her judgment. They are in fact two of the most prominent features changed when Cynthia pronounces her doom. His golden hair is also an association with the warm and moist elements that Henryson believes are the cosmic and physiological sources of youth and beauty. Instead of the gray garments of Saturn, Jupiter wears a garland around his head and has garments "full [gay] of grene" (l. 178). He is armed with "Ane burlie brand" and "ane groundin spear," "Of his father the wraith fra us to

weir" (l. 182). Jupiter is the planetary agent who defends man
against the ravages of time. As a productive and energizing force in
the universe, it is his job to defend life against temporal change and
to insure at least the continuation of living species, if not the
individual. Jupiter's protective function also has obvious Christian
associations. Just as Christ is the protector of man against the wrath
of the Father, Jupiter is the protector of man against the anger of
Saturn. But whether interpreted in a Christian or pagan sense he is
the cosmic life force, continuously at odds with change and decay.

The third figure in the planet portraits is Mars, "The God of Ire."
If the planets are to be grouped into benevolent and malicious
forces, Mars must fall into the latter group and therefore into
Saturn's camp. He is the god of "strife, debait, and all dissensioun"
(l. 184). He comes dressed in characteristic battle array:

> In hard harnes, hewmound, and habirgeoun,
> And on his hanche ane roustie fell fachioun,
> And in his hand he had ane roustie sword,
> Wrything his face with mony angrie word.
>
> (ll. 186–89)

While his armor is traditional and appropriate to his role as the god
of war and anger, Henryson has possibly added some ironic touches
in his description in his use of the word "rustie." Both Smith and
Wood say the word might be glossed as "bronze." Fox suggests the
word derives from the habit of not wiping the blade clean of blood.[34]
Meaning "covered with rust," the word is used in Gower and
Caxton specifically to show knightly inactivity. It is possible
however, that Henryson is making use of the dramatic comic figure
of war, the *miles gloriosus*, a stock figure in miracle and morality
plays. Derived from Plautus, the *miles gloriosus* was a braggart
soldier who came equipped with ragged battle dress and stormed
and blustered his way through a play to the delight of the audience.
In some ways the comedy in his role was closely related to that
produced by the ranting of the Herod figure in the mystery plays in
that it probably involved a great deal of simple slapstick. Comedy
was also generated by the comic contrast of the *miles gloriosus* with
what a true knight should be. The use of the lathe or rusty sword
and rusty armor later became a standard way of characterizing the
braggart soldier, as in Shakespeare's portrayal of Falstaff. It is

possible that Henryson is characterizing Mars by using elements of the *miles gloriosus* drawn from the drama.

The further characterization of Mars bears this out. He appears before the powerful Cupid

> Schaikand his sword, . . .
> With reid visage and grislie glowrand ene,
> And at his mouth ane bullar stude of fome. . . .
>
> (ll. 190–92)

The inappropriateness of this action would be similar to what Henryson might well have witnessed in the Scottish parliament, but it is also filled with the broad humor often used in the mystery plays. There is also the puzzling element of his blowing a horn and speaking "with mony bosteous brag." The horn has led Stearns to suggest that Henryson has blended Mars with traditional views of March, since the trumpet of March symbolized both the wind and the announcement of a new season.[35] But this trumpet could also have been associated with the presentation of the *miles gloriosus* in the drama. The bragging is of course malicious, but it is also a characteristic of the *miles gloriosus* as well. For Henryson to mention the bragging here is possible evidence of his attempt at comedy. If Henryson truly believed that those who followed the prognostications of astrology were not sensible, as suggested in the *Orpheus*, then it seems likely that this portrait of Mars could be ironic and that there may be irony in the other portrayals as well.

After Mars comes a benevolent force, "fair Phebus" who is the

> . . . lanterne and lamp of licht,
> Of man and beist, baith frute and flourisching,
> Tender nureis, and banischer of nicht. . . .
>
> (ll. 197–99)

His description, and in particular the word "Nureis," are indications that he is in the camp of Jupiter, as the sun is indeed in league with natural vegetative forces in the universe. Phoebus, however, is the offspring of Saturn and Venus, giving added emphasis to his power. He is after all the god who is credited with "of the warld causing, be his moving / And influence, lyfe in all eirdlie thing" (ll. 200–201). As in the description of Jupiter, the imagery used is that of light and heat. Phoebus is a "king royall" whose face is so bright that none

might behold it "for peirsing of his sicht" (l. 207). He rides in a
"goldin cart with fyrie bemis bricht" (l. 208). Phoebus' chariot is
drawn by four steeds, which Henryson describes in some detail:

> The first was soyr, with mane als reid as rois,
> Callit Eoye, into the orient;
> The secund steid to name hecht Ethios,
> Quhitlie and paill, and sum deill ascendent;
> The thrid Peros, richt hait and richt fervent;
> The feird was blak, callit Philologie,
> Quhilk rollis Phebus doun into the sey.
>
> (ll. 211–17)

Henryson's description of Phoebus' team has proved one of the most
interesting keys to his reading habits. Stearns argues that the names
of these horses show a mixture of Fulgentian and Ovidian
influences. The second name, Ethios, is found in Pseudo-Bede.
Editors have had a difficult time explaining the use of the name
"Philologie" in line 216. Skeat and Dickins have both amended the
name to read Philegoney. Gregory Smith amended the line to "And
callit Phlegonie." Both emendations were made on the assumption
that Henryson was using the Ovidian name Phlegon as his base.
Stearns believes that this name along with that of Ethios shows
Henryson's use of Pseudo-Bede's *De mundi coelestis terrestrisque
constitutione*, because both Fulgentian and Ovidian names are
used. Elliott believes that the line should be "and callit Philogey."
Fox attempts to refute Elliott's case and argues for the reading of the
line as it stands. He contends "Henryson may be following an
unknown source or he may be working from memory, perhaps from
memory of several different lists." [36]

Venus has been insulted along with Cupid, and she comes next
"Hir sonnis querrell for to defend, and mak / Hir awin complaint"
(ll. 219–20). At this point, the balance of the planet portraits
becomes uncertain. After the description of Phoebus should come
the introduction of a malevolent force, a member of the party of
Saturn. As an ally of the forces of generation, Venus would be out of
place. But Henryson's Venus seems to reflect both sides of love.
Although she comes in "ane nyce array," she is not an entirely
benevolent figure. Her clothing is divided: "The ane half grene, the
uther half sabill black" (l. 221). And moreover in her face "semit
greit variance." Sometimes she seems capable of perfect truth and
sometimes inconstance:

> Under smyling scho was dissimulait,
> Provocative with blenkis amorous,
> And suddanely changit and alterait,
> Angrie as ony serpent vennemous
>
> (ll. 224–28)

Henryson sums up this double nature of Venus in a line possibly borrowed from *The Book of the Duchess*: "With ane eye lauch, and with the uther weip" (l. 231). This nature is also responsible for the variance that appears in love, which is "sum tyme sweit, sum tyme bitter and sour" (l. 234). Cresseid has already experienced the sweet side of love, and indeed the sour side as well. Venus is "the principle of change." [37] This dual personality which Henryson describes places Venus in both camps. When she is laughing, truthful, and "grene," she is allied to the goals of Jupiter. When she is dissimulating, inconstant, and "black," she is allied to the goals of Saturn. Her ability to move to either side is partially due both to the dual nature of her character and to Henryson's use of the Boethian character of fortune in her portrayal. Fortune is described in terms of her shifting favor, alternately smiling and frowning, as the two sides of Venus demonstrate. Just as man's fortune may be changeable, so is the course of love, "now hait, now cauld." Venus exemplifies these changes.

That Henryson uses Venus in her malevolent sense is demonstrated by her complaint. It is also demonstrated by the fact that she is followed by a benevolent god, Mercury. He is a physician:

> Boxis he bair with fyne electuairis,
> And sugerit syropis for digestioun,
> Spycis belangand to the pothecairis,
> With mony hailsum sweit confectioun. . . .
>
> (ll. 246–49)

As a doctor he benefits mankind, thus belonging in the group with Jupiter and Phoebus, and he is a master with words. He is "richt eloquent" and full of rhetoric. He knows all the polite terms, and he is "With pen and ink to report all reddie" (l. 242). Even his red hood is "Lyke to ane poeit of the auld fassoun" (l. 245). The uses of his rhetorical abilities are also beneficial to man. One of his major activities is "Setting sangis and singand merilie" (l. 243). With both his medicine and his verse, he helps men to be of good humor.

He also dresses his part. Like Chaucer's Physician he appears
prosperous and honest:

> Doctour in phisick, cled in ane skarlot goun,
> And furrit weill, as sic ane aucht to be;
> Honest and gude, and not ane word culd lie.
>
> (ll. 250–52)

The association of his ethical qualities with his prosperous appearance is a technique Henryson may well have learned from Chaucer,
but the mere association of Mercury with the science of healing is
traditional.

The last portrait is that of Cynthia, the goddess of the moon.
Although less malevolent than Saturn she is still a member of his
group. She is associated with dark colors and coldness:

> Of colour blak, buskit with hornis twa,
> And in the nicht scho listis best appeir;
> Haw as the leid, of colour nathing cleir;
> For all hir licht scho borrowis at hir brother
> Titan, for of hir self scho hes nane uther.
>
> (ll. 255–59)

The duskiness of her color and her nocturnal habits make her a
symbol of temporal decay and human distress, just like Saturn and
Mars. As in the description of the other planets, dress matches
personality. Her clothes are gray and full of black spots. On her
breast is painted a churl "Beirand ane bunche of thornis on his bak, /
Quhilk for his thift micht clim na nar the hevin" (ll. 262–63), an
image symbolic of human tribulation and frustration. With Venus
appearing in her malevolent form, the hostile gods are now "more
potent than the benevolent ones." [38]

After Mercury has opened the court, Cupid steps forward to state
the charges. Cresseid, he contends, has done the gods great injury.
She has blamed Cupid and Venus for her unhappy state, whereas
Cupid contends she herself is to blame. Despite the fine treatment
they have accorded her, Cupid says:

> . . . hir leving unclene and lecherous
> Scho wald retorte in me and my mother,
> To quhome I schew my grace abone all uther.
>
> (ll. 285–87)

Cupid contends that her attempt to blame the gods for her own actions is a threat to them all: "Was never to goddes done sic violence" (l. 292). He therefore asks the help of all the assembled gods in punishing Cresseid.

In short order he has made his case, and, without waiting for a response from Cresseid, Mercury suggests that Cupid ask the highest and the lowest of their assembly to fix Cresseid's punishment. This choice leaves little room for mercy. The two gods chosen, Saturn and Cynthia, are both forces contrary to love, and their decision is speedy. They decide to match the punishment to the crime and give Cresseid a "siknes incurabill" so that she will be forever abominable to all lovers. Saturn delivers the first part of the sentence, which is organized in terms of the basic theory of humors. He places a frosty wand on her head and changes her moisture and heat into coldness and dryness; he deprives her of her fairness and her beautiful hair, and finally condemns her to penury instead of riches. The judgment is in keeping with his character and the nature of her crime. Henryson's narrator, however, laments that it should be so. He asks Saturn, "On fair Cresseid quhy hes thow na mercie, / Quhilk was sa sweit, gentill and amorous?" (ll. 325–26).

Cynthia's judgment parallels Saturn's. She too deprives Cresseid of her heat and her joy. She then goes on to inflict the disease: Cresseid's eyes are to be spotted with blood, her voice to be hoarse, her complexion to be overspread with black spots, and her face to be full of lumps. Henryson very likely associated leprosy with venereal disease.[39] If indeed he did, Cresseid's punishment would be a direct result of her physical excesses.

Cresseid's dream and its interpretation are important in understanding the nature of her punishment and Henryson's theme. Although her vision has been interpreted as an *oraculum* or prophetic dream, Ralph Hanna argues strongly that it is a simple *somnium*. Cresseid, he believes, is not in the proper state of mind for a prophetic dream, and her vision is merely a reflection of forces that have already shaped her life.[40] Hanna's argument is supported by medieval literature on the theory of dreams, especially Macrobius' commentary on the *Somnium Scipionis*, and it provides additional proof that Henryson was depicting Cresseid's movement toward ethical maturity.

When the court of gods vanishes, Cresseid awakens and discovers her state in a mirror. With characteristic understatement Henryson describes her reaction: "Gif scho in hart was wa aneuch God wait"

(l. 350). After the vision she has seen, Cresseid should be wiser. A
correct interpretation of her dream would reveal that her state is her
own responsibility, but she is still looking for someone to blame:

> . . . "Lo quhat it is," quod sche,
> "With fraward langage for to mufe and steir
> Our craibit goddis; and sa is sene on me!
> My blaspheming now have I bocht full deir. . . ."
> (ll. 351–54)

She believes that her fault was speaking her mind, not having the
wrong ideas from the start. She thinks that it is not her blaming the
gods but the fact that she told them she blamed them that is
responsible for her punishment. Ironically, line 354 is truer than
Cresseid realizes. She has paid dearly for her blaspheming, but she
does not realize that her blasphemy is in her physical and moral
excesses and her immaturity, not just in her verbal attack on the
gods.[41] There is uniformity of opinion on Henryson's originality in
his use of this disease as Cresseid's punishment. It seems to suit the
nature of Cresseid's sin in both its physical and moral implications.
As Fox has shown, it was not merely pejorative in its implications.
Lepers were believed to enjoy a special relationship with God.
Brody observes that because leprosy was considered a divine
affliction, it was believed that lepers were undergoing purgation for
their sins. Therefore, men of the Middle Ages viewed them with a
mixture of horror and respect for their special status.[42]

At this point, Henryson uses a masterful dramatic stroke to return
the narrative to the realistic plane of events. While Cresseid is
bemoaning her fate, a child knocks on the door to summon her to
supper. Somewhat like the knocking on the gate in *Macbeth*, this
realistic element brings the reader out of a world of visionary terror
and pity into the realm of everyday life. The child's speech also
gives Henryson the opportunity for added irony about Cresseid's
situation. Her father, the child relates, has been worried about her
long prayers. There is no need for such lengthy praying Calchas has
said, because "the goddis wait all your intent full weill" (l. 364).
Calchas has meant this remark to reassure Cresseid, but the gods
have indeed known her intent all too well.

Cresseid sends for her father and tells him all that has transpired.
Again, Henryson's narrative becomes very economical. In four

lines, Cresseid tells Calchas about her plight. Calchas' mourning occupies another stanza. After the initial shock, Cresseid begins to confront her problem. Still concerned about public opinion as she was when she would not go to church, she "wald not be kend." [43] She wraps herself in a mantle, puts on a beaver hat,[44] and goes incognito to a hospital at the edge of the city to finish her life. Even so, she does not escape recognition, for "sum knew hir weill" (l. 393). The other lepers' general regret for her is mixed with a special sympathy for her plight: Henryson ironically notes, "scho was of nobill kin; / With better will thairfoir they tuik hir in" (ll. 398–99).

The hospital is the setting for Cresseid's famous complaint, a major example of Henryson's artistic mastery. The metric and stanzaic pattern of her lament is different from that used in the other sections of the poem. Henryson sets the scene carefully: "The day passit and Phebus went to rest. / The cloudis blak ouerheled all the sky" (ll. 400–401). The weather and the night are both associated with the forces that have doomed Cresseid to her fate. Also symbolic is her location in the hospital: "ane dark corner of the hous" (l. 405), where she goes alone to lament her state. She begins with a most pessimistic appraisal of her situation: "O catiue Creisseid, now and euer mair / Gane is thy ioy and all thy mirth in eird" (ll. 408–9). She wishes she were under the ground where she could never again hear the name of Greece or Troy. She then begins to recount her former luxuries and to grieve over their loss.

For this section of the poem, Henryson turns again to the *ubi sunt* motif which he also employed in the *Fabillis*, "Thre Deid Pollis," and "The Ressoning betuix Aige and Yowth." He seems deeply indebted to "The Debate Between the Body and the Soul," a poem he may have used in "The Paddock and the Mouse." Cresseid laments the lost comforts of life at court and home:

> Quhair is thy chalmer wantounlie besene,
> With burely bed and bankouris browderit bene;
> Spycis and wyne to thy collatioun,
> The cowpis all of gold and silver schene,
> Thy sweit meitis servit in plaittis clene
> With saipheron sals of ane gude sessoun;
> Thy gay garmentis with mony gudely goun. . . .
>
> (ll. 416–22)

Then she laments the loss of the joys of nature:

> Quhair is thy garding with thir greissis gay
> And fresche flowris, quhilk the quene Floray
> Had paintit plesandly in everie pane. . . .

(ll. 425–27)

In all of these events, Cresseid shows her continued immaturity and self-pity. Most obviously in her lament of the loss of the comforts of home, she is showing that she prizes trivia. A person who has just witnessed her own condemnation at a court of the gods, as Cresseid has, ought to have her mind on things other than spices, wine, and gay garments. Even the joys of nature are hardly fit concerns for her at this point. Her overvaluing of the nature scenes she describes shows that she has still not come to a full realization of her offense and of the nature of her punishment.[45] She continues to ignore the charges of Cupid, which accurately explain her situation.

The third section of Cresseid's complaint is an honest appraisal of her condition. She bemoans her decayed fame, ruined voice, and disfigured face, a description marked by contrast with her former appearance. She has gone from "greit triumphand fame and hie honour" to "darknes dour" (ll. 434, 437). She has also lost her "cleir voice" and "lesand part." In this section is the most obvious description of her tale as a tragedy in the medieval sense. She has undergone a horrible change in fortune, and her change is the subject of this instructive tragedy. Cresseid perceives her situation as an object lesson for others.

In the fourth section of her complaint she warns all of the "ladyis fair of Troy and Grece" (l. 452) to understand her "miserie, quhilk nane may comprehend" (l. 453). She is also becoming more honest about the nature of her situation, for she warns them of "My greit mischeif, quhilk na man can amend" (l. 455). This is progress toward the full realization of her state that will result in some kind of salvation—psychological, moral, or even social. She is also objective enough to desire to teach the beautiful women she addresses a standard medieval lesson:

> Be war in tyme, approchis neir the end,
> And in your mynd ane mirrour mak of me:
> As I am now, peradventure that ye
> For all your micht may cum to that same end,
> Or ellis war, gif ony war may be.

(ll. 456–60)

This lesson was often associated with *ubi sunt* poems. This form of didactic literature carried the lesson that one should not place his faith in things of this world. And that is precisely the lesson Cresseid finds in her experience. She warns the women who listen about the real nature of their youth, fame, and beauty:

> Nocht is your fairnes bot ane faiding flour,
> Nocht is your famous laud and hie honour
> Bot wind inflat in uther mennis eiris. . . .
>
> (ll. 461–63)

In all of these lines, Cresseid is coming nearer an understanding of the temporal world in which she lives. "Fortoun is fikkill" she concludes. Her understanding, however, is not yet complete. What she still laments most are the temporal things she has to leave behind. The whole goal of the *ubi sunt* poem is to turn man's mind away from material values to spiritual values. Cresseid is beginning the turn, but she is still looking back wistfully; moreover, she is not yet fully aware of her own role in her downfall. So much has her concern been focused on what she has lost that she has not yet come to understand fully how the loss occurred. Her understanding and Henryson's object lesson are not yet complete.

Henryson makes it clear that Cresseid has achieved only partial understanding for she is "chydand with hir drerie destenye." After her complaint, she is approached by a leper lady who helps her to some acceptance of her destiny. She counsels:

> Quhy spurnis thow aganis the wall
> To sla thy self . . .
> I counsall the mak vertew of ane neid;
> Go leir to clap thy clapper to and fro,
> And leif efter the law of lipper leid.
>
> (ll. 475–76, 478–80)

This acceptance of her fate, which is forced on her, and her decision not to kill herself but to live out her life as the gods decree, are further steps toward the complete understanding she must achieve.[46] All of Cresseid's sins may be understood in Christian terms as types of pride, in her appearance, her possessions, and even her own will. Any attempt at suicide would be yet another form of pride in which she would place her own understanding of the world and her state above that of God. This is precisely the fault that Cresseid must overcome in order to understand the cause for her problems. Her acceptance of her leprosy and the fate that accompanies it is another step in subjugating her own ego to the purposes of the universe.

Henryson next makes an abrupt narrative shift. From Cresseid's decision to make the best of her life, he turns to the garrison of Troy which has just had a great victory over the forces of Greece. The army, led by Troilus, is returning to the city after the victory when the soldiers pass by the company of lepers in which Cresseid is to be found. In just ten lines, Henryson establishes the background for one of the most tightly drawn recognition scenes in British literature.[47] "Nobill Troylus" sees the lepers, but does not recognize Cresseid. As he was passing, "upon him scho kest up baith hir ene" (l. 498). It occurs to him that he might have seen her before, but "scho was in sic plye he knew hir nocht" (l. 501). Yet her face calls into mind the visage of Cresseid. Henryson takes special pains to explain how Troilus is reminded of his former lover without recognizing her even when looking straight at her:

> Na wonder was, suppois in mynd that he
> Tuik hir figure sa sone, and lo, now quhy:
> The idole of ane thing in cace may be
> Sa deip imprentit in the fantasy
> That it deludis the wittis outwardly. . . .
>
> (ll. 505–9)

Stearns has shown that Henryson is using principles of sound Aristotelian psychology.[48] It is, according to Aristotle, completely possible that the vague resemblance of Cresseid could have called into Troilus' mind the image of her.

After Troilus' remembrance of Cresseid, "Ane spark of lufe" springs into his heart, and "Within ane quhyle he changit mony hew" (ll. 512, 517). His love of Cresseid inspires him to an act of charity:

> For knichtlie pietie and memoriall
> Of fair Cresseid, ane gyrdill can he tak,
> Ane purs of gold and mony gay iowall,
> And in the skirt of Cresseid doun can swak. . . .
>
> (ll. 519–22)

This magnanimous act ultimately leads to Cresseid's self-knowledge and moral salvation. Troilus is acting out of selfless love and his good memories of Cresseid. It will be through this final act of love by Troilus that she is able to achieve true contrition.

Ironically, in this meeting, "not ane ane uther knew" (l. 518). It is not until all the lepers gather to divide up the alms that they find that Troilus has been unusually generous. When the treasure is discovered, Cresseid asks "Quhat Lord is yone,' quod sche, 'have ye na feill, / Hes done to us so greit humanitie?'" (ll. 533–34). When she is informed that it is Troilus, "thair stert ane bitter stound / Throwout hir hart, and fell doun to the ground" (ll. 538–39). It is the shock of finding that Troilus has been capable of such great charity for her which finally makes her aware of her own role in shaping her situation. It is at this point that her suffering "takes on the hue of purgation." [49] His love, fidelity, and charity contrast with her own lust, faithlessness, and selfishness. When she is able to say "O fals Cresseid and trew knicht Troylus" she has at last reached a stage of moral redemption. She herself is able to draw the contrast between their two natures with the same objectivity that marked the end of her complaint:

> For lufe of me thow keipt continence,
> Honest and chaist in conversatioun;
> Of all wemen protectour and defence
> Thou was, and helpit thair opinioun;
> My mynd in fleschelie foull affectioun
> Was inclynit to lustis lecherous. . . .
>
> (ll. 554–59)

Although Stearns believes the poem is antagonistic to courtly love in its theme, these lines express the perfect blend of courtly love and chivalry. According to Andreas a perfect courtly lover was to protect and defend all women in honor of his own beloved. [50] Cresseid's realization of Troilus' fidelity and, by his example, her knowledge of what she should have done, is the occasion for another warning. She now addresses lovers in general, advises them to choose their mates carefully, and cautions them to be careful who they trust.

She then turns again to self-accusation for the second time in this passage. She accuses herself of "greit unstabilnes" and she professes herself to have been "unconstant," and "untrew of fey." Her self-accusation is generated by self-knowledge, however, and she finally faces up to her responsibility in what may be the climactic

line of the poem: "Nane but my self as now I will accuse" (l. 574).[51]
At last Cresseid has reached maturity. She is able to realize the part
she has played in bringing about her situation. All of these good
sentiments must be followed by good actions, and Cresseid takes up
her pen to write her testament.

Cresseid's acceptance of personal responsibility has immense
implications for the way in which she looks at her past life. No
longer are there echoes of regret for her loss of youth and beauty.
No longer is there undue attachment to material things and to the
comforts of life at home or at court. She is instead quite resigned to
her human state: "Heir I beteiche my corps and carioun
with wormis and with taidis to be rent" (ll. 577–78). She
bequeaths her cup and clapper and ornament along with all her
riches to the lepers, an act of charity parallel to Troilus'. This shows
how far she has been morally redeemed. Only her ring is reserved
for Troilus as a remembrance. Her spirit is commended to Diana,
the goddess of chastity, "to walk with hir in waist woddis and wellis"
(l. 588). This is another act in her moral redemption. Her wish for an
ascetic afterlife is a mark of her character change.

Cresseid's finer moral sentiments are reflected in her bequest to
Troilus. Remorseful that she has only the ring which Troilus gave
her, she rues ever giving his gifts to Diomede:

> O Diomeid, thou hes baith broche and belt
> Quhilk Troylus gave me in takning
> Of his trew lufe." . . .

(ll. 589–91)

These are her dying words. After she has died, one of the lepers
takes off her ring and takes it to Troilus. There is no doubt that
Cresseid's moral redemption is total. She has been able to assume
her share of the blame for the problems she has created. She is no
longer looking for a scapegoat to help her avoid the problems of
personal responsibility.

Troilus' grief over Cresseid now seems appropriate indeed. When
he received the ring, "He swelt for wo, and fell doun in ane swoun"
(l. 599). The marble tomb that he orders for Cresseid is a fitting
monument not only to his love and the moral lesson to be derived
from her life, but also to her moral nature. Her epitaph is a
masterpiece of Henryson's concise style in the poem:

> Lo fair ladyis, Cresseid of Troy the toun
> Sumtyme countit the flour of womanheid,
> Under this stane, lait lipper, lyis deid.
>
> (ll. 607–9)

Henryson cannot pass the opportunity to again insert a warning to the ladies who read his poem. He addresses his conclusion to worthy women whom he exhorts to avoid mingling their love with deception. His poem becomes a plea for honesty in love, a theme with which most treatises on courtly love would take no exception. With the admonition that women bear in mind his advice, Henryson closes the poem.

The theme of the poem has been variously interpreted in Christian and pagan terms. Critics in the Christian school suggest that the world of the poem is supervised by a divine figure similar to the Christian God and that Cresseid must win her salvation in Christian terms. The critics who believe the poem deals with pagan values point to the Graeco-Roman origin of the deities in the parliament of the gods and suggest that Cresseid's redemption depends not on Christian values only but on broad human values that fit into any religious system. The treatment of courtly love in the poem is directly related to the thematic debate. There seems little question that Henryson employs the conventions of courtly love; the major question is what is his attitude toward them? If he believes that the values of courtly love are to be vindicated, then his attitude toward his heroine and Christianity is not the same as if he is attacking the courtly love conventions. Directly related to both of these questions is his treatment of Cresseid. Is he really the severe moralist condemning courtly love and showing that those who practice it are liable to incur the same fate as Cresseid's? Or is he sympathetic, extenuating as far as possible the foibles of Cresseid to try to provide a sympathetic viewpoint on her and her value system?

The most significant essay on Christian elements in the moral structure of the poem is E. M. W. Tillyard's analysis of Cresseid's plight.[52] Tillyard suggests that "the age of assured and static belief" appears in the Christian elements of the tale. He believes that the parliament of gods, far from being a simple introduction of pagan deities, has important Christian implications: "the Middle Ages looked on the stars as an organic part of God's creation and as the perpetual instruments and diffusers of his will."[53] As God's agents in the activities of men, the planets were punishing her for her transgressions against the Christian God by her adherence to the code of love. Cupid's curious preeminence can then be explained by the fact that he is the "oldest of the gods, the creator of order out of chaos, and hence in authority over the others." [54] The major development in Cresseid's characterization is from love of things of this world and commitment to a love code of personal satisfaction to contempt for worldly things and commitment to God. Tillyard also sees the poem as presenting a conflict between the codes of love and the church similar to that in *Le Morte D'Arthur*, but he argues that Henryson is not being unduly harsh with Cresseid.

Tillyard's position is perhaps the most conventional interpretation of the poem. Stearns explains that Cresseid's plight is "the wages of sin." Elliott also believes that the movement of the poem is complete once Cresseid has become " 'alive again unto God,' " and he concurs that Cupid represents divine Providence. MacQueen suggests that the allegory of the poem causes the reader to judge the religion of love in terms of Christian morality. He further argues that this allegorical interpretation would naturally have suggested itself to Henryson. [55] Other Christian interpretations imply a pejorative bias in Henryson's attitude toward his character. Stearns speaks of Henryson's stern morality and his "recognizably moral point of view" in the construction of the poem. Tatyana Moran maintains that Henryson's morality is harsh indeed. She believes that he intends Cresseid's leprosy to be "a grim warning to women who use their beauty for immoral purposes." She further believes that Henryson has no sympathy whatsoever for his heroine, but instead takes "a kind of sadistic pleasure in describing her degradation." [56]

Many of those who question the validity of Christian interpretations disagree on the nature of Cupid or on Henryson's attitude toward Cresseid. Spearing believes that Cresseid is treated harshly, and he agrees with Moran that there "is no suggestion of healing." Adamson argues that the Christian God does not appear in the poem, and Aswell believes that the "narrator and Cresseid both belong in a secular universe" while suggesting that Henryson's planet dieties are the natural forces of growth and decay. He goes on to explain that the poem shows a lack of divine Providence in a universe where each man must judge for himself. Dolores L. Noll attacks Tillyard's argument about the nature of Cupid and goes on to argue that the poem is set in a "make-believe love cosmos," the isolation of which precludes a relationship to a larger Christian world. . . ." She emphasizes that although the poem reflects patterns of medieval thought, these patterns do not necessarily reflect Christian premises. Lindsay believes that she is not a Christian tragic figure because her repentance involves only worldly matters.[57]

It seems undeniable, however, that in many ways Henryson's theme must be interpreted as Christian. Although there might have been a tendency by critics to exaggerate the Christian implications of the characterization of Cupid, the planets do have functions that are derived from and explicable in terms of Christian thought. There is no inconsistency between Aswell's argument that they are the forces of growth and decay, and Tillyard's assertion that they have Christian implications.[58] In medieval thought, the forces of growth and decay are the basic principles through which the Christian God governs the universe, as Tillyard explains. Although Henryson's attitude toward astrology is not always clear, it seems that he could hardly have avoided accepting some of the implications of such a common (and Christianized) part of his social ethos. If the planet portraits are Christian symbols in this more general sense, the position of Cupid becomes less important. As one of a group of vegetative forces, he need not be considered as the ancient figure of order which Tillyard would make him. Indeed, his primary position among the gods is not substantiated in the poem. He calls the gods to the parliament, but he is certainly not foremost. His title, "the king" is later applied to Phebus as well. When Saturn appears, Henryson's narrator tells us that he has little respect for Cupid. And once the gods have assembled, Cupid is not even in possession of the chair, which is turned over to Mercury. There is no need to believe that he is more important than any of the other gods simply because he calls them to judgment. He is merely the god most closely offended, but the offense touches or threatens them all, hence his calling the parliament. Once the pagan deities are understood to occupy the curiously ambiguous position which they had in late medieval thought, their role becomes clear. Non-Christian in origin, they had become Christianized as planets when astrology became an inextricable part of the medieval world view.

Noll emphasizes the importance of Henryson's courtly love in the poem, and Aswell points out that "Henryson causes the reader to think of the love-vision conventions" in the opening of the poem.[59]

Not only is the season the typical time of love poems, but the narrator himself speaks of love as a "votary both of 'courtly love' and concupiscence." [60] But it is also true that Henryson's treatment of the love conventions is sophisticated. Insofar as courtly love and its rules are understood as encouraging promiscuity and falsehood, Henryson attacks the code in the same manner as Chaucer. Courtly love, however, need not be interpreted as a system designed to permit only sexual satisfaction. By the fifteenth century, it appears that the code had become assimilated into the general social ethic in the period of courtship prior to marriage. As so established, it encouraged many of the same attitudes toward sexual relations as found in the church. Fidelity and honesty were emphasized over secrecy and falseness. It was not necessary to add these values to the code; they were already there. [61]

Henryson's concept of love, in fact, is very closely related to that of Andreas Capellanus. Capellanus advocates fidelity: "Thou shalt keep thyself chaste for the sake of her whom thou lovest." It is precisely this lack of fidelity that leads Cresseid to begin her affair with Diomede. Capellanus also advocates truth in love: "Be mindful completely to avoid falsehood." [62] This is the other great sin of which Cresseid is guilty. When she calls herself "fals Cresseid" she is referring to both her lack of chastity and her dishonesty. Henryson's references to Troilus as "noble" and "true," the typical means of describing him in the poem, provide the standards he applies to Cresseid in her actions under the code of love. Her inability to live up to those standards shows that she transgresses the laws of love. Lack of these two qualities is not only a sin in the code of courtly love, but also in Christianity. Cresseid's lack of chastity and her dishonesty are sins against both Cupid and God. Henryson has found moral elements common to both the courtly love and Christian systems. He has constructed a moral structure in which Cresseid's sins are double and in which her penance must be twofold. His emphasis on the code of courtly love does not imply adultery, immorality, and promiscuity; instead it implies fidelity and honesty. MacQueen explains the union effected between the standards of the church and those of the code of love by suggesting that both are "types or allegories of relationships which in themselves are seen and judged in terms of Christian morality." [63]

Moreover, allegory, specifically Christian allegory, is a vital part of the poem. Henryson may have intended it to be as important as in *Orpheus and Eurydice*. MacQueen suggests that the source of the allegory in both poems is derived from the commentaries of Nicholas of Trivet on the Orpheus story. Nicholas asserts that the Orpheus tale must be interpreted as a story about the attempt by reason and moral virtue to check the desires of appetite. Henryson's rationalism, which appears in both the *Fabillis* and *Orpheus*, would have made such an interpretation quite attractive. Troilus, Henryson suggests, represents virtue. Cresseid obviously represents appetite. The separation of the two leads appetite to acts of terrible excess. When they are finally reunited, neither can recognize the other "except through an act of charity, which in effect symbolizes divine grace." [64] This analysis helps to explain how the forms of courtly love became blended with the doctrines of the church. The allegorical habit of mind might have been so deeply ingrained in Henryson's thinking that it would have required a strong act of will for him to have ignored it. The allegorical significance of the weather in the prologue, the planet portraits, and Cresseid's disease are all in the pattern of the lesson Henryson wishes to teach. The bridge between the two systems of thought, whether allegorical or realistic, provides the unity of action and theme in Henryson's poem.

Finally, the treatment of Cresseid belies the "stern moralists" of both schools of criticism. As Grierson and Muir suggest "the keynote of the poem is sympathy." [65] Henryson is not being ironic in his sympathetic comments. Every indication is that he is trying to build sympathy in the minds of his audience. Moreover Cresseid does reach a state of moral salvation, as Tillyard suggests. To say that she has not been redeemed is to say that her suffering is pointless and that Henryson is taking nothing more than sadistic delight in her plight. Cresseid's suffering, however, leads to her redemption in terms of self-knowledge, knowledge of love, and charity.[66] Whether her repentance is Christian or not, Henryson suggests that it is valuable in aesthetic and human terms. When she understands the nature of her actions and sends her ring to Troilus, she has shown the ability to assume personal responsibility for her own conduct and for the welfare of others.

At one level Cresseid's character change need not be interpreted in Christian terms. The change from immaturity to maturity and wisdom is not simply a Christian phenomenon. But there can be little doubt that the elements that tempered Henryson's way of looking at the change she underwent were Christian. The pervasive nature of Christianity in medieval thought and in the poetry of

Henryson is such that a purely secular interpretation of the poem must disregard parts of the text and much of Henryson's schooling. Cresseid gains salvation through the basic steps in the Christian scheme of penance. Before sin can be atoned for, it must be recognized. Cresseid's punishment would be meaningless, as would any Christian penance without her recognition of the nature of the sin, the cause of the sin, and the means of true contrition. Her punishment is designed to bring her to an understanding of the nature of her selfishness and pride. With that knowledge, she may then gain the peace and understanding that come with genuine penance. She has satisfied not only the demands of Christian theology but also the morality of the love system that Henryson constructs, and there is satisfaction to be gained from her atonement to those laws as well. Cresseid has had to learn the nature of both sexual love and charity. As the tale of a woman who becomes a leper because she is unfaithful to her lover, this poem would be pessimistic indeed. As the story of a woman who learns the nature of love, both *eros* and *agape*, through suffering, it has an appeal that will last through the years.

CHAPTER 5

Orpheus and Eurydice *and the Shorter Poems*

I *Introduction*

BESIDES *The Testament* and the fables, Henryson wrote several shorter poems. The precise number is difficult to determine because of problems in attribution. Donald MacDonald has suggested that *The Thre Prestis of Peblis* should be included in the Henryson canon because of its similarity in style and theme to *The Morall Fabillis*.[1] Until there is additional evidence, MacDonald's case remains unproved, but there are poems now generally regarded as Henryson's on much slimmer proof. As a result, the Henryson canon is still subject to change. For instance, Ian Jamieson has challenged Smith's attribution of "The Want of Wyse Men" to Henryson.[2] The arguments are complicated by printing and manuscript practices and by the tendency of early printers and critics to consider the writings of the Chaucerians as an amorphous body of vaguely similar verse.

Nonetheless, it is possible to make some divisions among Henryson's shorter works. Of first importance is *Orpheus and Eurydice*. Although A. M. Kinghorn denounces it as inferior to *Sir Orfeo* and lacking in human interest,[3] the poem surely claims a secure position in medieval literature. Read in terms of its own Boethian philosophy, the poem shows a strongly developing human understanding on the part of the poet, along with a knowledge of medieval psychology and a commitment to early Renaissance rationalism. *Orpheus* demands individual attention, but the other shorter poems can be grouped into three categories.

The first group is the poems which deal with love. *Orpheus* could be included in this group. Among the others, two seem to belong here. "Robene and Makyne" combines some of the attitudes toward

love in the French *pastourelles* with those in the ballads. Lacking a
"Moralitas," it is the most direct of Henryson's poems in its
evaluations of love themes. Also included here is a poem that
overlaps with the next group, "The Bludy Serk." The narrative itself
seems to be devoted to the exploration of courtly love, but
Henryson appends a moral which gives it a religious interpretation.

The religious poems are among the most numerous. Outstanding
among them is the beautiful "Annunciation," perhaps the best of
Henryson's lyric efforts. In "Ane Prayer for the Pest," Henryson
directly addresses God in a fashion similar to that in "The Sheep and
the Dog" to request His help for those who suffer on earth. "The
Abbey Walk" is a meditative poem in a religious setting. Several of
the religious poems deal with death and the transitory nature of
earthly existence. Among them are "The Thre Deid Pollis," "The
Ressoning betuix Deth and Man," and two poems which have social
implications as well, "The Ressoning betuix Aige and Yowth" and
"The Prais of Aige." In the latter two poems, Henryson explores the
personal, social, and psychological implications of old age as well as
the religious nature of life on earth.

The third group of poems deals with social themes and
conventions. Some of the poems are merely exploratory, like the
two above and "The Garmont of Gud Ladeis." "The Garmont" has
affinities with the religious poems. Employing biblical sources, it
allegorically explores the proper conduct of a virtuous woman.
Other poems are critical and satirical in their intentions. "Aganis
Haisty Credence of Titlaris" is a criticism of backbiters, while "Sum
Practysis of Medecyne" takes to task the medical profession. "The
Want of Wyse Men" is a complaint against the foolishness of
Henryson's contemporaries. These poems are not devoid of
religious significance, but their primary emphasis is on social
problems, not theology.

Accurately dating the poems seems impossible at this point.[4] The
simplicity of the style of "Robene and Makyne" is at a pole opposite
from the fascinating wordplay of "Sum Practysis," but there is no
suggestion of a line of development. The poems we have inherited
must be only a part of Henryson's total production, and these
shorter poems are more likely genre poems than personal utter-
ances, as Ian Jamieson has shown.[5] By arguing for a line of
development among them, we might be misreading the poetry to
make dubious generalizations about the personality of the poet.

II   Orpheus and Eurydice

Perhaps none of Henryson's poems has been the subject of such widely diverse critical opinions as *Orpheus and Eurydice*. John Block Friedman, in his examination of the Orpheus tradition in the Middle Ages, commends Henryson for being able "to produce one of the most charming and memorable portraits of Orpheus to come out of the romance tradition." [6] At the other extreme, Maurice Lindsay believes that "Henryson's version of the Orpheus is so far inferior to the Middle English "Sir Orpheo" that it has little to commend it." [7] These varying points of view suggest the complexity of the poem and its use of medieval exegetical tradition as tempered by both romance convention and possibly Neoplatonism.

In its general form, the plot of the poem is the Virgilian Orpheus legend. Orpheus marries Eurydice, loses her when she is fleeing Aristaeus, searches her out, and attempts to bring her back to the world from Hades. He does not succeed because of his inability to keep from looking back at his wife. When he looks back, he violates the sole condition set for Eurydice's return by Queen Proserpina and loses his love. The poem is in rhyme royal, the same metric pattern as *The Testament of Cresseid*. Similar also to *The Testament* is the complaint, set off from the rest of the poem by its different stanzaic form; it consists of five ten-line stanzas rhyming *aabaabbcbc*.

There are three texts of the poem: the Chepman and Myllar text printed in 1508, the Asloan manuscript, around 1515, and the Bannatyne manuscript. G. Gregory Smith reprints the Chepman and Myllar text, but unfortunately it is incomplete, running to only 461 lines. There is some debate about the authenticity of the remaining two sources. The Asloan text is 578 lines, while the Bannatyne text contains 633 lines. H. Harvey Wood prints the Bannatyne text, but with some reservations about its authenticity. Since it follows the Asloan text by about 53 years, Wood believes that the Bannatyne expansions, which are primarily in the "Moralitas" are unreliable. He suggests they may have even been added by Bannatyne himself. MacQueen however has pointed out that there is no proof to support Wood's argument. [8]

There were at least three basic types of appeal in the Middle Ages for the Orpheus tale, and Henryson has made use of all of them. [9] First, it was an interesting story, derived ultimately from Virgil's

Georgics, and attractive simply for its artistic merit. In this sense, Henryson's narrative, apart from the "Moralitas," follows the tradition by providing a cleanly symmetrical tale, containing all the interest and excitement inherent in the myth.

Second, by the time of Henryson's poem, the Orpheus tale had become permeated with a set of romance conventions. Henryson made use of many of these, including love by reputation, Proserpina's role as queen of the fairies, the structure of Orpheus' complaint and appeals, and indeed the quest of Eurydice itself.[10] However, Henryson did not make his poem solely a romance. In arguing that Henryson may have been familiar with a version of *Sir Orfeo* similar to that in the Auchinleck manuscript, Carol Mills says that Henryson's primary concern was "the need to maintain the classical myth intact." [11]

The third aspect of the Orpheus tradition, and the one that may have had the strongest hold on Henryson's mind was the use of the tale to stimulate religious or philosophical meditation. The tale of Orpheus was another example, in the words of John Block Friedman, of the medieval Christian's "need to find Christian doctrine in the fables of the pagan gods." [12] The Christian aspects of the legend are clearly explained by the authorities Henryson cites in his "Moralitas." The tale, he tells us, is derived from Boethius, who included it in his *Consolation of Philosophy*. The lengthy "Moralitas" is based on the commentaries of Nicholas Trivet and William of Conches. In following this exegetical tradition, Henryson emphasizes the tropological level of interpretation, using the Orpheus legend to explore the human mind and to explain how to live a good life. In addition to the more traditional theological interpretation of the legend, Henryson has also incorporated Neoplatonism into his treatment of the legend. In exploring this level of Henryson's thinking, John MacQueen has argued that "there is ample evidence for a second level of allegory proper, based on Neoplatonic doctrine, metaphor, and numerology." [13] From this perspective, the poem becomes an allegorical analysis of the Soul of the World. Both the traditional tropological and Neoplatonic allegorical levels find extensive support in the text.

Henryson has combined all of these elements of the Orpheus tradition and possibly added another—that of political allegory, which may include references to contemporary Scottish affairs. The thematic texture of this poem is as rich as that in any of Henryson's other works. And in his use of character and plot to support this texture, Henryson has indeed produced a work that is a culmination of the entire Orpheus tradition.[14]

Orpheus is, according to Trivet, "pars intellectiua instructa sapientia et eloquencia."[15] Henryson calls him "the pairte intelletyfe / Off manis saule, and undirstanding fre, / And seperat fra sensualitie" (ll. 428–30). Henryson goes to great lengths to establish his hero's lineage. He begins with the mating of Jupiter and Memoria. The result is the nine muses: Euterpe, Melpomyne, Tersitor, Caliope, Clio, Herato, Polimo, Talia, and Urania. He notes that Caliope, "of all music maistress," was crowned queen by Phoebus who was Orpheus' father. Henryson's extra emphasis on Caliope among the muses is an attempt to enhance his protagonist's family background. Phoebus is, in the astrology of *The Testament of Cresseid*, one of the benevolent and life-nourishing forces among the gods. With all of Orpheus' genetic potential it is no wonder that Henryson relates:

> . . . he wes fair and wyse,
> gentill and gud, full of liberalitie,
> his fader god, and his progenetryse
> a goddess, finder of all armony. . . .
>
> (ll. 64–67)

Orpheus receives the best nourishment possible from his mother, and grows up to be a man of "statur large, and frely fair of face" (l. 72). His fame extends so far that Eurydice, queen of Thrace, sends a message asking him "to wed hir and be king."[16] At the level of Neoplatonism their union may represent "the immediate spiritual antecedents of human incarnation."[17] Her offer is significant because it establishes Orpheus' political position and, allegorically, his preeminence over the forces represented by Eurydice.

Eurydice represents:

> . . . our effectioun,
> Be fantesy oft movit up and doun;
> Quhile to ressone it castis the delyte,
> Quhyle to the flesche it settis the appetyte.
>
> (ll. 431–34)

Henryson's interpretation of Eurydice is consistent with Trivet's. She is passion, which offers itself willingly to the government of reason, as Eurydice offered her kingdom to Orpheus. Unfortunately, the attachment does not seem to be permanent. Reason cannot always retain its mastery over passion. Indeed, Eurydice's interest in him is carnal from the start. They seal their love affair with a kiss. Their happiness is built on "wardly Joy," the transience of which Henryson also showed in *The Testament of Cresseid*. The love affair and thereby the association between reason and passion is ultimately dissolved by passion's actions.

Eurydice strolls

> . . . furth in to a may mornyng,
> Bot with a madyn, untill a medow grene,
> To tak the air, and se the flouris spring. . . .
>
> (ll. 93–96)

As MacQueen has shown, the setting into which Eurydice walks is a typical courtly love setting,[18] but Henryson is using it as the scene of a dangerous and uncontrolled action of passion. This is also a possible vestige of the romance tradition. The landscape's conventional elements contrast sharply with the realism in Henryson's other landscapes in the poem. Once in the meadow, Eurydice is seen by Aristaeus, "a bustreouss hird" who attempts to ravish her. At this point the medieval interpretation of the tale departs abruptly from conventional Greek and Roman attitudes. Henryson follows Trivet in suggesting that Aristaeus is "gud vertew" (l. 436). His pursuit of Eurydice represents the attempt of virtue to control passion, but virtue, a quality complementary to reason, is unable to conquer passion. In her flight from Aristaeus, Eurydice steps on a snake. Her escape, according to Henryson, represents "this warldis vane plesans" (l. 439), and the serpent's sting is deadly sin, which causes mankind to lose heaven's bliss and the comforts of this life as well. After she is bitten, Proserpina carries her away.

Orpheus goes "haf out of mynd" and grievously laments his loss, structuring his complaint along lines remarkably similar to Cresseid's. In both cases the stanzaic structure differs from the rhyme royal of the overall poem. In both complaints, the thematic structure is typically medieval. He begins his lament with an address to his harp to help in the lament of one who "lossit hes in erd all his lyking" (l. 138). His harp serves as little solace, however, and he continues his lament with an evaluation of earthly pleasures that is similar to Cresseid's. He gives up his peace, play, and comforts of position including "my rob ryell, and all my riche array"

(l. 157). MacQueen takes special note of the numerological significance of this complaint and suggests that its structure represents the "five bodily senses." [19] Orpheus' abdication of his royal position is completely appropriate, since, allegorically, his whole kingdom was based on rule over the passions, that is, over Eurydice. He gives himself over to the woods with all of the discomforts of rustic life, including a lack of song.

Orpheus then turns his pleas to Phoebus and Jupiter. From Henryson's attitude in *The Testament of Cresseid*, it seems clear that he conceived of both of these gods as benevolent natural forces. A request for help to them would ordinarily be much more successful than an appeal to some of the less benevolent deities. Once his complaint has ended, Orpheus begins his search for Eurydice. He starts his journey down Watling street, representing the Milky Way, [20] and after he has sought for her throughout the cold regions, he finally comes to Jupiter. Thence he descends from his grandfather to Mars, then to Phoebus, who is saddened by his son's plight, but can offer no help. He comes next to Venus. Like the narrator in *The Testament of Cresseid*, he professes himself to be her "awin trew knyght" (l. 206). He then asks her advice, and she tells him "ye mone seik nedirmair" (l. 210), but Orpheus continues the search. He finally visits Mercury, who can give him no information about his wife, and in his descent he ignores the moon. [21]

Orpheus and Eurydice is one of the most encyclopedic poems Henryson wrote. In that regard, it is closer to *The Divine Comedy* or *The Canterbury Tales* than some of Henryson's other works. Besides permeating the portraits of the gods, this encyclopedic form appears in other elements of Orpheus' journey. As he is making his descent from heaven, "be the way sum melody he lerd" (l. 218). This melody is nothing less than the music of the spheres, the "armony of all this mappamound" (l. 223) which Henryson explains for four stanzas. After he has described the importance of the harmony of the spheres, he goes into detail about what Orpheus learned:

> Thair leirit he tonis proportionat,
> as duplare, triplare, and emetricus,
> enolius, and eik the quadruplait,
> Epoddeus rycht hard and curius. . . .

>   (ll. 226–29)

Orpheus' lesson becomes quite detailed, part of it based on
Boethius' *De musica*:

> ffirst diatesserone, full sueit, I wiss
> And dyapasone, semple and dowplait,
> And dyapenty, componyt with the dyss. . . .
>
> (ll. 233–35)

After this digression on music, Henryson introduces a bit of
biographical information which makes his intrusion into music
theory almost comic. "Off sic musik to wryt I do bot doit," he says,
"For in my lyfe I cowth nevir sing a noit" (ll. 240–42), a strange
admission for a man who goes into so much detail in his description
of the music of the spheres.

The encyclopedic nature of this poem is also evident in the rest of
Orpheus' journey. He finally ventures into hell to try to retrieve his
beloved. Henryson has effectively described hell, its horrors, and
the punishments meted out to sinners to enhance his moral theme.
Orpheus first meets Cerberus, which Henryson interprets as three
manners of death:

> The first is in the tendir yong bernage,
> The secound deid is in the middill age,
> The thrid is in greit eild quhen men ar tane.
>
> (ll. 465–67)

By playing on his harp, Orpheus manages to lull Cerberus to sleep.
He then passes to the river Styx and onto a boat on which three
sisters turn a wheel to which Ixion is tied. The three sisters are
Electo, Mygra, Thesiphone, the deities of vengeance. Henryson, however, follows Trivet in explaining that these three figures
represent "wickit thocht, ill word, and thrawart deid" (l. 478). The
wheel is actually the wheel of fortune which sometimes grants men
prosperity and sometimes poverty, and Ixion is a kind of worldly
man, "brukel and lecherouss" (l. 491). Like Eurydice, he is a
representative of appetite, and Henryson explores his attempted
seduction of Juno to illustrate the similarities between Ixion and the
heroine. That he is allowed to escape from his wheel when Orpheus
lulls the three sisters to sleep with his harp shows that

> . . . quhen ressoun and perfyte sapience
> playis upone the herp of eloquens,

> and persuadis our fleschly appetyte
> To leif the thocht of this wardly delyte,
> Than seissis of our hert the wicket will. . . .

(ll. 507–11)

Orpheus' next encounter is with Tantalus who is standing in the water unable to get a drink. In his "Moralitas" Henryson analyzes Tantalus' history in great detail. He explains that Tantalus' slaying of his own son to please the god of riches makes him a symbol of "men gredy and covetouss" (l. 532). Such men he contends are unable to sleep at night because they are so obsessed with their pursuit of wealth, a search as illusory as Tantalus' attempt to get a drink of water. Again Orpheus plays on his harp, the water stops, and Tantalus finally gets a drink. This passage signifies that man will no longer place his trust in the deceptions of avarice when

> . . . ressoun and intelligence
> Smytis upoun the herp of conscience,
> Schawand to ws quhat perrell on ilk syd
> That thai incur quhay will trest or confyd
> Into this warldis vane prosperitie. . . .

(ll. 545–49)

Further on, Orpheus goes through a particularly rough landscape full of "thornis thik and scherp," where he is cut and bruised. This is one of the realistic Scottish settings which are often judged to be one of Henryson's greatest strengths. In the midst of this dismal landscape, he meets Titius. Titius is pinned to the ground, while a bird sitting on his breast tears at his entrails. Titius is an example of intellectual pride, for "he set al his intentioun / To find the craft of divinatioun" (ll. 561–62), that is to learn things which are properly only God's concern. In his exposition of Titius' sin, Henryson makes his most explicit comments on astrology and those who believe in its principles

> Fra wichcraft, spaying, and sorsery,
> and superstitioun of astrology,
> Saif allanerly sic maner of thingis
> quhilk upoun trew and certane caussis hingis. . . .

(ll. 588–91)

Titius is guilty of a crime of passion: lack of restraint and lack of knowledge of his proper place in the universe. Orpheus comes to his rescue as well. When he plays his harp, the grip leaves and Titius is given some relief from his pain. This illustrates that when Orpheus plays his harp, he "biddis ho, / Till our desyre and fulich appetyte" (ll. 611–12).

In all three of these instances, Orpheus, or reason, has proved the solution for man's problem. Henryson's rationalistic philosophy bridges faith and reason.[22] Man is indeed bound to sin through his passion, but, if he will only use his rationality, he will be able to escape sin and its consequences. Henryson's emphasis on rationalism in the fables indicates that he is far more committed to exploring Trivet's philosophy and the ideals of Neoplatonism than merely for the purposes of this poem.

After Orpheus has passed through the outer realms of hell, he finally reaches the area where Pluto and Proserpina are holding court, yet another of the romance elements in the tale.[23] He finds their hall an intolerable place with a horrible stench. It is a "grundles deip dungeoun" where the "drink is pusonable." Even Kinghorn, who generally finds little to praise in this poem, is forced to concede this description is masterful.[24] This hell is "the realm of unsatisfied and uncontrolled appetite."[25] It is a completely appropriate place for Eurydice, but she is not alone. Among the multitudes, Orpheus finds "mony cairfull king and quene" (l. 317), including Hector, Priam, Alexander, Julius Caesar, Herod, Jesabel, Nabob, and others. Like Dante's hell, Henryson's inferno includes both pagan and Christian sinners. Orpheus goes directly to Pluto and his wife and asks permission to take Eurydice away. They are, in allegorical terms, compelled to grant desire to reason when the two are in accord. By reclaiming passion, reason "seikis up to contemplatioun" (l. 618). Yet Orpheus is disturbed by Eurydice's appearance and he exclaims "ffull wo is me to se yow changit thus" (l. 353), as he goes on to lament the change in her cheeks, lips, and "creistell ene." Pluto objects that her own languor is the cause of her degeneration, for she fares as well as any of those in hell. But, of course, passion is not self-sufficient; it must be reunited with reason.

Orpheus prepares to leave hell with his queen mindful of the one condition for her return which Proserpina has set: that he not look back on his journey out, i.e., that he have faith. Reason united with passion must also have faith to reach the heights of contemplation, but "blindit . . . with grit effectioun" (l. 388), he looks back at his beloved. Pluto then comes and returns her to hell.[26]

Orpheus is crushed by his experience. He falls into a swoon and, when he comes to, utters a bitter complaint. His complaint, however, is not against himself or Pluto or even Eurydice. It is instead against the laws of love:

> Quhat art thow, luve, how sall I the defyne?
> Bittir and sueit, crewall and merciable,
> plesand to sum, to uthir plent and pyne,
> Till sum constant, to uthir wariable;
> hart is thy law, thy bandis unbrekable. . . .
>
> (ll. 401–5)

Kenneth Gros Louis notes this is the type of complaint derived directly from the romance versions of the tale.[27] This is also the same kind of complaint which Cresseid uttered in her anguish immediately after learning that she had leprosy. It is the complaint of the immature. It is not love that is hard; indeed, Venus warned Orpheus not to continue to seek Eurydice. But when reason is overcome by passion, love is dangerous. Orpheus represents reason still under the influence of desire in this complaint. At one level, he has not been able to throw off desire, as Cresseid was eventually able to do, to obtain true maturity. At another level, MacQueen emphasizes that the characterization of Orpheus is permeated with elements of the Platonic formula and that "sometimes one might even suspect that Orpheus is himself an allegory of the Soul of the World."[28]

Orpheus and Eurydice has all the characteristics of an early work. It has indeed "a certain rawness which one associates with immaturity of conception."[29] The handling of character is not nearly so smooth as it is in *The Testament of Cresseid*. The "Moralitas" is much more intrusive than it is in *The Morall Fabillis*, and the breadth of human experience encompassed is smaller. In this poem, however, it is possible to see the basic elements which Henryson developed in his other major works.

The emphasis on passion versus reason, irresponsibility versus maturity, is the same as that developed in *The Testament of Cresseid* and *The Morall Fabillis*. Indeed, in his speeches on passion and the nature of love, Orpheus seems to foreshadow some of the passages about the narrator and some of Cresseid's dialogue *The Testament*. This same theme is developed much more subtly in some of the fables such as "The Paddock and the Mouse" and "The Preaching of the Swallow."

Orpheus and Eurydice is one of Henryson's most precisely organized poems,[30] but many of its structural devices also appear in his other works. The prologue is a device that Henryson employed in *The Morall Fabillis* and refined to excellence in *The Testament of Cresseid*. The complaint which Orpheus utters is similar in both content and structure to Cresseid's complaint. In both *Orpheus* and *The Testament of Cresseid* Henryson used a metric stanza different from that in the rest of the poem to emphasize both theme and characterization.

The possibilities of political allegory in *Orpheus* are strong. Friedman points out that "throughout the narrative Henryson has elaborated on the *de casibus* theme inherent in the myth." [31] Henryson may be taking an opportunity to relate his comments on the nature of true nobility to contemporary Scottish life. The prologue suggests political comment in its opening lines:

> The nobilnes and grit magnificens
> of prince and lord, quhai list to magnifie,
> his ancestre and lineall discens
> Suld first extoll, and his genologie,
> So that his harte he mycht inclyne thairby
> The moir to vertew and to worthiness,
> herrand reherss his elderis gentilnes.
>
> (ll. 1–7)

The emphasis on nobility and high social position is a characteristic of some of the didactic literature of the fifteenth century which attempted to revive chivalric ideals as standards for the nobility. The birth-worth debate in Medwall's *Fulgens and Lucres*, the didactic passages in Caxton's Malory, and the flood of chivalric handbooks are all symptoms of a society seeking ideals of noble conduct. In Scotland, where monarchs had been killed (purposefully or accidentally), and a kind of feudal anarchy had prevailed, the search for concepts of noble conduct was intensified, as shown in poems by Dunbar and romances such as *Rauf Coilyear*. The subject of nobility was particularly topical during the reign of James III. Henryson's reference to his worthy ancestors would be a reminder to James of the strength of character of his grandfather, James I, and the popularity of his father, James II.

Given the popular opinion of the King's character in 1475–1480, Henryson's subsequent comments would not have been too strong:

> It is contrair the Lawis of nature
> A gentill man to be degenerat,
> Nocht following of his progenitour. . . .
>
> (ll. 8–10)

While this same theoretical point is discussed in the manuals of chivalric conduct and in the romances, Henryson gives it a special touch which would apply to the Scottish monarch. His use of "progenitour" in line ten is more specific than most theoretical discussions become. The main "progenitour" who haunted James III was James II, who had shown promise of bringing peace and stability to Scotland. This line by itself, however, would not adequately substantiate the political comment, since Henryson could have used the singular form to keep from spoiling his rhyme. More specific references follow. Henryson notes that the main qualities of the "progenitour" are "the worthe rewll, and the lordly estait" (l. 11). These qualities at one level could be exercised by any noble, but they seem especially appropriate to the throne. Subsequent lines leave little doubt that Henryson is commenting on the monarch:

> A ryall rynk for to be rusticat
> Is bot a monsture in comparesoun,
> had in dispyt and full derisoun.
>
> (ll. 12–14)

The "ryall rynk" can apply of course to only one man. The "degenerate" nature of royalty during the reign of James III was a common topic, discussed in the parliament and attacked in poems such as *The Thre Prestis of Peblis*, *The Harp*, and Henryson's own fables.

Any such attack on a monarch could not be made openly. Henryson has to camouflage his comments by saying that the subject of his political introduction is "the grit lordis of grew," (l. 15) but, surprisingly, after such a long discussion of political degeneracy, they are not really shown to be degenerate. In fact they "set thair hairt, and all thair haill curage, / Thair faderis steppis Justly to persew" (ll. 16–17). A prologue in praise of ancient nobles needs no such lengthy discussion of royal shortcomings as a mere structural convention. The contrast between the conduct of the king and the great lords of Greece might have naturally suggested itself to Henryson.

The discussion of nobility does not stop with this simple dedication, as Henryson goes into detail about the qualities the lords of Greece possess, and which, by implication perhaps the king lacks. They are respectful of their high lineage and of their elders, and they show "all vertewis excellent" (l. 21). With this introduction, Henryson then turns to Orpheus' ancestry to allow his reader to understand how his hero could be capable of such noble deeds. The prologue suggests the poem is an object lesson in noble conduct, and such a lesson could hardly benefit the great lords of Greece; lessons are made primarily for those ignorant of what they teach. The main object of Henryson's lesson could be James himself. The antimonarchical tone set in this introduction is somewhat subdued in the rest of the poem. There are kings and queens who act foolishly, but none of the characters in the tale seems to be directly parallel to James. Orpheus, himself, is in many ways an example of kingly conduct that James might have emulated. If he represents reason, Henryson's rationalism would have suggested to him that some form of reason was the best guide a king could have. Orpheus' rationality would be a corrective to the problems that Henryson witnessed in his country. Besides this implicit standard for royal conduct, Henryson introduces passages that comment on the penalties for the misuse of office. Among the sinners he finds in hell are Julius Caesar, Herod, Nero, Pilot, Cresus, Pharoah, and Saul. These are among the

> . . . mony cairfull king and quene,
> With croun on heid, with brass full birnand,
> quhilk in thair lyfe full maisterfull had bene. . . .
>
> (ll. 317–19)

Their sins are all based in carnality. Caesar is condemned for his cruelty, Herod for lust, and Nero for general "Iniquitie." Pharoah and Saul get particular attention, and their sins are quite similar to James': Pharoah oppressed "godis folk," while Saul is condemned for his abuse of justice. All of them are heads of state who "have in some way failed in their duty as moral and spiritual leaders." [32]

That these references have topical significance is supported by the next passage that criticizes popes, cardinals, and bishops, anachronistic figures in Orpheus' hell. Their sins too are those widespread in Henryson's day. The bishops are particularly guilty of "wrang Intrusioun" (l. 341). Stearns believes that the political comment refers to the appointment of Henry Creichton as abbot of Dunfermline, despite the election of Alexander Thompson by the resident monks.[33] It is also possible that Henryson is referring to the outstanding example of such intrusion in his day, the investiture of William Scheves as archbishop of St. Andrews, which may also have been the subject of "The Trial of the Fox." If this is indeed the subject of Henryson's comment, that would place the *Orpheus* during or slightly after the mid-1470s, perhaps just before some of the fables which apparently became critical of the monarch.

Political comment is only one of the motives for Henryson's poem. He has combined politics with the theology, philosophy, and body of literary conventions which had developed around the Orpheus tale to produce a work with themes that have a broad and continuing appeal.

III *Love Poems*

After *Orpheus*, *The Testament*, and *The Morall Fabillis*, probably the best known of Henryson's works is "Robene and Makyne." The poem consists of sixteen stanzas of alternating tetrameter and trimeter, rhyming *a b a b a b a b*. The excellence of this poem has long been recognized even by those who do not appreciate Henryson's other works. In 1898, T. F. Henderson asserted that the "true individuality of Henryson is to be found not in such labored and ambitious efforts as *Orpheus* or *The Testament*, but in the wholly simple and ingenuous *Robene and Makyne*." Kinghorn praises its dramatic effects but believes it is Henryson's "lightest" poem.[34]

However, the poem is not as straightforward as it might seem, although the plot is quite simple. Robene, a country swain, is discovered sitting on a "gud grene hill, / Kepand a flok of fe" (ll. 1–2). Makyne approaches him, tells him that she has loved him "yeiris two or thre" and asks him to take pity on her. Robene objects that he knows nothing of love, but Makyne offers to be his teacher. She then provides him with an "*a b c*" of love in which she advises him to be "heynd, courtass, and fair of feir, / Wyse, hardy and fre" (ll. 19–20). Robene next explains that his sheep would object if they made love on the grass, so Makyne reinforces her plaint by promising "my hairt all haill, / Eik and my madinheid" (ll. 35–36). Robene still defers her offer and tells her that he will consider it if she will meet him there the next morning. Makyne continues to

plead and he continues to refuse until sunset. Not even her
profession that she is growing ill for lack of his love will move him.
When they part, Robene goes home light at heart, but Makyne goes
home with only her sorrow. Robene, however, is suddenly stricken
with lovesickness, and goes to Makeyne to offer her his heart, but
he is too late. She chides him with an old proverb: "The man that
will nocht quhen he may / sall haif nocht quhen he wald" (ll. 90–91).
The situations have now been reversed, and it is Robene who must
plead. He assures her that they will walk to the woods where "ma na
Janglour us espy," thereby insuring the secrecy of their liaison.
Makyne's reply is philosophical:

> . . . that warld is all away
> and quyt brocht till ane end,
> and nevir agane thairto perfay
> Sall it be as thow wend. . . .
>
> (ll. 105–8)

Despite Robene's further pleading Makyne will not be moved.
When they part this time, it is she who goes home light at heart and
he who must go back to his flock in sorrow over his beloved.

One of the major arguments about the poem concerns its debt to
the *pastourelle*. The conventions of the *pastourelle* are reflected in
the plot: a man, often a knight or poet, and a woman, usually either
a beautiful peasant or a noble lady, meet on a spring morning, and
the man implores the woman for her love. Sometimes the request is
granted, but most often, particularly in the Provençal *pastourelle*, it
is not. W. Powell Jones has attempted to show that the poem is
directly indebted to a *pastourelle* by Baudes. However, Janet Smith
has concluded that "among all the extant French *pastourelles*, not
one corresponds exactly to Henryson's 'Robene and Makyne.' "
Arthur K. Moore has noted several striking differences between the
pastourelle and Henryson's poem. He observes that the *pastourelle*
usually begins with a knight riding out on a spring morning in search
of love or adventure and the hero usually encounters a peasant girl
on the road. Moore also takes special note of the explicit sexual
description in the seduction scenes. He then argues that Henryson's
poem lacks the initial riding out, the class difference, and the
prurient interest. He concludes, therefore, that the *pastourelle* is
not the major influence on the poem and suggests that instead
Henryson made extensive use of the ballad. He points out that the

ballade stanza he employs is very close to the ballad form and that there are apparent verbal parallels between the poem and several ballads, including "Lord Thomas and Fair Annet." [35]

A major consideration in this debate is the system of love Henryson employs. In many respects it is the type of courtly love found in the French *pastourelles*. The setting and basic characterization are certainly in harmony with courtly love conventions, as they were developed in the fifteenth and sixteenth centuries. The season seems to be spring or summer, perfect for lovers, and Robene is portrayed as a shepherd watching his flock in a green meadow. The love Henryson describes is also compelling and shameless in its demands. Makyne uses little tact in her approach to Robene. She is forthright in her proposals just as is the traditional knight who encounters the maiden on the road. Like the love of the *pastourelles*, this love ostensibly has a set of rules and standards. Makyne tells Robene that he must be gracious, courteous, wise, and hardy to be a suitable lover. He must also be patient in his love to be a suitable partner for her. [36] A further similarity is to be found in that both this love and courtly love are specifically sexual instead of Platonic. Makyne promises Robene her maidenhead as well as her heart. This is also the kind of love which results in lovesickness, another traditional element in courtly love. When she first approaches Robene, Makyne tells him that she is afraid she will die if he does not grant her his love. When he gives her his final refusal she says, "I sicht, and that full sair" (l. 58). Her melancholy is contagious. This is precisely the same kind of language that Robene uses to describe his own lovesickness.

In all of these respects this type of love is typical of the *pastourelles*, but Henryson includes elements not characteristic of the French poems. For one thing, the situation is not quite typical, since the two characters are involved in an affair similar to that in *Venus and Adonis*. The philosophical note in Makyne's refusal of Robene's love is also atypical. If Henryson intended this poem as an allegory of the fading pleasures of youth, no "Moralitas" could have made his point more effectively. She says that not only love "is all away," but also the world. Her additional comment that it will never again be "as thou wend" is more profound than the traditional thematic fare of the *pastourelle*.

Henryson's blend of the love of the *pastourelle* with a more serious theme is only one cause of the difficulties in classifying this poem. Certainly there can be no question that he owes a debt to the conventions of the *pastourelle*, but in his use of these conventions, just as in his use of Chaucer, Henryson is not merely a slavish admirer. He borrows what suits his purposes, but he modifies the form to carry his own theme and to reflect his own interests. His originality in this work has led many modern readers to agree with Maurice Lindsay that it is "the finest of all of Henryson's minor poems." [37]

The second poem which deals with sexual love also examines religious love. "The Bludy Serk" is similar to *Orpheus* and "Robene and Makyne" in that its basic plot is associated with traditions of romance. It is also similar to "Robene and Makyne" in its metric and stanzaic pattern. The plot is a variant of *The Tale of the Emperor Frederick's Daughter*. A maiden is imprisoned in a dungeon by a horrible giant. Her father is a powerful king, but his age precludes his attempting to rescue her, and the giant refuses all ransom. Finally a young prince hears of her plight and comes to her father's kingdom. In a battle with the giant he wins but is mortally wounded. As he is dying, he asks the maiden to take his bloody shirt and "think on it, and syne on me, / quhen men cumis yow to wow" (ll. 77–78). She is so impressed by the prince's sacrifice that she remains celibate. The "Moralitas" informs us that the king is like the Trinity, the lady like man's soul, the giant like Lucifer, and the prince like Christ. Allegorically, the poem shows how man's soul is rescued from sin by Christ. George Peek argues that the difference between the narrative and the "Moralitas" suggests that Henryson "has really created two separate and distinct stories: one the story of a maiden's rescue and a knight's courage, and another which is an allegory of Christ's love for man and the necessity for man's response." [38]

Indeed, it is additional proof of Henryson's artistry that the poem can be appreciated at two different levels, but the interpretation of this tale as Christian allegory is not original to him. This same narrative is found in the *Gesta Romanorum*, a collection of stories drawn from various sources but all given specifically Christian morals. Henryson's use of a version of this tale close to those in the texts of the *Gesta Romanorum* is well established. In fact, it seems likely that he might have used the precise version in Harleian MS. 7333. Assuming that the Harley narrative was Henryson's source, Peek suggests that he made three major changes: "first the lack of names or identifying elements in the story; second the fact that the king still lives during his daughter's capture; and third, the fact that the lady is carried off and thrown into a dungeon rather than seduced by the evil one." Henryson also provides more details on characterization and more description, including grisly aspects of the appearance of the giant.[39] All of the differences between his poem and the Harley version indicate that Henryson was interested in intensifying the drama of the poem while maintaining its moral intact. Although "The Bludy Serk" is also a genre poem insofar as it demonstrates Henryson's strong reliance on a structured body of literary conventions, it further shows Henryson's ability to blend and modify convention for the purposes of his art.

IV *Religious Poems*

Two of the most prevalent themes in Henryson's religious poems are aging and death. "The Ressoning betuix Aige and Yowth" and "The Prais of Aige" take the first theme for their subject. Probably the outstanding antecedent of these two poems is *The Parlement of the Thre Ages*. This poem opens with a pastoral setting in which representatives of the three ages of man debate which period in man's life is best. The claims of Youth are physical vitality and the pleasures of the senses. Middle Age can claim personal accomplishment, while Old Age knows the transitory nature of things and can claim wisdom. The debate form employed here is traditional in discussions of the fleeting nature of the pleasures of this world, as seen in the closely related "Debate Between the Body and the Soul." The implications of this poem are more important for Henryson's "Thre Deid Pollis" and "The Ressoning betuix Death and Man." In the debate between body and soul, the body lists its pleasures and accuses the soul of negligence in its lack of concern for its own welfare in the pursuit of pleasure. The soul, in its reply, emphasizes the lack of substance in the pleasures of the body, and suggests instead that it is the body that has been negligent in its lack of concern for the welfare of the soul. The poem includes gruesome descriptions of the physical decay of the body and the torments that await the soul when it is finally carried off by devils. Henryson's familiarity with "The Debate" seems likely from parallels already established with portions of *The Morall Fabillis*.

Henryson's four poems on the transitory nature of life and mortality are written directly from this tradition. "The Ressoning betuix Aige and Yowth" begins with a nature prologue similar to that in *The Parlement of the Thre Ages*. Although the "mornyng myld" with its "perly droppis of the balmy schowris" seems an incongruous setting for the kind of debate that is to follow, it is a scene, as Jamieson suggests, directly in the tradition of the earlier debate.[40] The narrator who describes the morning sees a figure with characteristics traditionally associated with age. He is a "cative on ane clud cumand" who has "cheikis clene and lyart lokis hoir" (ll. 10–11). The two start their debate, and Yowth makes his case. He is strong and fair, and he has confidence that "my fegour will not faid" (l. 23). He is happy with "luvis law," and his wits are keen. He had no reason to believe that he will not be so forever. He ends each of his stanzas with the refrain "O yowth, be glaid in to thy flowris grene" (l. 8).

Aige is no less pressing in his case. From personal experience, just like the old man in *The Parlement of the Three Ages*, he knows that the pleasures of youth do not last. He tells Yowth that soon he shall be bald, his strength shall fail, and his courage will depart. He offers Yowth the example of his own appearance, if there is any doubt about his word. His constant refrain is in counterpoint to that of Yowth: " 'O yowth, thy flowris fadis fellone sone.' " His admonition is repeated at the end of the poem.

As the old man leaves, Yowth, who has been the first-person narrator, remains behind and thinks about what he has witnessed. The poem ends with a repetition of both refrains and the suggestion that both are to some extent true. In his ambiguous conclusion, Henryson again reflects the conventions of *The Parlement of the Three Ages*. In this tradition, to some extent each of the various ages has its own pleasures. Henryson's poem gains greater impact from its brevity, but there can be little doubt that it is a product of this tradition.

So too is "The Prais of Aige." While the lines of descent are not quite clear, it is a part of the general tradition of *The Parlement* and even shares some of the philosophy of the more somber "Debate Between the Body and the Soul." It also begins with the traditional natural setting. An old man is discovered singing under a rose bush, and the narrator is moved to joy by his song. The singer says he would not be young again were he given the chance, for the world is false and "full of variance." Freedom has fled, and covetousness is now king. Youth must further put up with the raging of the blood and great vanity. No, the singer concludes, it is better to be old.

The theme of this poem is similar to that of the religious poems which inspired Henryson's other works in this group, but Henryson

introduces another tradition here, that of the social complaint.
These forms will be treated in more detail when we deal with the
third class of shorter poems, but earlier works in the tradition
include "On the Retinues of Great People" and "On the Evil Times
of Edward II." They usually deal with social injustices afflicting the
poet and others in his society.[41] "The Prais of Aige" certainly
borrows from the complaint in its description of social conditions:

> ~reuth is all tynt, gyle has the gouvernance
> Wrechitnes has wroht all welthis wele to wo;
> Fredome is tynt, and flemyt the lordis fro,
> And covatise is all the cause of this. . . .
>
> (ll. 11–14)

These general social ills are part of the cause that the old man is glad
his youth is gone: "The more of age the nerar hevynnis blisse" (l.
16). This portion of the old man's complaint is not the only way in
which Henryson blends two traditions. Most social complaints
conclude with a plea for change or a prayer to God for help, which is
the type of ending Henryson uses here:

> Quhat have we here bot grace us to defend?
> The quhilk god grant us for to mend oure mys,
> That to his glore he may oure saulis send;
> The more of age the nerar hevynnis blisse. . . .
>
> (ll. 29–32)

This conclusion is another of the devices Henryson uses to merge
the tradition of religious poems on aging and the transitory nature of
things of this world with the complaint. His originality in this poem
is not to be found in independent creation but in the synthetic
genius which can find similarities in two different traditions.

Henryson's other two poems in this group are more directly in
the *memento mori* tradition of "The Debate Between the Body and
the Soul," "Ubi sunt qui ante nos fuerunt?" and "Whan I Think on
Thyngis Thre." "The Thre Deid Pollis" relies particularly on the
shock effect inherent in the earlier traditions. Besides the impact of
the sheer physical grotesquerie of three talking skulls, the poem
depends for its effects on the shock which results from the abstract
contemplation of death. In "Ubi sunt" this effect is achieved by a
series of questions arranged in the pattern "Where are they who
were here before us?" The poem does not answer the series of

questions it poses, but relies instead on the reader's imagination to
drive home the theme of the transitory nature of life. "Whan I Think
on Thingis Three" is a first-person narrative in which the poet
reveals his own trepidation at the prospect of death. The list of such
poems could easily be multiplied by inclusion of other lyrics such as
"Timor mortis conturbat me."

Henryson's "Thre Deid Pollis" uses numerous elements in this
tradition. It begins with a message to "sinfull man" who is in this
mortal sea. In the third line, the reader learns that he is being
addressed by the skulls themselves. Their descriptions include
some of the gruesome details to be found in earlier lyrics: they have
"holkit ene . . . [and] peilit pollis bair" (l. 4). Immediately after
their descriptions, they inform the reader that they were once as he
is now. Their warning is generalized in the assertion that all men
must suffer death, which is uncertain in its arrival. They then turn
their comments especially to "wantone yowth" and "lusty gallandis
gay" and tell them "Thy example heir be us it may be sene" (l. 24).
But they spare no one in their grim statements. The "ladeis quhyt,"
along with "King & quene" and "febill aige," are also told that their
states will change. There will be no help when the end comes, not
from science, "art, musik, or . . . astronomye" (l. 46). They warn
men especially against the effects of pride. The only solution is "for
our sawlis to pray in general / To Iesus chryst" (ll. 59–60). This is the
same theme to be encountered throughout earlier works in this
tradition.

While "The Thre Deid Pollis" is a monologue, "The Ressoning
betuix Deth and Man" is a dialogue. Death addresses man in the
first stanza and tells him to heed the fate of all earthly things. "Paip,
empriour, king, barroun, & knycht" cannot withstand his power.
Man at first does not know who is addressing him and shows his
pride in refusing to yield; he even threatens Death. Death identifies
himself and repeats his warning. Man, suddenly humbled, repents
himself of his sensuality and especially his pride, the same sin which
receives the most emphasis in "The Thre Deid Pollis." The next
comment by Death emphasizes man's ignorance and his transitory
nature and emphasizes again that there is no escape, "Thocht thow
war paip, Empriour, and king all thre" (l. 40). Man's last speech
professes his humility and ends with a prayer for mercy similar to
that in the preceding poem: "Jesus, on the, with peteous voce, I
cry, / Mercy on me to haif on domisday" (ll. 47–48).

"The Abbey Walk" is a meditative poem which relies less on

shock effect than the poems above. Although this poem is often interpreted as biographical in its references to the abbey, which is supposed to be the Dunfermline establishment Henryson would have known, Jamieson points out that the poem follows conventions as well established as those in the mortality poems. He mentions in particular *Deo Gracias* and *A Lamentacion beate marie*, both of which have passages in which a character sees or overhears something instructive or miraculous in a church. He further adds that in one *chanson d'aventure*, the narrator finds a meditative inscription written on a wall.[42]

Henryson's poem contains a combination of these elements. The narrator, walking in an abbey, sees on a wall an inscription which begins: "off quhat estait, man, that thow be, / Obey and thank thy god of all" (ll. 7–8). The rest of the inscription occupies the remainder of the poem. Its warnings are parallel to those in the other poems. Kingdom and great empire shall not endure; gold will eventually desert man. The inscription then tells the story of Job, in medieval typology, a representative of Christ. In relating Job's misfortunes, the poem makes the point that man should "Blame nocht thy Lord, sa is his will; / Spurn nocht thy fute aganis the wall" (ll. 29–30). The poem goes on to affirm God's justice and mercy and asserts:

> This changeing and grit variance
> off erdly staitis up and doun
> Is nocht bot causualitie and chance,
> as sum men sayis, without ressoun,
> Bot be the grit provisioun
> of god aboif that rewll the sall. . . .
>
> (11. 41–46)

It too ends with an admonition to forego vanity and worldly interests and repeats the refrain "obey and thank thy god of all" (1. 56). Henryson has once again chosen a traditional form to develop his interests in the theme of mortality.

Without doubt, the most beautiful of Henryson's religious poems is "The Annunciation." Even those who tire of Henryson's didacticism find it appealing. Kinghorn, for instance, says that its vital diction makes it one of Henryson's strongest efforts.[43] It too, however, relies on a poetic tradition. Besides the Gospel of St. Luke, it owes a debt to other annunciation poems, as John Stephens has shown.[44]

In one sense this poem is about love just as much as "Robene and Makyne"; it even begins with a description of the powers of love, one of Henryson's most original touches in this poem.[45] Love, the poet tells us, is "forcy as deith," and makes everything easy. One of the greatest examples of love, he relates, is to be found in Gabriel's message to Mary. The second stanza is an exposition of the message; Mary listens in silence while Gabriel makes the annunciation. Henryson believes it is the law of love, as well, which generates miraculous events, including the miraculous conception of Christ, which he emphasizes along with biblical history.[46] It is the divinity of Mary and the love and grace of God, he asserts, that make possible the salvation of all mankind. Finally, the poet addresses the Virgin and asks her to make him as chaste as she herself is.

Much of the vitality of the poem is due to its style. Although it contains numerous elements of the alliterative tradition, the sparkle of Henryson's diction is partially due to the slightly more aureate vocabulary he displays. Lines 25–29 exemplify his blending of the two major traditions of Scottish poetry:

> Thir tithingis tauld, the messinger
> Till hevin agane he glidis:
> That princes pure, withoutyn peir,
> Full plesandly applidis,
> And birth with barne abidis.

The alliteration of stops (/t/, /g/, /p/, /p/, and /b/ respectively) along with the stress patterns, represent the tradition of older Scottish poetry, while the aureate diction along with the rhyme are the elements of post-Chaucerian glamour.

The subtle thematic structure of the poem is also noteworthy. Although this poem contains some of the conventional religious sentiments embodied in the mortality poems and earlier poems on the annunciation, they are less blatantly didactic.[47] Most modern readers find Henryson's discourse on love, specifically *caritas*, a palatable means of expressing his sentiments. With its comprehensive treatment of love and its stylistic interest, this poem has become one of the favorites among Henryson's works.

The final poem in this group also contains elements of social comment, like "The Prais of Aige" and "The Abbey Walk." "Ane Prayer for the Pest" consists of eleven stanzas rhyming *a b a b b c b c* It begins with an address to God and a request that He "Haif mercy of us" (l. 5). Yet even though Henryson affirms that God "dois no wrang to puneiss our offens" (l. 6), there is a strong implication that God should exercise more mercy than he has heretofore. The people, represented by the poet, beg God on bended knees to relent his wrath. They are "richt glaid thow puneiss our tresspass / be ony kind of uthir tribulatioun" (ll. 17–18), but this punishment is too severe. The poet requests that God use drought, sickness, or hunger instead, and even feels impelled to remind God to "Remmember, Lord, how deir thow hes us bocht" (l. 41). If God will only help them, they will mend their ways. Their sin, after all, has not been entirely their own fault. If the government authorities were not so corrupt, such great sin would not have spread through the land. In an abrupt shift of his stanzaic form in stanza nine, Henryson begins his final plea:

> Superne/ Lucerne/ guberne/ this pestilens,
> preserve/ and serve/ that we not sterve thairin.
> Declyne/ that pyne/ be thy Devyne prudens.
>
> (ll. 65–66)

These lines echo Dunbar and illustrate Henryson's own abilities as an aureate poet. In his conclusion, Henryson again asks help in correcting the misdeeds of his people and promises to reform if God will only take pity on them.

This poem makes extensive use of the conventions of social complaints. As in most such poems, the narrator makes himself a spokesman for the people at large, a device employed in "On the Retinues of Great People" and "On the Evil Times of Edward II." As a spokesman for the people, Henryson is, however, unusually audacious. In poems dealing strictly with social problems, the poet may take it on himself to question governmental policies; Henryson, more courageously, questions divine policies. In his reminder to God about the value and dignity of man and in his description of the state of his fellows, there is an implicit questioning of divine Providence. This same tone is to be found in "The Sheep and the Dog," where the poor sheep asks God how he can see injustice in the world and not act against it.

The poem is also similar to social complaints in its bifurcation of society into two groups, the oppressed and the oppressors. Henryson is quite daring in vaguely suggesting that God is punishing the wrong group. It is the oppressed, the poor, who must pay because the oppressors, the governments, do not do their job. It is the upper classes, after all, who encourage the kind of corruption and degradation for which the whole society is now being punished.

Henryson's religious poems span the spectrum of medieval types both in their themes and structures. Some, like "The Annunciation," are strictly concerned with theological matters, while others, like "The Prais of Aige," have a substantial element of social comment. Some, like "The Ressoning betuix Aige and Yowth," are similar to the fables in their diction and metric structure; others, such as "The Annunciation" and "Ane Prayer for the Pest," are more ornate in their language and form. Henryson's poems in this group are all firmly grounded in medieval poetic traditions, but their variety in theme and form shows the wide range of his accomplishment.

V Poems on Social Themes

Henryson's shorter social poems have more in common with complaint and instructional verse than with satire. There is some humor in these poems, but behind it lies the most severe judgment of those who take advantage of their fellows. One of the poems that best illustrates this kind of dark humor is "Sum Practysis of Medecyne."

The poem consists of nine stanzas of tetrameter and pentameter lines with a tail rhyme. It is not, unusual for Henryson to mix metric patterns, but the variation in this poem exceeds that in his other works. More striking still is the diction. In no other poem does Henryson rely so much on words either coined or derived from Latinate and native sources.[48] The following lines from "Dia Culcakit" are typical:

> Cape cukmaid and crop the colleraige,
> and medecyne for the maw, and ye cowth mak it,
> with sueit satlingis and sowrokis, The sop of the sege,
> The crud of my culome, with your teith crakit. . . .
>
> (ll. 27–30)

This atypical diction has not as yet been completely analyzed. At least one speculation is that it is based partially on students' Latin, as well as on more traditional sources.[49]

In structure the poem consists of a two-stanza introduction, four stanzas of prescriptions, and a one-stanza conclusion. The introduction begins with a direct address to the reader by the physician-speaker:

> Guk, guk, gud day, ser, gaip quhill ye get it,
> Sic greting may gane weill gud laik in your hude
> Ye wald deir me, I trow, becauss I am dottit,
> To ruffill me with a ryme. . . .
>
> (ll. 1–4)

The narrator continues with his claims of his expertise. His "prettik in pottingary" is unsurpassed, and he brags about how effective his cures will be.

After this expansive introduction, the narrator next turns to the cures themselves. The prescription for cholic, also quoted above, is laden with both colloquial and Latinate mumbo-jumbo. The medical gibberish is not the only satirical element in the cure, however, for when it is all summed up, the physician says

> Put all thir in ane pan, with peper and pik,
> Syne sottin to thiss,
> The count of ane sow kiss, For the collik.
> Is nocht bettir, I wiss
>
> (ll. 36–39)

The bawdy humor in the final element in the prescription is repeated in other cures. *Dia Custrum* prescribes

> The lug of ane lyoun, the guse of ane gryce;
> ane unce of ane oster poik at the nether parte,
> annoyntit with nurice doung . . .
>
> (ll. 70–72)

In his use of such ridiculous cures, Henryson is satirizing the practice of quacks who try to impress the patient with their ersatz knowledge.

So too in the conclusion he recommends:

> Bot luk quhen ye gadder thir gressis & gerss,
> outhir sawrand or sour,
> That it be in ane gude oure: Ane uthir manis erss.
> It is ane mirk mirrour
>
> (ll. 87–90)

The scatology and bawdry are both as unusual in Henryson's poetry
as the uncommon diction. They serve, however, to heighten the
sense of the ridiculous by their sharp juxtaposition with what proper
cures should be and with the dignity usually attendant to the
medical profession.

That much of his practice is quackery even the speaker is aware.
In his final advice to his reader, he explains that he has no more
time, but he advises the reader to look at his work. The result of
such diligent study he contends is that all men "sall bliss yow, or
ellis bittirly yow ban" (l. 85). Although the physician is generally
regarded with respect in medieval literature, there is no doubt that
Henryson was making an attack found in the estates satires of poets
such as Gower, Langland, Skelton, and Dunbar. Traditionally, in
estates satire, doctors are connected with their love of money and
their strict, undesirable cures. Henryson is certainly working in that
tradition.[50]

Henryson temporarily departs from satire in "The Garmont of
Gud Ladeis" which combines elements of social instruction with the
themes of religious poetry. The poem consists of ten stanzas of
alternating tetrameter and trimeter. Between the initial introductory stanza and the conclusion, the remaining eight stanzas are a
description of the garments the poet would use to dress his beloved.
They have allegorical significance, each item standing for some
feminine virture. Janet Smith is convinced that the source is Olivier
de La Marche's *Triumphe des Dames*, written around 1500. Recent
investigations by Jamieson have thrown doubt on this source,
however, partially because Marche's poem seems too late. In any
case, "The Garmont" is the expression of the same general spirit
found in Marche's work, another anonymous poem (which might
have been based on Henryson's), and a poem by Gilbert Haye.[51]
There may also be a debt to a biblical source, 1 Timothy 2:9–11. As
much as any of the other shorter poems, "The Garmont" is
traditional.

The brief introduction expresses the desire on the part of the
author to have his lady wear the garments he lists. She must have
honor as her hood, "garneist with governance." Her shift must be
chastity woven with shame and dread, while her girdle should be
constance mixed with love. Her gown, belt, mantle, hat, and other
garments have similar allegorical functions. The result is a list of
feminine virtues that would produce a godly, faithful, virtuous
woman. This goal of the list of virtues is little different from that of

the poetic tradition described above or from such works as *The Book of the Knight of the Tower*. All of these works have the object of producing virtuous wives and mothers who would avoid the temptations of fine clothes, fickleness in taste, infidelity, and gossiping. The woman Henryson clothes would fit precisely such a mold.

One of the outstanding strengths of this poem is its concreteness. It also shares, says Ridley, the "color, and pace of a ballad." [52] Because of its debt to ballad stanza in its structure, it is a fitting companion to "The Bloody Serk." Henryson's use of specifics in "The Garmont" is one of the ways his poem shows an advance over its analogues and possible sources.

"The Want of Wyse Men" is nine stanzas of pentameter rhyming *a b a b b c*. In this group, it has generated the most controversy concerning attribution. It is attributed to Henryson in neither of the early texts, but in one manuscript, MS. 19.1.16 of the National Library of Scotland, it is printed along with *Orpheus and Eurydice* without a separate heading. Moreover, thematic similarities between this poem and "The Sheep and the Dog" suggest that the poem is Henryson's.

The thematic elements here are not common only to Henryson's works, however; they appear often in the poetry of the Middle Ages. As a work of social criticism, this poem reflects the major conventions of medieval complaint. It begins with an expression of despair about the state of the world. The poet would like to find "sum clerk of connyng" to interpret matters for him so that he can understand why "this warld be turnyt up so doun" (1. 3). There is no faithfulness, wealth, or real wisdom; in fact, the stanza ends with the proverbial expression "Sen want of wyse men makis fulis to sit on binkis" (1.8) which will become the refrain. He remembers that there was a time when the world was well-regulated and "regnyt reule, & resone held his rynkis" (1. 14), but now even "nobilitee is thralde" (1. 15). Along with it is exiled "ald noble corage" (1. 33), justice, equity, and wisdom. There is in the poem a kind of wistfulness about the "good old days" when such virtues were held in esteem. At the present time, however, the poet believes that "law is bot wilfulness" (1. 49) and "Vyce is bot vertew" (1. 59).

All of these complaints are reflected in earlier poems. "On the Evil Times of Edward II" complains that justice has fled, while "On the Retinues of Great People" implies that the nobility is degenerate because of its disregard of the peasants. In other poems as well there is a sense not just that a particular situation is wrong or unjust, but that corruption is so widespread that the whole world has become degenerate. In this respect these poems share a kind of apocalyptic tone with religious poems such as *Piers Plowman*.

Like other complaints, the poem ends with an appeal. While the desperation of some poets led them to the point of despair, in this poem Henryson suggests that the state of things has not passed beyond the point of correction. It will require the power of God, however, to set things right, and so his appeal is directed to Him:

> O Lord of lordis, god & gouvernour,
> Makar & movar, bath of mare & lesse,
> Quhais power, wisedome, & honoure,
> Is infynite, salbe, & ewir wes,
> As in the principall mencioun of the messe,
> All thir sayd thingis reforme as thou best thinkis. . . .
>
> (ll. 65–70)

There is strong contrast between the appeal in this poem and that in "Ane Prayer for the Pest." Here the poet is less inclined to question and correct God. Here too, the poet is using a conventional kind of appeal in a traditional complaint.

The emphasis on the glories of previous years in this poem coincides with the revival of nostalgic feelings about the past in England as well. Caxton in particular was concerned about the degradation of modern knights, as he explains in the preface of his edition of Malory. His feeling for chivalry was an attempt to find a means of correcting social degeneration. Doubtless, Henryson too wished for a way to improve his society.

"Aganis Haisty Credence of Titlaris," the last of the shorter poems, has much in common with "The Want of Wyse Men" and some of Dunbar's satires. Dunbar and other courtiers would have likely been more aware than Henryson of the vicissitudes of court life and the dangers of talebearers. These scandalmongers were part of the same degenerate upper class described in earlier complaints, but they became especially dangerous as England and Scotland began a period of consolidation of governmental power and disparate feudal courts gave way to a single national court. As the knight was displaced by the courtier and a man's power was gained not through his sword but through his personal friendships, backbiters and court gossips exercised increasingly greater influence, often grounded on base flattery and falsehood. It is to such power that the poem objects.

The beginning carries a message in some ways typical of Henryson. The rank, foul, talebearers are lacking in "cheritie" the quality Henryson emphasizes in *The Morall Fabillis* and *The Testament of Cresseid*. Part of the responsibility for the evil done by these men must be that of the lord to whom gossip is presented, he contends. Such a powerful man should "awyse him weill" (l. 5) when he is presented with gossip or scandalous stories. Henryson goes on to point out the specific kinds of judgments that should be made. The first consideration is whether a tale is true or not. A lord should decide if the information is being furnished out of love or envy. In any case, the parties who have offended should be called to make lawful defense, which the lord should hear with an open mind. He warns that it is no worship for a noble lord to give hasty credence to such tales; it is in fact, against reason for him to believe such things until he knows all the facts. He continues to berate the talebearers, and calls them "moir perrellus than ony pestillence" (l. 30). In the last three stanzas, Henryson addresses the lords, the backbiters themselves, and a more general audience. He asks the lords once again to be cautious about any information that backbiters bring to them. He condemns the wicked tongue to hell because of its danger and lack of conscience. He finally expounds on the dangers of backbiters who "Thre personis severall . . . slayis with ane wowrd" (l. 51), and concludes with a prayer that God grant the lords grace not to give scandalmongers their quick belief.

There is in the poem a personal tone which could reflect some of Henryson's own experience with courtiers. But all of the attitudes in the poem can be explained by reference to the conventional complaints regarding vicious courtiers. Traditionally, such gossips at court always hurt the innocent, and they are most formidable when they gain the ear of a powerful lord. There is no reason to assume more personal involvement in this poem than in any of the others.

Judged against the conventions of the Middle Ages, Henryson's shorter poems are no disappointment. The poet clearly employs medieval traditions in the creation of his shorter works. Sometimes indeed he modifies them or combines them with other traditions but the elements of conventional rhetoric and structure are easily recognizable nonetheless. Once again, however, Henryson has adapted some of the conventions in ways that permit his own particular genius its reign as well. In a poem such as "Sum Practysis of Medecyne," traditional medieval satire on a prominent member of the estates group has been blended with brilliant language derived from native elements, medical Latin, and perhaps students' Latin, to enliven a conventional form. Certainly "The Annunciation" shows this same flair. But it is again primarily through his style that Henryson lifts his work beyond the ordinary medieval poem on the subject into the realm of majesty.

Henryson's use of convention should not be considered the mark of an inferior muse. Much of the literature of the late Middle Ages is after all traditional literature. Both Chaucer and Malory make extensive use of sources, and their genius may be described as synthetic and stylistic. Henryson is in many ways much the same. Most of his plots and subjects are derived from or suggested by other pieces of literature, and many of the conventions he employs are derived from literary traditions. In the shorter poems he continues his use of the generic forms of the period.

CHAPTER 6

Henryson and Later Poetry

HENRYSON'S accomplishment and his importance for Middle Scots verse can hardly be overestimated. He forged a group of exceptional poems that has become an inspiration to later poets, and, by his eclecticism, he infused Scottish verse with some of the best elements of other cultures and literatures. Perhaps most important of all, he brought to Scottish poetry the broad sympathetic understanding which is a mark of all great writing.

Through the *Fabillis* he explored a wide variety of social classes and types of individuals. Perhaps no other single work in all of Scottish literature contains a greater range of characters. *Orpheus and Eurydice* provided Scottish poetry with a model blend of intellectual and emotional appeal. Although not as imposing in its structure or development, *Orpheus* is based on a design similar to Dante's. *The Testament of Cresseid* continues the tradition of learning established in his other poems, but shows the finest human sympathy for the fate of the fallen heroine. Along with *Orpheus*, it explores psychological development of character, especially with regard to love and maturity. The shorter poems exemplify Henryson's debt to medieval traditions, but they also show the synthetic genius which marks the best poetry of all ages.

Henryson's general strengths are now widely recognized. His love and understanding of his fellowman are perhaps the foremost qualities in his verse that have attracted generations of readers. He was not just "a good person to know," [1] but he was a man who apparently achieved true charity at least in his poetry. For the medieval church, *caritas*, the general love of one's fellowman, was a virtue always to be pursued. Henryson's *caritas* seems to remain directly connected with the religious attitudes and didactic techniques that were its roots. His style, which is outstanding among the Makars, also shows the influence of instructional literature. He generally avoids the flash of aureation for the plainer but still

striking colloquialisms of the native Scots tradition, the Latin in the
common vocabulary, and his own occasional coinages. The simplicity of his style has sometimes led him to be undervalued, but his
work shows the deeper complexity of finely polished plain and
middle style.

Henryson's rationalism and use of classical resources should also
not be overlooked. As a precursor of the Renaissance, he shows
evidence of the humanistic love of classical learning which was to
mark the literary production of the later period. But his learning is
never obtrusive, though it is always evident. His rationalism,
particularly in its reliance on right reason and the fashion in which it
is blended into his theology, looks backward to the twelfth century
and forward to the seventeenth. The rational element in Henryson's
theology is one of the most distinctive aspects of his thought.

With all of the reasons for Henryson's importance and lasting
value as a poet, his relative neglect by later generations appears all
the more remarkable. Doubtless he exercised considerable influence through Thynne's edition of Chaucer. We now know that
Heywood was apparently influenced by him in *A Woman Killed
with Kindness*,[2] but it is impossible to tell for certain how many
literary men believed *The Testament of Cresseid* to be Chaucer's
and how many found their concept of Cresseid's character was
shaped by Henryson's poem as well as the *Troilus*. For the most
part, however, after his death he was known as the author of
"Robene and Makyne"[3] one of the pastorals in the development of
a tradition that led to *The Shepherd's Calender*. It is true that he
was well known to many of his contemporaries: Dunbar, for
instance, lists him along with the notice of his death in his poem on
the Makars. His influence on Dunbar, however, seems relatively
slight. Perhaps more affected was Gavin Douglas, translator of the
Aeneid; in Douglas' heavily alliterative description of winter
(Prologue, VII), Wittig contends that one is "forcibly reminded of
Henryson's verse portrait of Saturn."[4] Beyond this, however, all of
the Makars were affected by Henryson's impact on the development
of the Middle Scots language. Henryson's style was closer to
common speech in its diction for the most part than Dunbar's. The
language and metric forms he uses largely reflect the same "homely
realism" as his use of descriptive detail. In his preservation of
colloquial elements in literary Middle Scots, Henryson provided a
standard for later generations to emulate. It is a language similar to
his, not Dunbar's, that appears in poems of Ramsay and Burns.

In both language and subject matter, Henryson appears to have influenced Allan Ramsay. The strength of Ramsay's verse is largely in the direct and precise nature of his diction. Much of the force of Ramsay's word choice can be attributed to his knowledge and imitation of older poems such as those he published in *Ever Green*. Among these poems were Henryson's "Robene and Makyne" and two of the fables. Such influence, generalized though it might have been, also appears as Wittig suggests in the art "of suggesting the tenderness that underlies the hard outer surface," [5] a quality which Ramsay clearly shows in his apostrophe to his book and in some of his poems based on folk sources. Insofar as Ramsay attempts to find roots in the Scottish peasantry, he makes use of techniques which he also admired in Henryson.

Probably the most famous culmination of the tradition of Henryson is to be found in the work of Robert Burns. Burns uses the same kind of blunt, clear diction; although he is often archaic he seldom tends to use euphemisms or Latin decorations. Perhaps most important is Burns' interest in similar subjects, treated in a similar manner. "To A Louse" and "To A Mouse" both share with Henryson's fables distrust of pretension, championing of the underdog, pity, and sad, wise understanding. Burns would have had available to him "The Lion and the Mouse" and a variant version of "The Two Mice" in Ramsay's *Ever Green*. Similarities between the tone and structure of Burns' fables and those of Henryson make it clear that Burns was profoundly influenced by the tradition which also inspired Henryson. The general similarities in disposition are unmistakable, as is the interest in folklore and native traditions. The contempt for hypocrisy, especially in members of religious orders, marks the social satire of both. Throughout the poetry of both there is also a democractic spirit often coupled with a direct approach to God. As Lindsay has shown, there seems little doubt that Burns was specifically influenced by Henryson.[6]

Henryson's emphasis on the dignity of the lower classes even appears in the novels of Sir Walter Scott, but it is not his influence on the nineteenth century that is outstanding. Henryson's impact on the present seems sure to bring forth even more remarkable results in the future. It was not until 1865 that David Laing published his landmark edition of Henryson's poems and reviewed the Henryson canon along with all the evidence relative to his biography. Although Laing was carried too far into the realm of speculation in his attempt to identify facts about the author's life, his work was invaluable. Appreciation of Henryson gradually began to increase, and, with the work of G. Gregory Smith on the Scottish Text Society edition of the poet's works in 1908, a more important place for him seemed assured. Unfortunately, critical acceptance was late in coming, partially because he has been overshadowed by Dunbar. In 1916, in fact, Neilson and Webster could write "it is doubtful whether there is in the whole of English literature a case of neglected genius so remarkable as that of Henryson." [7]

The neglect of Henryson's writings has been much remedied already. Numerous editions of the works, three major volumes of criticism, and a large number of articles have helped to make the public familiar with his genius. As his renown has spread so, likely, will his influence. In his edition of Henryson's poems Hugh MacDiarmid takes note of Henryson's neglect and corrects his own error in creating the battle cry of the recent Scottish Renaissance. When modern Scottish literature was trying to escape "quaintness" and "provinciality," he coined a phrase to give young writers a goal: "Not Burns—Dunbar!" MacDiarmid admits his mistake and asserts: "I can now wish that in the early twenties I had chosen Henryson rather than Dunbar." [8] Such too are the sentiments expressed by many modern critics and students of Scottish literature. Dunbar, despite his brilliance, does not wear nearly so well as Henryson. The sparkle of Dunbar's satires is attractive, but it is no match for the mature wisdom of Henryson's fables.

But in addition to being a master of wisdom literature, Henryson has many other gifts. In his description of the court of the gods in *The Testament of Cresseid*, there is as much stylistic brilliance as to be found in any of his Scottish contemporaries or successors. In both grandiose descriptions of the heavens and their inhabitants and realistic portrayals of poverty and disease, Henryson has an eye for details that capture the reader's imagination.

The salient characteristic of his verse is not its folksy wisdom or its stylistic brilliance; instead it is his humane love of his fellowman. If at times he seems stern, it is because he cares how other human beings affect one another. He is not a student of speculative ethics; for him ethics and morality must be judged by their human results. And it is this concrete sense of morality that is the key to Henryson's synthetic genius. He adopts from the changing climate of ideas surrounding him those elements which fit his world view, and in the poetry that world view is built on love. He accepts medieval notions of God and charity, but he accepts them not simply as matters of faith; rather it is because they have practical human results. If avarice is bad, he judges it so not because it is one of an abstract list of Seven Deadly Sins but because it results in permanent damage to the greedy person and those he victimizes. He uses a similar basis for judging lechery; Cresseid's sins are not merely sins because the church so pronounced them. She has in fact done considerable harm to her lover and herself and must be judged by natural laws no more charitably than she is judged by Henryson's court of the gods.

The ease with which Henryson introduces elements of the new humanism into his medieval values is not surprising. With their emphasis on specific human acts and the importance of human values and ideas, the new humanists are very close to Henryson's sense of ethics in his mature works. Like the doctrine of charity found in medieval religious thought, the tenets of humanistic thought became an integral part of the climate of ideas during the period of Henryson's birth and maturity.

Henryson has several roles in the history of British culture and literature. He is a major link between the Scottish literary tradition and the influences of England and the Continent. He was perhaps the most skillful poet writing in Britain during a century when England and Scotland alike were being changed by intellectual and spiritual forces which culminated in the Renaissance. He has become a source of pride and tradition for later generations of Scottish poets in search of their heritage. Finally, he is an excellent poet, capable of verses which touch both intellect and emotions; and his gift for poetry transcends the boundaries of time and place.

Notes and References

Chapter One

1. J. Grant, *History of the Burgh and Parish Schools of Scotland* (London, 1876), pp. 1–75.

2. John MacQueen, *Robert Henryson* (Oxford, 1967), pp. 12–15. See also Charles Sears Baldwin, *Medieval Rhetoric and Poetic* (New York, 1928), pp. 74–98.

3. MacQueen, pp. 5–7.

4. Charles Elliott, ed., *Robert Henryson, Poems*, 2d ed. (Oxford, 1975), p. xxiv.

5. R. D. S. Jack, *The Italian Influence on Scottish Literauture* (Edinburgh, 1972), p. 8; John MacQueen, "Neoplatonism and Orphism in Fifteenth-Century Scotland," *Scottish Studies* 20 (1976), 69–89.

6. Cited in David Laing, ed., *The Poems and Fables of Robert Henryson* (Edinburgh, 1865), pp. xviii–xix.

7. H. Harvey Wood, ed., *The Poems and Fables of Robert Henryson*, 2d ed. (Edinburgh, 1958), p. 137, l. 242. Wood's text will be used for *Orpheus*, the minor poems, and three of the fables. W. Tod Ritchie's edition of *The Bannatyne Manuscript* (Edinburgh, 1928–1930) will be used for the first ten fables, and Denton Fox's edition of *The Testament of Cresseid* (London, 1968) will be cited for references to that poem. As the notes will make clear, I have made some changes in spelling, punctuation, and capitalization in the latter two works.

8. Laing, pp. xiii–xiv.

9. John MacQueen, "The Literature of Fifteenth-Century Scotland," in *Scottish Society in the Fifteenth Century*, ed. Jennifer M. Brown (London, 1977), p. 204.

10. *The Kinaston Manuscript* (Bodl. Ms. Add. C. 287), as reproduced by G. Gregory Smith in *The Poems of Robert Henryson* (Edinburgh, 1914), pp. ciii–civ.

11. Kurt Wittig, *The Scottish Tradition in Literature* (Edinburgh, 1958), p. 49.

12. Marshall W. Stearns, *Robert Henryson* (New York, 1949), p. 14. For additional comment about the period, see Ranald Nicholson, *Scotland: The Later Middle Ages* (Edinburgh, 1974), pp. 184ff.

13. E. W. M. Balfour Melville, *James I, King of Scots* (London, 1936), p. 251.

14. Caroline Bingham, *The Stewart Kingdom of Scotland* (London, 1974), p. 120.

15. Nicholson, p. 575.

16. For more information on the sexual irregularities and personal excesses in abbeys and monasteries, see G. G. Coulton, *Scottish Abbeys and Social Life* (Cambridge, 1933), pp. 216–17, and Nicholson, pp. 459ff.

17. MacQueen, *Robert Henryson*, p. 2.

Chapter Two

1. G. Gregory Smith, "The Transition Period," in *Periods of European Literature* (Edinburgh, 1900), IV, 42.

2. Florence Ridley, "A Plea for the Middle Scots," in *The Learned and the Lewed*, ed. Larry D. Benson (Cambridge, Mass., 1974), p. 196. Although Ridley is a strong proponent of the independence of the Makars, she also provides a history of the term "Scottish Chaucerian," while disputing its validity. See especially pp. 175–81.

3. Ronald Marken, "Chaucer and Henryson: A Comparison," *Discourse* 7 (1964), 381. In his comparison of the two poets, Marken concludes, "Henryson's *Testament* has served as a foil to accentuate the immortal greatness of its predecessor" (p. 387). Other treatments of Henryson's debt to Chaucer include H. Harvey Wood's *Two Scots Chaucerians* (London, 1967); pp. 7–23, and Ian Robinson's *Chaucer and the English Tradition* (Cambridge, 1972), pp. 234–35, 242–44.

4. Besides Ridley, see especially Marshall W. Stearns, "Henryson and Chaucer," *Modern Language Quarterly* 6 (1945), 271–84.

5. J. A. Burrow, *Ricardian Poetry* (New Haven, 1971), especially pp. 1-10.

6. Smith, *Poems*, p. lxxxix; see also Elliott, p. x.

7. See Marken, p. 383, and A. C. Spearing, *Criticism and Medieval Poetry* (London, 1964), pp. 118–44.

8. Stephen Hawes, *The Pastime of Pleasure* (London, 1865), p. 38; chap. 11, ll. 18–19. For comment on this definition and its representative nature, see H. S. Bennett, *Chaucer and the Fifteenth Century* (New York, 1961), p. 130.

9. See Tom Scott, *Dunbar* (Edinburgh, 1966), p. 36, and G. Gregory Smith, ed., *Specimens of Middle Scots* (Edinburgh, 1902), p. lxi.

10. Wittig, p. 63; for comment on how Henryson's use of more common language affects his imagery, see Isabel Hyde, "Poetic Imagery: A Point of Comparison between Henryson and Dunbar," *Studies in Scottish Literature* 2 (1965), 183–97.

11. Wood, *Poems and Fables*, p. xv.

12. Jill Mann, *Chaucer and Medieval Estates Satire* (Cambridge, 1973), especially pp. 1–16.

13. Burrow, p. 111.

14. See Donald Howard, *The Idea of the Canterbury Tales* (Berkeley, 1976), pp. 30–45.

15. Nevill Coghill, *The Poet Chaucer* (London, 1967), p. 90.

16. Marshall W. Stearns, "Robert Henryson and the Aristotelian Tradition of Psychology," *Studies in Philology* 41 (1944), 499.

17. There has, however, recently been debate about the precise extent of Chaucer's commitment to chivalry. The traditional point of view is represented by Nevill Coghill, *Chaucer's Idea of What is Noble* (London, 1971), pp. 8–10, while the view that Chaucer is more critical of chivalry and the romance is explained by Paul T. Thurston, *Artistic Ambivalence in Chaucer's Knight's Tale* (Gainesville, Fla., 1968).

18. See Robert L Kindrick, "Lion or Cat: Henryson's Characterization of James III," in *Studies in Scottish Literature XIV* (Columbia, S.C., 1979), pp. 123–36.

19. See Smith, *Poems* pp. 27–28, and Wood, *Poems and Fables*, p. 244.

20. J. Y. Simpson, "Antiquarian Notices of Leprosy and Leper Hospitals in Scotland and England," *Edinburgh Medical and Surgical Journal* 56 (1841), 301–30; 57 (1842), 121–56, 294–429.

21. Gussie Hecht Tannehaus, "Bede's *De schematibus et tropis*—A Translation," *Quarterly Journal of Speech* 48 (1962), 250–52; reprinted in *Readings in Medieval Rhetoric*, ed. Jospeh M. Miller, Michael H. Prosser, and Thomas W. Benson (Bloomington, Indiana, 1973), pp. 96–122.

22. D. W. Robertson, *A Preface to Chaucer* (Princeton, 1962); see also Dorothy Bethurum, ed., *Critical Approaches to Medieval Literature* (New York, 1960) and Francis L. Utley, "Robertsonianism Redivivus," *Romance Philology* 19 (1965), 150–60.

23. See Robertson, pp. 286–317.

24. See, for instance, Guibert de Nogent, "A Book About the Way A Sermon Ought to be Given," and Honorius of Autun, "Concerning the Exile of the Soul and Its Fatherland; Also Called About the Arts," both in Miller, Prosser, and Benson, pp. 170–72 and 204–5, respectively.

25. Robert S. Haller, trans., *Literary Criticism of Dante Alighieri* (Lincoln, Nebr., 1973); see also Harry Caplan, "The Four Senses of Scriptural Interpretation and the Mediaeval Theory of Preaching," *Speculum* 4 (1929), 282–90, and Robertson, pp. 292–93.

26. Haller, p. 112.

27. Ibid.

28. Ibid., p. 113.

29. See Robertson, pp. 289ff.

30. Ibid., p. 304

31. Geoffrey de Vinsauf, "The New Poetics," in *Three Medieval Rhetorics*, ed. James J. Murphy (Berkeley, 1974), p. 38.

32. Robertson, pp. 138–40.

33. Bennett, p. 126; see also Robinson, pp. 242–43.

34. A description of some of these traditional themes will be found in

Caplan and in G. R. Owst, *Literature and Pulpit in Medieval England* (Oxford, 1966), pp. 56–110.

35. Bennett, pp. 124–30.

36. Smith, *Poems*, p. xlvii; Stearns, *Robert Henryson*, pp. 69, 57–59, 79–80.

37. John Speirs, *The Scots Literary Tradition*, 2d ed. (London, 1962), p. 46; see also *Late Medieval Scots Poetry*, ed. Tom Scott (New York, 1967), pp. 7–8.

38. Smith, *Specimens*, pp. xi–xviii, and Fox, "The Scottish Chaucerians," p. 166. See also Angus McIntosh, "The Dialectology of Mediaeval Scots: Some Possible Approaches to Its Study," *Scottish Literary Journal*, supp. no. 6 (1978), 38–44.

39. Smith, *Specimens*, pp. xi–xii; Wood, *Poems and Fables*, pp. xxxiii–xxxiv.

40. A. M. Kinghorn, ed., *The Middle Scots Poets* (London, 1970), p. 27; Wittig, p. 63.

41. An essential article for understanding the pronunciation of Middle Scots is Adam J. Aitken, "How to Pronounce Older Scots," in *Bards and Makars*, ed. Adam J. Aitken, Matthew P. McDiarmid, and Derick S. Thomson (Glasgow, 1977), pp. 1–21. A convenient guide is also available in David Murison, *The Guid Scots Tongue* (Edinburgh, 1977).

42. The following table is based on Aitken, p. 3.

43. For more information, see Smith, *Specimens*, pp. xviii–xlix. Murison, and Elizabeth Eddy, "Middle English and Middle Scots," *Ralph—For Medieval and Renaissance Teaching* 4 (1977), 1, 6.

44. Smith, *Specimens*, pp. lx–lxv, and David Murison, "Linguistic Relationships in Medieval Scotland," in *The Scottish Tradition*, ed. G. W. S. Barrow (Edinburgh, 1974), p. 77.

45. T. F. Henderson, *Scottish Vernacular Literature*, 3d ed. (Edinburgh, 1910), p. 131.

46. See Maurice Lindsay, *History of Scottish Literature* (London, 1977), pp. 24–25.

47. Wood, *Poems and Fables*, p. xvi.

48. Stearns, *Robert Henryson*, p. 107.

49. Wittig, p. 18.

50. Ibid., p. 50.

51. Francisque-Michel, *A Critical Enquiry into the Scottish Language* (Edinburgh, 1882), pp. xxx–xxxi; see also Smith, *Specimens*, pp. lv–lx.

52. Smith, *Poems*, p. lvi; W. Powell Jones, "A Source for Henryson's Robene and Makyne?," *Modern Language Notes* 46 (1931), 457–58.

53. Janet Smith, *The French Background of Middle Scots Literature* (Edinburgh, 1934), p. 59.

54. A sample of the arguments on this issue will be found in Robertson, pp. 391–503; E. Talbot Donaldson, *Speaking of Chaucer* (New York, 1970), pp. 154–63; D. W. Robertson, "The Concept of Courtly Love as an

Impediment to the Understanding of Medieval Texts," and John F. Benton, "Clio and Venus: An Historical View of Medieval Love," both in F. X. Newman, ed., *The Meaning of Courtly Love* (Albany, N.Y., 1968), pp. 1–18 and 19–42, respectively; and Francis L. Utley, "Must We Abandon the Concept of Courtly Love," *Medievalia et Humanistica*, no. 3 (Cleveland, 1972), pp. 299–324.

55. Gaston Paris, "Lancelot du Lac, II. Le Conte de la Charette," *Romania* 12 (1883), 459–534. A description of the earlier literature on courtly love is to be found in Roger Boase, *The Origin and Meaning of Courtly Love* (Manchester, 1977), especially pp. 5–18.

56. See John C. Moore, *Love in Twelfth-Century France* (Philadelphia, 1972), pp. 1–46.

57. In addition to Paris and Newman, see Tom Peete Cross and William A. Nitze, *Lancelot and Guinevere: A Study on the Origins of Courtly Love* (Chicago, 1930); C. S. Lewis, *The Allegory of Love* (Oxford, 1958); A. J. Denomy, *The Heresy of Courtly Love* (New York, 1947); Denis de Rougement, *Love in the Western World* (New York, 1956); Moshé Lazar, *Amour courtois et "fin'amors" dans la litterature du XIIe siecle* (Paris, 1946); Peter Dronke, *Medieval Latin and the Rise of European Love Lyric* (Oxford, 1965); and Joan M. Ferrante and George D. Economou, eds., *In Pursuit of Perfection* (Port Washington, N.Y., 1975).

58. Ferrante and Economou, "Introduction," p. 3. See also Moore, pp. 2–3 and 131–55.

59. Ferrante and Economou, "Introduction," p. 5. See also Newman, p. 7.

60. "Ab 'alen tir vas me l'aire," in *Medieval Song*, trans. James J. Wilhelm (New York, 1971), p. 167.

61. Andreas Capellanus, *The Art of Courtly Love*, trans. John Jay Perry (New York, 1941), pp. 106.

62. Paris, 518; Lewis pp. 2ff.

63. Andreas, p. 51.

64. George Economou, "The Two Venuses and Courtly Love," in Ferrante and Economou, p. 24.

65. Lewis, pp. 18–20.

66. Rougement, pp. 294–95.

67. Andreas, p. 31.

68. Denomy, p. 29.

69. On the development of love in the romance and its potential conflict with public duty, see Joan M. Ferrante, "The Conflict of Lyric Conventions and Romance Form," in Ferrante and Economou, pp. 135–78. For comment on parody and the decline of courtly love, see June Hall Martin, *Love's Fools* (London, 1972) and Saul N. Brody, "The Comic Rejection of Courtly Love," in Ferrante and Economou, pp. 221–61.

70. Charles Muscatine, *Chaucer and the French Tradition* (Berkeley, 1966), especially pp. 12–57.

71. John MacQueen, "Neoplatonism and Orphism in Fifteenth-Century Scotland," *Scottish Studies* 20 (1976), pp. 69–89.

72. R. D. S. Jack, *The Italian Influence on Scottish Literature* (Edinburgh, 1972), p. 4.

73. John Durkan, "The Beginnings of Humanism in Scotland," *Innes Review* 4 (1953), 7.

74. MacQueen, "Neoplatonism and Orphism," especially pp. 86–87.

75. Jack, pp. 8–14.

76. Ibid., p. 8.

77. MacQueen, "Neoplatonism and Orphism," p. 87.

Chapter Three

1. H. Harvey Wood, "Robert Henryson," in *Edinburgh Essays on Scots Literature* (Edinburgh, 1933), p. 9.

2. Kinghorn, p. 25.

3. George Clark, "Henryson and Aesop: The Fable Transformed," *ELH* 43 (1976), 17.

4. Stearns, *Robert Henryson*, p. 107.

5. David K. Crowne, "A Date for the Composition of Henryson's Fables," *Journal of English and Germanic Philology* 61 (1962), 589.

6. MacQueen, *Robert Henryson*, pp. 189–99.

7. Smith, *Poems*, pp. xxvii–xlv.

8. A. R. Diebler, *Henrisone's Fabeldichtungen* (Halle, 1885), pp. 45–46; MacQueen, *Robert Henryson*, pp. 215–18.

9. Crowne, pp. 588–89.

10. Nicholson, pp. 508–9; but see also R. J. Lyall, "Politics and Poetry in Fifteenth and Sixteenth Century Scotland," *Scottish Literary Journal* 3 (1976), 5–27. In attacking the argument that there are specific references to James in the *Fabillis*, Lyall emphasizes their traditional nature.

11. Crowne, p. 589; MacQueen, *Robert Henryson*, p. 193.

12. Crowne, p. 589.

13. Mary Rowlands, "The Fables of Robert Henryson," *Dalhousie Review* 39 (1959–1960), 491.

14. MacQueen, *Robert Henryson*, p. 191; Smith, *Poems*, pp. xxx–xliv; Crowne, pp. 583–86.

15. MacQueen, *Robert Henryson*, p. 207.

16. Donald MacDonald, "Henryson and Chaucer: Cock and Fox," *Texas Studies in Literature and Language* 8 (1966), 460–61. MacDonald has also explored Chaucer's influence on Henryson's use of proverbs, "Chaucer's Influence on Henryson's *Fables*," *Medium Aevum* 39 (1970), 21–27.

17. Diebler, p. 46.

18. MacQueen, *Robert Henryson*, pp. 215–16.

19. I. W. A. Jamieson, "A Further Source for Henryson's *Fabillis*," *Notes and Queries* 14 (1969), 403–5.

20. Denton Fox, "Henryson and Caxton," *Journal of English and Germanic Philology* 67 (1968), 592–93.

21. Smith, *Poems*, pp. xl–xliii.

22. MacQueen, *Robert Henryson*, p. 212.

23. Smith, *Poems*, p. xli.

24. Fox, "Henryson and Caxton," p. 587.

25. Donald MacDonald, "Narrative Art in Henryson's *Fables*," *Studies in Scottish Literature* 3 (1965), 102–5.

26. MacQueen, *Robert Henryson*, pp. 219–20.

27. Fox, "Henryson and Caxton," p. 589.

28. *The Bannatyne Manuscript*, ed. W. Tod Ritchie (Edinburgh, 1930), p. 206. Since MacQueen has established the importance of this manuscript (*Robert Henryson*, pp. 218–20), it will be the source of all citations for the prologue and the first ten fables. I have somewhat regularized the conventions of punctuation, capitalization, and spelling, particularly with regard to the use of *u*, *v*, þ, ȝ, and long *s*.

29. Clark, p. 2.

30. MacQueen, *Robert Henryson*, pp. 95, 99.

31. Ibid., p. 96.

32. Matthew P. McDiarmid, "Robert Henryson in His Poems," in *Bards and Makars*, p. 27.

33. Henderson, p. 126.

34. See Clark, p. 8.

35. Denton Fox, "Henryson's Fables," *ELH* 29 (1962), 343; see also Stearns, *Robert Henryson*, pp. 108–9.

36. Fox, "Henryson's Fables," p. 343.

37. MacQueen, *Robert Henryson*, p. 100; Fox, "Henryson's Fables," pp. 338–39; James Kinsley, *Scottish Poetry* (London, 1955). p. 18; Wittig, p. 40; Wood, *Poems and Fables*, p. xv; Speirs, p. 42, n.; see also McDiarmid, p. 29.

38. MacQueen, *Robert Henryson*, pp. 107, 100–105; but see also Clark, p. 9.

39. Rowlands, p. 492.

40. Clark, p. 10.

41. Harold E. Toliver, "Robert Henryson; From Moralitas to Irony," *English Studies* 46 (1965), 301.

42. MacQueen, *Robert Henryson*, p. 118.

43. Wittig, pp. 47–48; on the balance between beast and human characteristics, see Daniel M. Murtaugh, "Henryson's Animals," *Texas Studies in Literature and Langauge* 14 (1972), 405–21.

44. MacQueen, *Robert Henryson*, p. 121.

45. Ibid., p. 124.

46. Stearns, *Robert Henryson*, p. 36.

47. W. S. Reid, "The Middle Class Factor in the Scottish Reformation," *Church History* 16 (1947), 140–2.

48. MacQueen even suggests that this poem, *The Harp*, could have been written by Henryson in "The Literature of Fifteenth Century Scotland," in Jennifer M. Brown, *Scottish Society in the Fifteenth Century*, p. 209.

49. Stearns, *Robert Henryson*, p. 124.

50. Stearns even suggests that he might have had a legal background, *Robert Henryson*, p. 32.

51. See Wittig, p. 50.

52. Wood, *Poems and Fables*, p. 241.

53. MacQueen, *Robert Henryson*, p. 131.

54. Ibid., p. 133.

55. Ibid., p. 134.

56. Donald MacDonald, "Henryson and the *Thre Prestis of Peblis*," *Neophilologus* 51 (1967), 168–77.

57. MacDonald, "Henryson and Chaucer," pp. 454–59.

58. MacQueen, *Robert Henryson*, p. 135.

59. Toliver, p. 302.

60. MacDonald, "Narrative Art," pp. 107–8.

61. Diebler's suggestion that the fable dates from 1482–1484 accords well with this interpretation.

62. MacDonald, "Henryson and Chaucer," p. 101.

63. John B. Friedman, "Henryson, the Friars, and the *Confessio Reynardi*," *Journal of English and Germanic Philology* 66 (1967), 550.

64. MacQueen, *Robert Henryson*, pp. 147–48.

65. Lindsay, p. 40.

66. R. Sutherland, ed., *The Romaunt of the Rose and Le Roman de la Rose* (Berkeley, 1968), pp. 127–29.

67. Mann, pp. 37–54.

68. Friedman, pp. 554–55.

69. MacQueen, *Robert Henryson*, pp. 145–46.

70. Friedman, p. 553.

71. Ibid.

72. *The* Exempla *of Jacques de Vitry*, ed. T. F. Crane (London, 1800), p. 125; for added comment see Friedman, p. 553.

73. MacQueen, *Robert Henryson*, p. 145.

74. Ibid., p. 146.

75. He even suggests that the fox might represent the dispossessed Highland gentry, pp. 116–18.

76. MacQueen, *Robert Henryson*, pp. 149–51.

77. Stearns believes the fox to be Angus of the Isles because of his father's reputation (pp. 19–20). However, the other circumstances of Angus' life do not fit.

78. See Nicholson, pp. 468–69.

79. MacQueen, *Robert Henryson*, p. 153.

80. Another point of view is represented by Denton Fox, who has called

this a "conversational and apparently rambling discourse on God, man, and the world" in "Henryson's *Fables*," p. 349.

81. MacQueen, *Robert Henryson*, p. 154.

82. J. A. Burrow, "Henryson: The Preaching of the Swallow," *Essays in Criticism* 25 (1975), 31–32.

83. Clark, p. 14.

84. Smith, *Poems*, p. 28.

85. See MacQueen, *Robert Henryson*, p. 163.

86. Ibid., p. 160.

87. Kinsley, p. 20.

88. Clark, p. 16.

89. Burrow, "Henryson: *The Preaching*", p. 25.

90. A. C. Spearing, *Medieval Dream-Poetry* (Cambridge, 1976), pp. 188–89.

91. MacQueen also notes parallels with Mercury from *The Testament of Cresseid*, p. 169. For a statement on Henryson's use of conventional elements, see Nicolai Von Kreisler, "Henryson's Visionary Fable: Tradition and Craftsmanship in *The Lyoun and the Mous*," *Texas Studies in Literature and Language* 15 (1973), 391–95.

92. MacQueen, *Robert Henryson*, p. 168.

93. The role of James III in Scottish politics has become the subject of considerable scholarly controversy. The traditional point of vew about his reign is found in Nicholson, pp. 397–530 and W. Croft Dickinson, and Archibald A. M. Duncan, *Scotland from the Earliest Times to 1603*, 3d ed. (Oxford, 1977), pp. 235–48. However, James' political acumen and his role in Henryson's poetry have been reappraised by Norman A. T. Macdougall, "The Sources: A Reappraisal of the Legend," and Jennifer M. Brown, "The Exercise of Power," both in Brown's *Scottish Society in the Fifteenth Century*, pp. 10–32 and 33–65, respectively; and by Lyall, especially pp. 24–26. See also Von Kreisler, pp. 398–99 and Kindrick, pp. 123–36.

94. Stearns, *Robert Henryson*, p. 117.

95. In Bassandyne, these rebels are even more explicitly described as "rurall men" (l. 1068).

96. Stearns, *Robert Henryson*, p. 17.

97. Nicholson, p. 509.

98. MacQueen, "The Literature of Fifteenth Century Scotland," p. 199.

99. MacQueen, *Robert Henryson*, p. 171.

100. The remaining fables are not found in the Bannatyne manuscript. The text used here will be Bassandyne, as edited by H. Harvey Wood in *The Poems and Fables of Robert Henryson*, p. 78, ll. 2259–60 and 2266–67.

101. Stearns, *Robert Henryson*, pp. 120–21.

102. MacQueen, *Robert Henryson*, p. 173.

103. Stearns, *Robert Henryson*, pp. 111–12.

104. Anthony W. Jenkins, "Henryson's *The Fox, the Wolf, and the Cadger* Again," *Studies in Scottish Literature* 4 (1966), 107.

105. Stearns, *Robert Henryson*, p. 112.

106. See Lindsay, p. 41.

107. MacQueen, *Robert Henryson*, p. 184.

108. See Nicholson, pp. 501–4. But see also Dickinson, pp. 240–41 for an argument that the "favourites" are a myth.

109. I. W. A. Jamieson, "Henryson's *Taill of the Wolf and the Wedder*," *Studies in Scottish Literature* 6 (1969), 251–52.

110. MacDonald, "Narrative Art," pp. 103–5.

Chapter Four

1. Kinghorn, p. 24; Marken, p. 384; Robinson, p. 244; Henderson, p. 124.

2. Spearing, "*The Testament of Cresseid* and the High Concise Style," in *Criticism and Medieval Poetry*, p. 121; Elliott, p. xvi; Fox, *The Testament of Cresseid* (London, 1968), p. 1; see also Jane Adamson, "Henryson's *Testament of Cresseid*: 'Frye' and 'Cauld,'" *Critical Review* (Melbourne), 18 (1976), 39.

3. B. J. Whiting, "A Probable Allusion to Henryson's 'Testament of Cresseid,'" *Modern Language Review* 40 (1945), 46–47; Fox, *Testament*, p. 18.

4. Eleanor Long, "Robert Henryson's 'Uther Quair,'" *Comitatus* 5 (1972), 97–101.

5. For a good discussion of the types of problems encountered, see Denton Fox, "The 1663 Anderson Edition of Henryson's *Testament of Cresseid*," *Studies in Scottish Literature* 8 (1970), 75–76, and "Manuscripts and Prints of Scots Poetry in the Sixteenth Century," *Bards and Makars*, pp. 156–71.

6. For more information on Henryson's debt to Chaucer, contrast Marken, especially p. 387, with Ridley, "A Plea," pp. 183–96. See also Adamson, p. 52, and Del Chessell, "In the Dark Time: Henryson's *Testament of Cresseid*," *Critical Review* (Melbourne), 12 (1969), 61.

7. There are several good editions of this poem, but the best is Fox's *Testament of Cresseid* (London, 1968), from which all subsequent quotations will be drawn. For the convenience of the reader, I have regularized the spelling, particularly with regard to *u*, *v*, and 3.

8. Spearing, "High Concise Style," p. 120; E. M. W. Tillyard, "Henryson: *The Testament of Cresseid 1470?*" in *Five Poems 1470–1870* (London, 1948), p. 7; Edwin Muir, "Robert Henryson," in *Essays on Literature and Society*, rev. ed. (London, 1965), p. 18; Elliott, p. xvii.

9. Elliott, p. xiii.

10. Fox, *Testament*, p. 22.

11. Ridley, "A Plea," p. 196.

12. Stearns, *Robert Henryson*, p. 54.

13. Saul N. Brody, *The Disease of the Soul* (Ithaca, N.Y., 1974), pp. 144–46.

14. See Simpson, especially vol. 57 (1842), 121–56 and 394–429, and Brody, p. 51.

15. Stearns, *Robert Henryson*, p. 49.

16. Ibid., p. 50.

17. On Henryson's narrator and his role in the poem, see C. W. Jentoft, "Henryson as Authentic 'Chaucerian,' " *Studies in Scottish Literature* 10 (1972), 94–102; Lee W. Patterson, "Christian and Pagan in *The Testament of Cresseid*," *Philological Quarterly* 52 (1973), 713–14; John McNamara, "Language as Action in Henryson's *Testament of Cresseid*," in *Bards and Makars*, pp. 45–48; Chessell, p. 63; and Adamson, p. 42.

18. For a third point of view, that he approaches Cresseid's plight with a spirit of "tragic toughness," see Adamson, p. 39.

19. On Henryson's treatment of the theme of patience in Boethian terms, see Craig McDonald, "Venus and the Goddess Fortune in *The Testament of Cresseid*," *Scottish Literary Journal* 4 (1977), 23, and McDiarmid in *Bards and Makars*, pp. 35–37. But for comment that the narrator lacks patience, see Patterson, pp. 713–14.

20. Fox, *Testament*, p. 21.

21. See Tillyard, p. 7; Fox, *Testament*, pp. 50, 56.

22. Fox, *Testament*, pp. 50–51.

23. Fox, *Testament*, pp. 49–57; MacQueen, *Robert Henryson*, pp. 50–53; Adamson, pp. 41–43.

24. See Brody, pp. 36–38.

25. E. Duncan Aswell, "The Role of Fortune in *The Testament of Cresseid*," *Philological Quarterly* 46 (1967), 485.

26. Fox, *Testament*, pp. 22–23.

27. See Economou in Ferrante and Economou, pp. 24–25.

28. Tillyard, pp. 16–17.

29. MacQueen, *Robert Henryson*, pp. 69–71; Aswell, p. 475. See also Thomas W. Craik, "The Substance and Structure of *The Testament of Cresseid*: A Hypothesis," in *Bards and Makars*, p. 25.

30. H. S. Bennett, ed., *The Parlement of Foules* (Oxford, 1957), pp. 3–4.

31. Tillyard, p. 16.

32. MacQueen, *Robert Henryson*, pp. 72–73.

33. Larry D. Benson, *Art and Tradition in* Sir Gawain and the Green Knight (New Brunswick, N.J., 1965), p. 65.

34. Smith, *Poems*, p. 48; Wood, *Poems and Fables*, p. 255; Fox, *Testament*, p. 102.

35. Stearns, *Robert Henryson*, p. 83.

36. Fox, *Testament*, pp. 104–5; Marshall W. Stearns, "Robert Henryson and the Fulgentian Horse," *Modern Language Notes* 54 (1939), 45; W. W. Skeat, *Chaucerian and Other Pieces* (Oxford, 1897), p. 334; Bruce Dickins, ed., *The Testament of Cresseid*, rev. ed. (London, 1943), pp. 45–46; Smith, *Poems*, p. 48; Charles Elliott, "Two Notes on Henryson's Testament of Cresseid," *Journal of English and Germanic Philology* 54 (1955), 247–54.

37. Aswell, p. 478; see also Economou, pp. 24–25.

38. Adamson, p. 48.

39. See Brody, pp. 176–77.

40. Ralph Hanna, III, "Cresseid's Dream and Henryson's *Testament*," *Chaucer and Middle English Studies in Honour of Rossell Hope Robbins*, ed. Beryl Rowland (Kent, Ohio, 1974), p. 295.

41. Fox suggests three causes of Cresseid's leprosy; for a summary, see *Testament*, p. 54. See also Craig McDonald, p. 20.

42. Fox, *Testament*, p. 41, and Brody, pp. 60–61.

43. For comment on her concern for public opinion, see Patterson, especially p. 712.

44. On the significance of the beaver hat, see Fox, *Testament*, p. 116.

45. MacQueen, *Robert Henryson*, pp. 85–86.

46. See Adamson, p. 51.

47. Craik, p. 22.

48. Stearns, *Robert Henryson*, pp. 97–105.

49. Elliott, *Poems*, p. xvi.

50. Stearns, *Robert Henryson*, p. 63; Andreas, p. 94.

51. For a contrasting point of view on this line, see Adamson, pp. 54–55.

52. Tillyard, especially pp. 12–28.

53. Ibid., p. 20.

54. Ibid., pp. 15–16.

55. Stearns, *Robert Henryson*, p. 63; Elliott, *Poems*, p. xvi; MacQueen, *Robert Henryson*, p. 93.

56. Stearns, *Robert Henryson*, p. 63; Tatyana Moran, "The Meeting of the Lovers in 'The Testament of Cresseid,' " *Notes and Queries* 10 (1963), 11–12.

57. Spearing, "High Concise Style," p. 144; Aswell, pp. 485–86; Dolores L. Noll, "*The Testament of Cresseid*: Are Christian Interpretations Valid?," *Studies in Scottish Literature* 9 (1971), 24; see also Adamson, p. 54, and Lindsay, pp. 43–44.

58. Tillyard, p. 20; Aswell, p. 475.

59. Aswell, p. 485.

60. Fox, *Testament*, p. 56.

61. See Economou, pp. 19–20.

62. Andreas, p. 81.

63. MacQueen, *Robert Henryson*, p. 93.

64. Ibid., p. 91.

65. H. J. C. Grierson, "Robert Henryson," *Essays and Addresses* (London, 1940), p. 113; Muir, p. 19.

66. Fox, *Testament*, pp. 56–58.

Chapter Five

1. Donald MacDonald, "Henryson and *The Thre Prestis of Peblis*," pp. 174–76.

2. I. W. A. Jamieson, "The Minor Poems of Robert Henryson," *Studies in Scottish Literature* 9 (1971), 126, n.

3. A. M. Kinghorn, "The Minor Poems of Robert Henryson," *Studies in Scottish Literature* 3 (1965), 32.

4. Jamieson, "Minor Poems," p. 126.

5. Ibid., pp. 146–47.

6. John Block Friedman, *Orpheus in the Middle Ages* (Cambridge, Mass., 1970), p. 196.

7. Lindsay, p. 44.

8. Wood, *Poems and Fables*, p. xxvii; MacQueen, *Robert Henryson*, pp. 26–27.

9. Smith, *Poems*, pp. l–lv.

10. Friedman, *Orpheus*, pp. 196–202.

11. Carol Mills, "Romance Convention of Robert Henryson's *Orpheus and Eurydice*," in *Bards and Makars*, p. 58.

12. Friedman, *Orpheus*, p. 2.

13. MacQueen, "Neoplatonism and Orphism," p. 69; but for a view that the "Moralitias" provides an "optional" meaning, see Dorena Allen Wright, "Henryson's *Orpheus and Eurydice* and the Tradition of the Muses," *Medium Aevum* 40 (1971), 41–47.

14. Kenneth R. R. Gros Louis, "Robert Henryson's *Orpheus and Eurydice* and the Orpheus Traditions of the Middle Ages," *Speculum* 41 (1966), 643–45.

15. Wood, *Poems and Fables*, p. 264.

16. For added comment on this scene, see Friedman, *Orpheus*, pp. 197–98.

17. MacQueen, "Neoplatonism and Orphism," p. 77.

18. MacQueen, *Robert Henryson*, p. 33.

19. MacQueen, "Neoplatonism and Orphism," p. 82.

20. Wood, *Poems and Fables*, p. 259.

21. See MacQueen, "Neoplatonism and Orphism," pp. 79–81.

22. MacQueen, *Robert Henryson*, pp. 42–44.

23. See Friedman, *Orpheus*, p. 198.

24. Kinghorn, "Minor Poems," p. 33.

25. MacQueen, *Robert Henryson*, p. 35.

26. See MacQueen, *Robert Henryson*, p. 35.

27. Gros Louis, p. 653.

28. MacQueen, "Neoplatonism and Orphism," p. 75.

29. Kinghorn, "Minor Poems," p. 33.

30. See MacQueen, "Neoplatonism and Orphism," pp. 70–75.

31. Friedman, *Orpheus*, p. 206.

32. MacQueen, *Robert Henryson*, p. 38.

33. Stearns, *Robert Henryson*, pp. 26–27.

34. Henderson, p. 125; Kinghorn, "Minor Poems," p. 31.

35. Jones, pp. 457–58; Janet Smith, p. 43; Arthur K. Moore, "Robene and Makyne," *Modern Language Review* 43 (1948), 400–403.

36. Considering her initial boldness, her admonition to have patience may strike a modern reader as ironic.

37. Lindsay, p. 46.

38. George S. Peek, "Robert Henryson's View of Original Sin in 'The Bludy Serk,'" *Studies in Scottish Literature* 10 (1973), 200.

39. Florence Ridley, "Middle Scots Writers," *A Manual of the Writings in Middle English*, ed. Albert Hartung (New Haven, 1973), IV, 981.

40. Jamieson, "Minor Poems," p. 128.

41. See John Peter, *Complaint and Satire* (Oxford, 1956), especially pp. 60–103.

42. Jamieson, "Minor Poems," pp. 132–34.

43. Kinghorn, "Minor Poems," pp. 36–37.

44. John Stephens, "Devotion and Wit in Henryson's 'The Annunciation,'" *English Studies* 51 (1970), 323–31.

45. Jamieson, "Minor Poems," p. 143.

46. Charles A. Hallett, "Theme and Structure in Henryson's 'The Annunciation,'" *Studies in Scottish Literature* 10 (1973), 166.

47. Hallett, p. 172.

48. Wood, *Poems and Fables*, pp. 268–69.

49. Kinghorn, "Minor Poems," pp. 38–39.

50. Mann, p. 98; on the traditions of medieval burlesque and flyting in this poem, see also Denton Fox, "Henryson's 'Sum Practysis of Medecyne,'" *Studies in Philology* 69 (1972), 453–60.

51. Janet Smith, p. 100; Jamieson, "Minor Poems," p. 135.

52. Ridley, "Middle Scots Writers," p. 982.

Chapter Six

1. Maurice Lindsay, *A Book of Scottish Verse* (Oxford, 1967), p. xvii.

2. John J. McDermott, "Henryson's *Testament of Cresseid* and Heywood's *A Woman Killed with Kindness*," *Renaissance Quarterly* 10 (1967), 16–21.

3. Henderson, pp. 118–19.

4. Wittig, p. 79.

5. Ibid., p. 167.

6. Maurice Lindsay, *Robert Burns* (London, 1968), p. 129.

7. W. A. Neilson and K. G. T. Webster, *Chief British Poets of the Fourteenth and Fifteenth Centuries* (Boston, 1916), p. v.

8. Hugh MacDiarmid, ed., *Henryson* (Baltimore, 1973), p. 9.

Selected Bibliography

PRIMARY SOURCES

1. Manuscripts

Most of the manuscripts containing Henryson's verse have been printed for the Scottish Text Society. Following are the most important.

CRAIGIE, W.A., ed. *The Asloan Manuscript.* 2 vols. Edinburgh: William Blackwood, 1923–1925.

————. *The Maitland Folio Manuscript.* 2 vols. Edinburgh: William Blackwood, 1919–1927.

RITCHIE W. TOD, ed. *The Bannatyne Manuscript.* 4 vols. Edinburgh: William Blackwood, 1928–1934.

STEVENSON, G., ed. *Pieces from the Makculloch and the Gray Manuscripts.* Edinburgh: William Blackwood, 1918.

In addition, Harleian Manuscript 3865 of the fables has been edited by Diebler in *Henrisone's Fabeln* and relevant portions of the Kinaston Manuscript are reprinted in G. Gregory Smith's *Poems of Robert Henryson* (pp. xcv-clxii), both cited below.

2. Early Editions (Listed chronologically under editor or printer)

CHEPMAN W., and MYLLAR, A. *Porteous of Noblenes and Ten Other Rare Tracts.* Edinburgh, 1508. Two fragments of *Orpheus*, containing only 461 lines of the text.

THYNNE, W. *The Workes of Geffray Chaucer.* London, 1532. The best known text of *The Testament of Cresseid* (appended as a sixth book of *Troilus and Criseyde*) in the Renaissance.

CHARTERIS, HENRY. *The Morall Fabillis of Esope the Phrygian.* Edinburgh, 1570. A useful edition of the fables, printed by Robert Lekpreuik.

BASSANDYNE, THOMAS. *The Morall Fables of Esope.* Edinburgh, 1571. The most complete early edition of the fables.

SMITH, RICHARD. *The Fabulous Tales of Esope the Phrygian.* London, 1577. An Elizabethan "appreciation" of Henryson's poems.

CHARTERIS, HENRY. *The Testament of Cresseid.* Edinburgh, 1593. The best early text of the poem.

SMITH, ROBERT. *Fabillis of Isope.* Edinburgh, 1599. A lost edition, known only through inventory records.

HART, ANDRO. *The Morall Fables*. Edinburgh, 1621. A corrupt text useful only as a check on other readings.

ANDERSON, ANDREW. *The Testament of Cresseid*. Edinburgh, 1663. A useful text recently reevaluated by Denton Fox.

3. Major Modern Editions (Listed chronologically under editor)

LAING, DAVID. *The Poems and Fables*. Edinburgh: William Paterson, 1865. First collected edition of the poems; the introduction contains extensive biographical data.

DIEBLER, A. R. *Henrisone's Fabeln*. Halle: Erhardt Karras, 1885. A useful edition of the fables.

SMITH, G. GREGORY *The Poems of Robert Henryson*. Edinburgh: William Blackwood for the Scottish Text Society, 1906, 1908, 1914. Landmark three-volume edition of the poems with excellent (though dated) introduction and notes.

WOOD, H. HARVEY *Poems and Fables of Robert Henryson*. Edinburgh: Oliver and Boyd, 1933, Rev. 1958. The standard one-volume edition of Henryson's works.

ELLIOTT, CHARLES. *Poems*. Oxford: The Clarendon Press, 1963, Rev. 1975. A very good edition with a helpful but brief introduction.

FOX, DENTON. *The Testament of Cresseid*. London: Thomas Nelson, 1968. An excellent edition of this poem with an extremely helpful introduction and notes.

McDIARMID, HUGH. *Henryson*. Baltimore: Penguin, 1973. A good selection of the poetry with very little critical apparatus.

SECONDARY SOURCES

ADAMSON, JANE. "Henryson's *Testament of Cresseid*: 'Frye' and 'Cauld.' " *Critical Review* (Melbourne), 18 (1976), 39–60. An argument that Henryson portrays Cresseid's fate from the perspective of a "tragic toughness," showing neither scorn nor excessive sympathy.

ASWELL, E. DUNCAN. "The Role of Fortune in *The Testament of Cresseid*," *Philological Quarterly* 46 (1967), 471–87. An explanation that Henryson may seem "harsh and unyielding" to many modern readers because he shows that Cresseid must learn the ways of Fortune in human life.

BAUMAN, RICHARD. "The Folktale and Oral Tradition in the Fables of Robert Henryson." *Fabula* 6 (1963), 108–24. An analysis which emphasizes the folk elements in the fables, sometimes at the expense of Henryson's learning.

BENNETT, J. A. W. "Henryson's *Testament*: a flawed masterpiece." *Scottish Literary Journal* 1 (1974), 1–16. An analysis of *The Testament of Cresseid* based on the assumption that Henryson "misread" Chaucer.

BONE, GAVIN. "The Source of Henryson's 'Fox, Wolf, and Cadger.' " *Review of English Studies*, 10 (1934), 319–20. An argument that a passage in Caxton's *Reynard* is the source of Henryson's fable.

BROWN, JENNIFER M. ed. *Scottish Society in the Fifteenth Century*. London: Edward Arnold, 1977. A very helpful source of background material on Henryson's society, particularly in the essays by Norman A. T. Macdougall, Jennifer Brown, and John MacQueen.

BURROW, J. A. "Henryson: *The Preaching of the Swallow*." *Essays in Criticism* 25 (1975), 25–37. An argument that the major theme of "The Preaching of the Swallow" is prudence, which also provides a key to understanding the structure of the tale.

CHESSELL, DEL. "In the Dark Time: Henryson's *Testament of Cresseid*." *Critical Review* (Melbourne), 12 (1969), 61–72. An analysis of *The Testament* in terms of Cresseid's movement toward self-knowledge.

CLARK, GEORGE. "Henryson and Aesop: The Fable Transformed." *ELH* 43 (1976), 1–18. An examination of "The Cock and the Jasp" and "The Preaching of the Swallow" to show that Henryson transformed the Aesopian fable through greater attention to time and place.

CRAIK, THOMAS W. "The Substance and Structure of *The Testament of Cresseid*: A Hypothesis." In *Bards and Makars*, ed. Adam J. Aitken, Matthew P. McDiarmid, and Derick S. Thomson, pp. 22–26. Glasgow: University of Glasgow, 1977. An evaluation of *The Testament* as a tragic "alternative ending" to *Troilus and Criseyde*.

CROWNE, DAVID K. "A Date for the Composition of Henryson's Fables." *Journal of English and Germanic Philology* 61 (1962), 583–90. A quite solid but occasionally overconfident attempt to date the fables.

CRUTTWELL, PATRICK. "Two Scots Poets: Dunbar and Henryson. "In *The Age of Chaucer*, ed. Boris Ford, rev. ed., pp. 173–85. Baltimore: Penguin Books, 1969. A brief review of the general interests and techniques of both poets.

DIEBLER, A. R. *Henrisone's Fabeldichtungen*. Halle: Erhardt Karras, 1885. A valuable, though neglected, commentary on the fables and their sources.

DUNCAN, DOUGLAS. "Henryson's *Testament of Cresseid*." *Essays in Criticism* 11 (1961), 128–35. An argument that Henryson questions the ways of Providence in *The Testament*.

ELLIOTT, CHARLES. "*Sparth, Glebard* and *Bowranbane*." *Notes and Queries* 9 (1962), 86–87. An attempt to identify three animals from "The Trial of the Fox."

————. "Two Notes on Henryson's *Testament of Cresseid*." *Journal of English and Germanic Philology* 54 (1955), 241–54. An attempt to clarify two major textual problems, the "Esperus-esperance" controversy and the problem about the name of Phoebus' horse.

FOX, DENTON. "Henryson and Caxton." *Journal of English and Germanic Philology* 67 (1968), 586–93. An argument that Henryson need not have known or used Caxton's *Aesop* or *Reynard*.

————. "Henryson's *Fables*." *ELH* 39 (1962), 337–56. A valuable explanation of the relationships between Henryson's tale and "Moralitas" with special reference to "The Cock and the Jasp" and "The Preaching of the Swallow."

————. "Henryson's 'Sum Practysis of Medecyne.' " *Studies in Philology* 69 (1972), 453–60. An exploration of the influence of traditions of medieval medical burlesque and flyting on "Sum Practysis."

————. "The Scottish Chaucerians." In *Chaucer and Chaucerians*, ed. D. S. Brewer, pp. 164–200. University, Alabama: University of Alabama Press, 1964. An analysis of the Makars as "Scottish Chaucerians" with an emphasis on their Scottish roots.

FRIEDMAN, JOHN BLOCK. "Henryson, the Friars, and the *Confessio Reynardi*." *Journal of English and Germanic Philology* 66 (1967), 550–61. An attempt to show that "The Fox and the Wolf" was influenced by antimendicant tracts and is itself a *confessio Reynardi*.

————. *Orpheus in the Middle Ages*. Cambridge; Harvard University Press, 1970. An examination of the Orpheus traditions with a lenghty section on *Orpheus and Eurydice* showing how it is a culmination of various approaches to the legend.

GEDDIE, WILLIAM. *A Bibliography of Middle Scots Poetry*. Edinburgh: Scottish Text Society, 1912. A standard and still impressive work, which provides an excellent listing of earlier editions and scholarship.

GRIERSON, H. J. C. "Robert Henryson." In *Essays and Addresses*. London: Chatto and Windus, 1940, pp. 203–12. An appreciation of Henryson's poetry against the background of English and Scottish verse.

GROS LOUIS, KENNETH R. "Robert Henryson's *Orpheus and Eurydice* and the Orpheus Tradition of the Middle Ages." *Speculum* 41 (1966), 643–55. An argument that *Orpheus and Eurydice* is the culmination of two traditions of Orpheus legends.

HALLETT, CHARLES A. "Theme and Structure in Henryson's 'The Annunciation.' " *Studies in Scottish Literature* 10 (1973), 165–74. An analysis of the three-part structure of "The Annunciation," showing that Henryson deals with the theme of individual salvation in very personal terms.

HANNA, RALPH. "Cresseid,'s Dream and Henryson's *Testament*." In *Chaucer and Middle English Studies in Honour of Rossell Hope Robbins*, ed. Beryl Rowland, pp. 288–97. Kent, Ohio: Kent State University Press, 1974. An evaluation of Cresseid's dream as a *somnium*, in which she sees the cause of her distress as she would like to think it exists.

HARTH, SIDNEY. "Henryson Reinterpreted." *Essays in Criticism* 11 (1961), 471–80. A response to Duncan's article in which the author argues that Henryson does not deal with great questions of mercy or justice in *The Testament*.

HEIDTMANN, PETER. "A Bibliography of Henryson, Dunbar, and Douglas, 1912–1968." *Chaucer Review* 5 (1970), 75–82. A sound guide with few omissions, intended to supplement Geddie; now superseded by Ridley.

HUME, KATHRYN. "Leprosy or Syphillis in Henryson's *Testament of Cresseid.*" *English Language Notes* 6 (1969), 242–45. An examination of Cresseid's disease with reference to both alternatives.

HYDE, ISABEL. "Poetic Imagery: A Point of Comparison between Henryson and Dunbar." *Studies in Scottish Literature* 2 (1965), 183–97. An examination of the imagery of both poets in which the conclusion is drawn that Dunbar borrowed little from Henryson.

JAMIESON, I. W. A. "A Further Source for Henryson's 'Fabillis.' " *Notes and Queries* 14 (1967), 403–5. An evaluation of Henryson's use of the *Fabulae* of Odo of Cheriton.

_____. "Henryson's 'Fabillis': An Essay Towards a Revaluation." In *Words: Wai-Te Atu Studies in Literature*, no. 2, ed. P. T. Hoffman, D. F. McKenzie, and Peter Robb, pp. 20–31. Wellington, New Zealand, 1966. An attempt to reevaluate the fables through their sources.

_____. "Henryson's *Taill of the Wolf and the Wedder.*" *Studies in Scottish Literature* 6 (1969), 248–57. An examination of the sources of the tale to show that Henryson constructed his "Moralitas" as a rhetorical device to shock the reader.

_____. "The Minor Poems of Robert Henryson." *Studies in Scottish Literature* 9 (1971–1972), 125–47. An examination of the minor poems as genre works, with excellent guides to Henryson's use of medieval tradition.

JENKINS, ANTHONY W. "Henryson's *The Fox, the Wolf, and the Cadger* Again." *Studies in Scottish Literature* 4 (1966), 107–12. An explanation of the relationship between the fable and the Meon text of the *Roman de Renart.*

JENTOFT, C. W. "Henryson as Authentic 'Chaucerian': Narrator, Character, and Courtly Love in *The Testament of Cresseid.*" *Studies in Scottish Literature* 10 (1972), 94–102. A study of Chaucer's influence on Henryson's narrator and the poem's courtly morality.

JONES, W. POWELL. "A Source for Henryson's *Robene and Makyne?*" *Modern Language Notes* 46 (1931), 457–58. An inconclusive attempt to establish a *pastourelle* by Baudes de la Kakerie as the source for "Robene and Makyne."

KINDRICK. ROBERT, L. "Lion or Cat?: Henryson's Characterization of James III." In *Studies in Scottish Literature XIV.* Columbia, South Carolina: University of South Carolina Press, 1979, pp. 123–36. An examination of Henryson's political satire in the fables to show that he is basically a proponent of monarchy even though he has an ambivalent attitude toward James.

KINGHORN, A. M. "The Minor Poems of Robert Henryson." *Studies in Scottish Literature* 3 (1965), 30–40. An evaluation of the minor poems in terms of the poet's learning and personality.

LARKEY, SANFORD V. "Leprosy in Medieval Romance: a Note on Robert Henryson's *Testament of Cresseid.*" *Bulletin of the History of Medicine* 25 (1958), 77–80. A brief comment on Henryson's use of medical detail.

LONG, ELEANOR R. "Robert Henryson's 'Uther Quair.'" *Comitatus* 3 (1972), 97–101. An attempt to trace the influence of Guido delle Colonne's *Historia* on *The Testament* through a lost moral treatise.

LYALL, R. J. "Politics and Poetry in Fifteenth and Sixteenth Century Scotland." *Scottish Literary Journal* 3 (1976), 5–27. An argument that many of the putative references to James III in Middle Scots poetry, including Henryson's, are in fact based on a tradition of political "advice" and must be viewed cautiously.

MARKEN, RONALD. "Chaucer and Henryson: A Comparison." *Discourse* 7 (1964), 381–87. A comparison of artistry, tone, and authorial attitude in *Troilus and Criseyde* and *The Testament*, to Henryson's detriment.

McDERMOTT, JOHN J. "Henryson's *Testament of Cresseid* and Heywood's *A Woman Killed with Kindness*." *Renaissance Quarterly* 20 (1967), 16–21. An explanation of the influence of *The Testament*, with which Heywood was familiar, on the plot and characterization of *A Woman Killed with Kindness*.

McDONALD, CRAIG. "Venus and the Goddess Fortune in *The Testament of Cresseid*." *Scottish Literary Journal* 4 (1977), 14–24. An analysis of the court of the gods to show how Henryson treats Boethian themes.

MacDONALD, DONALD. "Chaucer's Influence on Henryson's *Fables*: The Use of Proverbs and Sententiae." *Medium Aevum* 39 (1970), 21–27. An examination of Henryson's use of proverbs in the fables to show that his techniques of using them are specifically Chaucerian.

———. "Henryson and Chaucer: Cock and Fox." *Texas Studies in Literature and Language* 8 (1966), 451–61. An examination of Henryson's borrowings from "The Nun's Priest's Tale" in "The Cock and the Fox."

———. "Henryson and the *Thre Prestis of Peblis*." *Neophilologus* 51 (1967), 168–77. An interesting but as yet inconclusive attempt to bring the *Thre Prestis* into the Henryson canon.

———. "Narrative Art in Henryson's *Fables*." *Studies in Scottish Literature* 3 (1965), 101–13. A study of Henryson's expansion of his sources, with particular reference to "The Wolf and the Wether" and "The Cock and the Fox."

McDIARMID, MATTHEW P. "Robert Henryson in His Poems." In *Bards and Makars*, pp. 27–40. An examination of Henryson's attempt to place "reason at peace with desire" in his poetry.

McNAMARA, JOHN. "Divine Justice in Henryson's *Testament of Cresseid*." *Studies in Scottish Literature* 11 (1973), 99–107. An argument that the gods are just because Cresseid is redeemed by her punishment.

———. "Language as Action in Henryson's *Testament of Cresseid*." In *Bards and Makars*, pp. 41–51. An analysis of the use of language and metalanguage to provide added dimensions for *The Testament*.

MacQUEEN, JOHN. "Neoplatonism and Orphism in Fifteenth-Century Scotland." *Scottish Studies* 20 (1976), 69–89. An analysis of the influence of Neoplatonism of the Quattrocento on *Orpheus and Eurydice.*

———. *Robert Henryson.* Oxford: Clarendon Press, 1967. An invaluable study of Henryson and his poetry which attempts to trace the development of his humanism through his educational and literary background.

———. "The Text of Henryson's *Morall Fabillis." Innes Review* 14 (1963), 3–9. A study which establishes the importance of the Bannatyne Manuscript as a text for the fables.

MILLS, CAROL. "Romance Convention of Robert Henryson's *Orpheus and Eurydice."* In *Bards and Makars,* pp. 52–60. An argument that Henryson knew a version of *Sir Orfeo* similar to that in the Auchinleck Manuscript but used it primarily for ornamentation.

MOORE, ARTHUR K. " 'Robene and Makyne.' " *Modern Language Review* 43 (1948), 400–403. An argument that Henryson did not borrow directly from the *pastourelle.*

MORAN, TATYANA. "The Meeting of the Lovers in 'The Testament of Cresseid.' " *Notes and Queries* 10 (1963), 11–12. A brief note on the recognition scene.

———. "The Testament of Cresseid and the *Book of Troylus." Litera* 6 (1959), 18–24. A discussion of Henryson's use of Chaucer.

MUDGE, E. L. "The Fifteenth Century Critic." *College English* 5 (1943), 154–55. A study of Henryson's social criticism in "On the Want of Wyse Men."

MUIR, EDWIN. "Robert Henryson." In *Essays on Literature and Society.* Rev. ed. London: Hogarth Press, 1965. Pp. 10–21. An attempt to appraise the relative balance of social influences and individual talent in Henryson's verse.

MURTAUGH, DANIEL M. "Henryson's Animals." *Texas Studies in Literature and Language* 14 (1972), 405–21. A study of Henryson's use of irony in the byplay between human and animal characteristics in the fables.

NOLL, DOLORES L. *"The Testament of Cresseid:* Are Christian Interpretations Valid?" *Studies in Scottish Literature* 9 (1971), 16–25. An analysis of *The Testament* as a poem built on the premises of courtly love.

PARR, JOHNSTONE. "Cresseid's Leprosy Again." *Modern Language Notes* 60 (1945), 487–91. An argument that Henryson's depiction of Cresseid's disease could be based on a textbook description.

PATTERSON, LEE W. "Christian and Pagan in *The Testament of Cresseid." Philological Quarterly* 52 (1973), 696–714. A study of Cresseid's development from a sense of shame to guilt and a better understanding of her flaws.

PEEK, GEORGE S. "Robert Henryson's View of Original Sin in 'The Bludy Serk.' " *Studies in Scottish Literature* 10 (1973), 199–206. A study of Henryson's three major changes from the version of the tale in Harleian MS. 7333.

RIDLEY, FLORENCE. "Middle Scots Writers." In *A Manual of the Writings in Middle English*, ed. Albert Hartung, IV, 961–1060, 1123–84. New Haven: Connecticut Academy of Arts and Sciences, 1973. An excellent bibliographical guide to the Makars.

———. "A Plea for the Middle Scots." In *The Learned and the Lewed*, Larry D. Benson, pp. 175–96. Cambridge: Harvard University Press, 1974. A study of *The Testament of Cresseid* to show Henryson's originality and to attack the designation of him as a "Scottish Chaucerian."

ROSSI, SERGIO. "L'annunciazione di Robert Henryson." *Aevum* 29 (1955), 70–81. A text and brief analysis of "The Annunciation."

———. *Robert Henryson*. Milan: Carlo Marzorati, 1955. A survey of Henryson's work with particular reference to his humanism.

ROWLAND, BERYL. "The 'seiknes incurabill' in Henryson's *Testament of Cresseid*." *English Language Notes* 1 (1964), 175–77. An argument that Cresseid's disease is syphillis.

ROWLANDS, MARY. "The Fables of Robert Henryson." *Dalhousie Review* 39 (1959–1960), 491–502. An evaluation of the social concerns of the fables.

———. "Robert Henryson and the Scottish Courts of Law." *Aberdeen University Review* 39 (1962), 219–26. An examination of Henryson's attitudes toward courts, particularly in "The Sheep and the Dog."

SPEARING, A. C. "*The Testament of Cresseid* and the High Concise Style." In *Criticism and Medieval Poetry*. London: Edward Arnold, 1964. Pp. 118–44. A valuable essay, emphasizing Henryson's brevity and control in *The Testament*.

STEARNS, MARSHALL W. "Henryson and Chaucer." *Modern Language Quarterly* 6 (1945), 271–84. An examination of *The Testament* to show that Henryson was deeply indebted to Chaucer.

———. "Henryson and the Political Scene." *Studies in Philology* 40 (1943), 280–89. An explanation of Henryson's political commentary on events pertaining to the nobles and the court of James III.

———. "A Note on Henryson and Lydgate." *Modern Language Notes* 60 (1945), 101–3. A study of Henryson's use of Lydgate, particularly in the planet portraits.

———. "A Note on Robert Henryson's Allusions to Religion and Law." *Modern Language Notes* 59 (1944), 257–64. A study of social comment, particularly in the fables.

———. "The Planet Portraits of Robert Henryson." *PMLA* 49 (1944), 911–27. A study of Henryson's use of sources and traditions in this section of *The Testament*.

———. *Robert Henryson*. New York: Columbia Press, 1949. A study of Henryson's verse which focuses on political and social comment, incorporating many of the essays listed here.

———. "Robert Henryson and the Fulgentian Horse." *Modern Language*

Notes 54 (1939), 239–45. An evaluation of the "Philologie" debate in *The Testament* and an attempt to establish Henryson's debt to Pseudo-Bede.

———. "Robert Henryson and the Leper Cresseid." *Modern Language Notes* 49 (1944), 265–69. An analysis of *The Testament* with an emphasis on Henryson's stern morality.

———. "Robert Henryson and the Socio-Economic Scene." *ELH* 10 (1943), 285–93. An examination of the social and economic background of the fables showing that Henryson champions the poor.

STRAUSS, JENNIFER. "To Speak Once More of Cresseid: Henryson's *Testament* Re-considered." *Scottish Literary Journal* 4 (1977), 5–13. A study of the planetary gods to show that they represent forces in Cresseid's life as she moves toward a sense of responsibility.

TILLYARD, E. M. W. "Henryson: *The Testament of Cresseid* 1470?" In *Five Poems 1470–1870.* London: Chatto and Windus, 1948. Pp. 5–29. Probably the most important argument that *The Testament of Cresseid* is based on Christian principles.

TOLIVER, HAROLD E. "Robert Henryson: From *Moralitas* to Irony," *English Studies* 46 (1965), 300–309. An argument that the use of the "Moralitas" provides another dimension to Henryson's work sometimes leading, as in *The Testament*, to sympathetic irony.

VON KREISLER, NICOLAI. "Henryson's Visionary Fable: Tradition and Craftsmanship in *The Lyoun and the Mous.*" *Texas Studies in Literature and Language* 15 (1973), 391–403. A study of Henryson's use of the conventions of visionary literature to disguise his political satire.

WHITING, B. J. "A Probable Allusion to Henryson's 'Testament of Cresseid.'" *Modern Language Review* 40 (1945), 46–47. A study of the role of *The Spektakle of Lufe* in dating *The Testament*.

WOOD, H. HARVEY. "Robert Henryson." In *Edinburgh Essays on Scots Literature.* Edinburgh: Oliver and Boyd, 1933. Pp. 1–26. A general survey of Henryson's poetry with an emphasis on his artistry.

———. *Two Scots Chaucerians.* Writers and Their Work no. 201. London: Longmans, Green, 1967. A good, brief introduction to Henryson's poetry.

WRIGHT, DORENA ALLEN. "Henryson's *Orpheus and Eurydice* and the Tradition of the Muses." *Medium Aevum* 40 (1971), 41–47. An argument that Henryson's "Moralitas" for *Orpheus* provides an optional meaning, "not the obligatory key" for the whole poem.

Index